W9-AHH-698

This book is presented to you by the
Rotary Club of Chilliwack, the Chilliwack
Learning Society and The Book Man

Chilliwack
Learning
Society

Rotary
Club of Chilliwack

THE BOOK MAN

THIS CRAZY TIME

by TZEPORAH BERMAN

with MARK LEIREN-YOUNG

"If you've ever uttered the word 'can't,' you need to pick up *This Crazy Time*. Tzeporah Berman's inspirational journey from accidental logging activist to international climate champ will show you how a fearless dreamer can help safeguard millions of acres of old-growth forests and tackle the biggest challenge of our time: climate change. You'll walk away with an honorary MBA in changing the world. How will you put yours to use?" Adria Vasil, author of the Ecoholic series

"In *This Crazy Time*, Tzeporah Berman brings the inflated rhetoric of the environmental debate down to earth and puts a passionate and empathetic human face on the defining global challenge of our time. Her journey from the front lines of logging blockades to the hot seats of corporate boardrooms is told with remarkable intimacy and rare self-reflection, tracing the central arc of the environmental movement as a whole over the past twenty years. In times growing crazier with each day's weather, we need her thoughtful leadership more than ever." Chris Turner, author of *The Leap* and *The Geography of Hope*

"Over the past twenty years the environmental debate has been loud, raucous and increasingly prominent. And Tzeporah Berman has been right there in the thick of it. Berman is a key leader and, in this book, a thoughtful interpreter of significant events. Let her be your guide to some of the most exciting, and important, moments in recent Canadian history." Rick Smith, executive director of Environmental Defence; co-author of *Slow Death by Rubber Duck*

"Tzeporah Berman is a modern environmental hero, and this fascinating book shares her exciting history, and the even more exciting thinking that it's given rise to. If we get out of our ecological woes, she'll be a big reason." Bill McKibben, author of *Eaarth* and founder of 350.org

"Tzeporah's inspiring and humorous story about her development as an environmental activist has significance far beyond the successful struggle against old-growth clear-cutting. If governments remain unwilling to enact effective climate policies, the obvious next step is for civil actions that engage the public while slowing or preventing investments that facilitate fossil fuel combustion (coal plants, oil pipelines, freeways). Who better to lead that charge?" Mark Jaccard, member of the Intergovernmental Panel on Climate Change and author of *Hot Air: Meeting Canada's Climate Change Challenge*

"Our global environmental crisis is going critical. It's easy to lose hope. Tzeporah Berman is one of the few people with the insight, experience and guts to show us a way forward that actually might work. *This Crazy Time* seamlessly blends hard-won practical tips on how to build a mass movement for change with deeply moving stories of Berman's own successes and failures in the high-stakes world of international environmental campaigning. It shows how each of us—by working with others and marrying courage with political and business smarts—can change the world, for real and for good. This is a fabulous book. It will give you goose-bumps, make you laugh and leave you in tears. And you won't put it down till the last page." Thomas Homer-Dixon, author of *The Upside of Down*

"Tzeporah Berman's true-life exploits make a great read. From Paris Hilton to rock concerts in forest blockades, she manages to share a very personal take on the state of our planet with the highs and lows of life as one of our strongest eco-campaigners." Elizabeth May, Green Party Member of Parliament

"Tzeporah Berman is a Canadian environmental hero and national treasure. In *This Crazy Time* she takes us on a very personal and fascinating journey through her life as an environmental activist. Berman provides us with gripping front-line accounts of her involvement in saving Clayoquot Sound, and her campaigns with ForestEthics, PowerUp Canada and Greenpeace International. Throughout her journey we learn how she constantly struggles to balance family life with her role as an environmental activist. Tzeporah Berman has a profound understanding of the environment. At times besieged by critics from both within and outside of the environmental movement, she manages to remain focused on her primary objective: the introduction of environmental policy that preserves natural habitat and biodiversity, while recognizing the need for economic stability. *This Crazy Time* is a must-read for those on any side of a particular environmental issue. Tzeporah Berman emphasizes the power of dialogue and the importance of compromise for reaching lasting solutions to environmental problems. And she leaves the reader with a sense of optimism that each and every one of us can make a difference." Andrew Weaver, Professor and Canada Research Chair in Climate Modelling and Analysis; author of *Keeping our Cool: Canada in a Warming World*

"You can call Tzeporah Berman a crazy, tree-hugging, jailbird, eco-terrorist. But in today's world it's just about the only honest job around. Save a vital rainforest, or clear-cut its giant redwoods into newsprint, packaging and toilet paper. Are we kidding? Our tragedy is that we aren't all chained to a tree." William Marsden, author of *Fools Rule: Inside the Failed Politics of Climate Change*

"If you've ever wondered how ordinary people become the extraordinary people who change the world, read this book. Here is a memoir that will convince you Canada's forests are a global treasure, but more importantly, reminds each and every one of us that we have the power to act on our beliefs. Fast-paced, frank and often surprisingly funny, *This Crazy Time* is a primer for a more impassioned world." J.B. MacKinnon, co-author of *The 100-Mile Diet*

"Tzeporah Berman has risked life and liberty in what is ultimately the greatest cause: the future of this planet. Sad, alarming, witty and bold, *This Crazy Time* takes us inside the war against those who are so recklessly and ruthlessly destroying the earth while most of us sleep."
Ronald Wright, author of *A Short History of Progress*

THIS CRAZY TIME

TZEPORAH BERMAN

BERMAN

with MARK LEIREN-YOUNG

THIS CRAZY TIME

LIVING OUR ENVIRONMENTAL CHALLENGE

Alfred A. Knopf Canada

PUBLISHED BY ALFRED A. KNOPF CANADA

Copyright © 2011 Tzeporah Berman and Mark Leiren-Young

www.randomhouse.ca

Knopf Canada and colophon are registered trademarks.

Library and Archives Canada Cataloguing in Publication

Berman, Tzeporah, 1969–
This crazy time : living our environmental challenge / Tzeporah Berman with
Mark Leiren-Young.

Includes bibliographical references and index.
Issued also in electronic format.

ISBN 978-0-307-39978-6

1. Berman, Tzeporah, 1969–. 2. Women environmentalists—Canada—Biography.
3. Women conservationists—Canada—Biography. I. Leiren-Young, Mark II. Title.

GE195.9.B47 2011   333.72082'0971   C2011-902539-6

MIX
From responsible
sources
FSC® C102091

Text design by Andrew Roberts
Cover image: Dreamstime.com

Printed and bound in the United States of America

2 4 6 8 9 7 5 3 1

Optimism is the only moral choice. It's an option, first of all, it's not a given. If you run out of hope at the end of the day, you always have the choice of getting up in the morning and putting it on again, like a sweater. You have to keep trying to find hope. I think it's immoral to do otherwise, because the minute you say, "I can't do a thing about it. This world is going to hell in a handbasket and it's beyond me to change it." The minute you say that, you're essentially saying, "I'm gonna stop trying. . . ." If you give up hope and stop trying to fix what's wrong, you're handing to your children—and mine and everybody else's—a worse world than the one you found. And I can't live with that.

BARBARA KINGSOLVER,
INTERVIEWED ON *WRITERS AND COMPANY*, CBC RADIO

CONTENTS

PART IV: **CLIMATE RECKONING**

PREFACE

THE STORIES IN THIS BOOK represent moments and events that were important for me, but they are part of complex and multi-faceted campaigns that I can only begin to describe here. I specifically want to recognize the importance of indigenous leadership in this work and make clear that while I can and do discuss my direct engagement with First Nations and try to understand and incorporate human rights and sovereignty issues, I know that I have not done justice to their courageous and critical initiatives. Although I've tried to tell my tale with every attempt at accuracy and have benefited from the contributions of essential colleagues in creating this record, errors of fact, omissions and mistakes in the book are mine.

Social change doesn't happen because of the work of just one individual. We often want to believe that it does because we seem hardwired to the notion of heroes, and it seems simpler to visit our hopes, disappointments or accolades on one person. While an individual can make a huge impact, societal change is brought about because society moves, and that movement forward takes the work of many people, in so many ways, visible and not. Success, clarity and game-changing moments in the campaigns I describe resulted from the efforts of numerous individuals and organizations. I recognize many of them in the acknowledgements, but there are thousands more who contributed to this work. I dedicate this book to them and to all of you who are helping to achieve a cleaner, saner and safer world.

Tzeporah Berman
Amsterdam
June 2011

INTRODUCTION

First they ignore you, then they ridicule you, then they fight you, then you win.

Mahatma Gandhi, paraphrasing labour organizer
Nicolas Klein's speech to garment manufacturers, 1918

"CAN YOU COME HOME SOON?" my son asks as we sit talking into our computers on different sides of the world. Then, before I can answer, he adds, "Have you saved the polar bears yet?"

Sitting at a cast-iron table at a café on the edge of an Amsterdam canal, I'm wondering about this crazy time we live in and what it's going to take to create a world where a child doesn't grow up worried about the fate of the polar bears, let alone his own fate.

I've just finished my first week of work at Greenpeace International as the co-director of the global climate and energy programme. Every day I'm inspired and humbled by the knowledge, commitment and diversity of experience crammed into the perpetually buzzing four-storey building on the outskirts of Amsterdam. I'm excited by the opportunity to share an office with more than a hundred brilliant, passionate people working at all hours, in many languages, determined to overcome cultural differences, time differences and enormous odds to patch together environmental strategies with thousands of others who are working in similar offices and other organizations around the world. I am also afraid of suffocating in the red tape of an organization this big, overwhelmed by the scale of the problems we face and, after nineteen years of professional activism, I still have moments of wondering when my life will go back to normal.

But this is the new normal for many of us in the twenty-first century.

I'm supposed to be en route to Bangkok to meet with Greenpeace staff from across Asia, but protests against the Thai government closed most of the city, so we moved the meeting to Hong Kong. Then the flight to Hong Kong was grounded, so now I have a stolen day to try to wrap my head around the recent changes in my life, the scale of the problems we're facing and my new job trying to "save the polar bears."

Thousands of miles away, on an isolated island off the west coast of Canada, Quinn waits for my response. I look at his eager face on the screen and find myself second-guessing the decision to shortly take my kids from their home that's a few hundred yards up the hill from their six-room school on an organic farm to this crazy, vibrating city that never seems to sleep.

As I spend my days and nights at the office, I worry that I don't have what it takes to do this new job—to help coordinate hundreds of climate and energy campaigners and organizers from dozens of countries, whose aim is nothing less than an energy revolution. Our mission isn't "just" to stop global warming, it's to protect what's left of the world's pristine places and ensure what's known as "climate justice": fair agreements over energy use between developed and developing countries.

The most amazing, inspiring and frustrating thing isn't that we can't address these issues, it's that we can and don't. The experts keep telling us we have a way through this, that we have the technology to change the way we deal with our energy needs. The Princeton professors Stephen Pacala and Robert Socolow wrote in *Science* in 2004: "Humanity already possesses the fundamental scientific, technical and industrial know-how to solve the carbon and climate problem. We are not dealing with a failure of technology, a failure of industry, a failure of human ability. We are dealing with a failure of social and political will."[1]

That's why, even with this big a mission and the blizzard of e-mails and calls every day from people in India, China, Brazil, Australia, Canada and the United States, most of the time I think I'm clear on what needs to happen. We don't need to be rocket scientists, we don't need to build a new widget—we need to find ways to organize, to demand that our elected officials and major corporations put in place the policies and laws that will regulate pollution, reduce our dependence on fossil fuels and stimulate the use of existing clean technologies. After years of doing this work, I can usually draw on some lesson, experience or campaign and focus on making a decision, giving advice or designing a plan.

Then, out of nowhere, there are moments when I feel as if I'm twenty again and making it up as I go along, almost paralyzed by the scale of the change required and by the realization that I'm suddenly helping to direct the climate campaign of one of the largest environmental organizations in the world. My lowest points come when I think about the impact this responsibility will have on my boys, how much travelling I'll have to do, how much time we'll be apart.

"How many days left before you come home, Mommy?" asks Forrest, when we start our nightly talk on Skype. Forrest is twelve.

Then Quinn, who is eight, takes over the computer. "Forrest cried for an hour yesterday, but he told me not to tell you."

As I picture Forrest crying, I'm less concerned about whether I can mediate the internal dispute over Greenpeace's position on energy from biomass, or whether we can launch a legal challenge against a new coal plant in the Czech Republic than I am that I can't crawl under the covers and read him a bedtime story in which everyone lives happily ever after.

But this is the moment when change finally has a chance. Today, "green is the new black," and everyone from Paris Hilton to Bill Gates wants to do what they can to fight climate change. Every business from Coca-Cola to Walmart to your corner store is trying to figure out how to capture the socially conscious market, but not necessarily how to reduce their ecological footprint. Yet we are living in a world where everybody at least claims to want to do something to help—whether by recycling more or consuming less. Individuals, corporations and governments are all more open than they've ever been to exploring solutions, and investment in clean technologies is at an all-time high.

In 2009 Europe developed more renewable energy than energy from coal, oil or nuclear power. After decades of receiving blank looks or shameless laughter from politicians and corporate leaders whom I have lobbied on environmental issues, I knew the message had finally sunk in when US President Barack Obama declared, "Our future on this planet depends on our willingness to address the challenge posed by carbon pollution."[2] Then Jiang Bing, head of China's National Energy Administration, announced Beijing's plans to spend 5 trillion yuan, or about US$738 billion, over the next decade to develop cleaner sources of energy.[3]

We've come a long way from the days of solar panels and windmills being the pipe dream of some West Coast hippies. Tipping points are moments when opinions and decisions shift quickly and dramatically—when new concepts, theories or ideas spread like wildfire. Tipping points create political space and opportunity for change.[4] The changing market for clean energy and world leaders' recognition of the need to address environmental challenges has created a tipping point that truly gives us an opportunity to re-envision the world.

That's why I returned to Greenpeace International, after leaving the organization a decade ago. I took this position in a city halfway around the world from our home on Cortes Island knowing it would mean less baking, less gardening, less Lego, fewer games of Go Fish and Battleship, fewer bedtime stories and more heartbreaking calls like these.

When I look at my children, I am frequently haunted by the words of experts like Dr. James Hansen, who recently stepped down as NASA's top climate scientist, who warns that the earth's climate is reaching a stage beyond which climate change will spiral out of control. We are already seeing a rise in violent storms, droughts in some parts of the world and floods in others leading to escalating food costs, water scarcity, ocean acidification and economic instability.[5]

The number that should be haunting every parent and inspiring every choice we make—not just in the shopping mall, but in the voting booth—is 350. That's the parts per million of carbon dioxide that scientists say our atmosphere can safely process. We're currently at almost 390 parts per million. Study after terrifying study has shown that if we don't get that level back down to 350, we will be unable to avoid apocalyptic consequences such as the floods in Sri Lanka that recently displaced a million people or the devastating fires in

Russia. This is a crazy time we are living in. We simply can't afford to keep spewing junk into our atmosphere, where it is building up and smothering the planet. Yet for decades we have been burning our way through oil and coal and treating our atmosphere like an ashtray. Now, according to the United Nations, the economic implications, including the impact on water, food and human dislocation, make climate change the greatest challenge humanity has ever faced.[6]

Dr. Hansen wrote in 2010 (which, by the way, tied 2005 as the hottest year since humanity started keeping stats on the planet's temperature in 1880),[7] "The predominant moral issue of the twenty-first century, almost surely, will be climate change, comparable to Nazism faced by Churchill in the twentieth century and slavery faced by Lincoln in the nineteenth century. Our fossil fuel addiction, if unabated, threatens our children and grandchildren, and most species on the planet."[8]

The situation is serious enough that in 2007 the *Bulletin of the Atomic Scientists,* the keepers of the global "Doomsday Clock,"[9] moved the hands two minutes closer to midnight because of the dangers posed by climate change.[10]

The US general Wesley Clark warns that "energy security is crucial to national security."[11] We know this from watching wars fought over oil, or from experiencing how vulnerable our society is when energy prices skyrocket and millions of people simply can't afford to get from A to B, or the price of staples like rice and flour rises dramatically.

And the organization Christian Aid is predicting that by 2050 more than one billion people will be forced out of their homes by climate change, creating an unprecedented number of global refugees.[12]

If peak oil, security issues and clearly fragile economic systems that depend on finite resources aren't enough to get your attention, we also now know that fossil fuel use has been linked to everything from mercury poisoning, to asthma, to changing patterns of infections and insect-borne diseases, and skyrocketing mortality rates due to heat waves, reduced water and threatened food security. The medical journal *The Lancet*'s Health Commission in 2009 warned: "Climate change is the biggest global health threat of the twenty-first century."[13]

Michael McGeehin, director of the Division of Environmental Hazards and Health Effects at the Center for Disease Control and

Prevention (CDC) in the United States, agrees. "Heat waves are a public health disaster. They kill, and they kill the most vulnerable members of our society. The fact that climate change is going to increase the number and intensity of heat waves is something we need to prepare for."[14] Even Jeroen van der Veer, the chief executive of Royal Dutch Shell, has given speeches saying, "Regardless of which route we choose, the world's current predicament limits our maneuvering room. We are experiencing a step-change in the growth rate of energy demand due to population growth and economic development, and Shell estimates that after 2015 supplies of easy-to-access oil and gas will no longer keep up with demand."[15] Of course, the CEO of Shell is not therefore seriously advocating that we transform our energy systems to depend on renewable energy instead of fossil fuels. In fact, Shell and most of the other major oil and gas companies seem hell-bent on literally going to the ends of the earth (strip-mining for oil in the Canadian tar sands or deep-water drilling in the fragile Arctic) to get at what's left. My point is that regardless of your opinion of the solution or your impetus for change, there is a growing recognition from all corners of society that we need to change how society functions and fuels itself, and something's gotta give.

I'm not interested in spending time convincing anyone that global warming is happening. I am invested in convincing you that we need to make major changes in our lives and the laws and policies that govern our societies in order to reduce our dependence on dirty energy and protect the earth's living systems. Even the most devout climate change deniers know our consumerist lifestyle is unsustainable because it's based on dirty, dangerous and finite resources, such as coal and oil, instead of on those that we know are renewable, like sun and wind.

It doesn't take a climate scientist to realize there isn't enough oil left for everyone in India and China to live like North Americans. Regardless of whether you accept the science behind climate change, or the clear health risks, there are other economic and national security reasons that should worry you.

The need to ensure access and equity in emerging economies should be a pretty strong motivator. The carbon footprint of the poorest one billion people is around 3 percent of the world's total footprint, yet climate change affects these communities the most.[16] The past one hundred years have been a frenzy of development and pollution. We've benefited in many ways, but now we're starting to live the repercussions. It's as if we've thrown a massive party in our parents' house and have to clean up the mess in the living room before Mom and Dad get home—except in this case it's our grandchildren's house that we've trashed.

From a big-picture perspective, the solutions seem clear, and we are already seeing them emerge in many places around the world.[17] We need to dramatically reduce our dependence on finite resources and dirty fossil fuels. We need to rebuild our society so we're not dependent on food that was farmed on one continent, processed at the other end of the planet and then shipped to the consumer. We need to move to a sustainable economy driven by renewable resources, in which the value of clean air, clean water and biodiversity are taken into account when we make economic and political calculations.

And what's the worst thing that happens if we act to change the way industrial society is fuelled and then it turns out that NASA, the CEO of Shell, a four-star general, the United Nations and pretty much every scientist and government on the planet were wrong about climate change? We end up with renewable energy systems, more local food production, cleaner air, cleaner water, more vibrant communities, fewer species going extinct, fewer people dying of cancer and respiratory diseases, millions of new clean energy jobs and increased global security.

My favourite cartoon about climate change is by Joel Pett from *USA Today*. It shows the audience at a symposium looking at a PowerPoint list of objectives: "energy independence, preserve rainforests, sustainability, green jobs, livable cities, renewables, clean water, air and healthy children." Meanwhile, at the back of the room, one cranky guy asks, "What if it's a big hoax and we create a better world for nothing?"

So this isn't a book to convince you of the dangers of climate change. There are many excellent books out there (pretty exhaustively referenced here if you want to access them) that will do that and scare your socks off.[18] This is a book that will, I hope, help you to get off your butt so you can kick some—starting with your nearest politician's. So, in the following chapters I will share with you—in the belief that stories are and always have been helpful signposts and guides from which we can find direction for ourselves too—some stories of why and how I have engaged with these issues, what has worked and what hasn't. Hopefully, in the process I will give you some ideas of how you too can engage—at whatever level you choose—in some of the defining issues of our age.

SITTING IN THIS CAFÉ, I am acutely aware that I am living a "before and after" moment—one of those moments in our personal and collective history when things change so dramatically that we define our lives in terms of "before" and "after." In history we describe eras as either BC and AD, or BCE and CE. In my personal history, the birth of my children divides my life into chapters. I frequently find myself referring to "before Forrest" or "after Quinn."

As an environmental activist, I've had several moments that changed what I do, how I do it and why. In the summer of 1993 I was twenty-four and sitting in an overcrowded courtroom in Victoria, British Columbia, anticipating the judge's verdict on the Clayoquot Sound demonstrations. Forty-four people were sitting on the benches, waiting to be sentenced, expecting that sentence to be community service hours for the crime of blockading the logging trucks in Canada's old-growth temperate rainforests, sometimes for barely ten minutes. Teenagers, moms, grandmas—a lot of grandmas—took part. We realized something strange was going on when dozens of uniformed sheriffs filed in and lined the walls.

Once the sheriffs entered, the judge started his sentencing. He would state a name, the person would stand, and he would decree the number of days the defendant was to serve in prison. As he said each name, a sheriff would handcuff the prisoner and take him or her out the back door. Everyone started crying. One young mother turned to me and said, "Oh my God, what am I going to do? Take care of my daughter."

As I sat there, stunned, and watched this scene play out, my lawyer came over and said, "The Crown is arguing for a jail sentence of six years for you."

Six years?

The government saw me as one of the leaders of the protests, and they were determined to make an example out of me.

I went outside the courthouse to catch my breath. Another lawyer I'd never met came over to me, still wearing his ceremonial robes, and said, "I just caught the tail end of that. Do you know what was happening in the courtroom next to you?"

I didn't. I was trying to handle both my own shock and the chaos of sudden responsibility for these people, their belongings and their kids.

He told me that next door a man who was arrested with a sawed-off shotgun, who'd confessed that he'd been walking around Victoria looking for young girls to kill, had been given no jail time. But in our courtroom, professors, tradespeople and grandmothers advocating for peace and public dialogue were being handcuffed and taken to prison.

I called my friend and fellow organizer, Valerie Langer, who was back in Tofino, a small town on the edge of the remote rainforests of Clayoquot Sound. "They're all going to jail. They're sending them all to jail. All the grandmothers, all the mothers."

As I babbled in shock, Valerie managed to make a horrific day even worse when she said, "The logging started again today."

Greenpeace Canada had just run a poll, and the stats showed that 86 percent of Canadians didn't support the logging of Clayoquot Sound.[19] We'd managed to get our message out: this old-growth rainforest on the west coast of Vancouver Island, one of the few intact temperate rainforests on our planet, mattered, and this logging shouldn't be allowed to happen. And now some of the leaders of our community were going to jail for trying to stop it.

Democracy was not working. Protesting was not working. Public awareness and outrage were simply not enough. We needed a new strategy. We had to find out who was buying all this wood, and stop them. That moment changed the way we fought for the forests. The "markets campaign" was born.

Not long after that event and its outcome, I joined Greenpeace International for the first time to learn everything I could about how to run an environmental campaign. I trained with the best campaigners in the world, and for the next ten years, worked to apply what I had learned to try to save Canada's ancient forests and help transform the marketplace so manufacturers and consumers would demand ecologically responsible wood and paper products. Along the way I helped create ForestEthics, another independent non-profit environmental organization, to do this work.

Over the past two decades, it's been an intense journey. I've fought some of the largest corporations anywhere and challenged heads of state on national television. I've chased Canada's leaders around the world as they tried to sell environmental disaster as economic progress. I've mingled with movie stars and rock stars and supermodels—something I'd never imagined happening to me—discussing the importance of going green. I've been vilified by some corporations, courted to share a stage with others and helped colleagues from many organizations pull together to negotiate "the world's biggest forest protection deal,"[20] the Canadian Boreal Forest Agreement, which has been described as a historic success story by some and a dangerous sellout by others.

Until about three or four years ago I thought I had figured out a pretty effective means to make positive change. We were making some headway on persuading companies to produce greener products, and governments around the world to protect more ancient forests. Of course, I was concerned about global warming, but it wasn't what I directly worked on. And then the reports started crossing my desk showing how much of the forests I had devoted my life to protecting were now being devastated by beetle infestations or fires—direct results of a warming climate.

In 2007 I was invited to the United Nations international climate negotiations in Bali to talk about the impacts of global warming on our forests and the impact logging was having on global warming. The conference brought together thirty thousand people from every country in the world. I delivered my speech, and then went to the opening of the climate negotiations. That's where the secretary-general of the United Nations, Ban Ki-moon, said something that spun my world around: "The situation is so desperately serious that any delay could push us past the tipping point, beyond which the ecological, financial and human costs would increase dramatically. We are at a crossroad. One path leads to a comprehensive climate change agreement, the other to oblivion. The choice is clear."

I was sitting there, taking notes, and I turned to the woman next to me and asked, "Did he just say 'oblivion'?"

It wasn't long ago that if, as an environmentalist, and especially as a woman, I used the word "crisis," I was called "hysterical." I've been called an "enemy of the state," an "eco-terrorist" and "a whacked-out nature worshipper who prays to the moon" for saying things that were nowhere near as extreme as what the secretary-general of the United Nations had just said. Oblivion?

Then something amazing happened. The woman beside me from the Congo Basin started keening—moaning and crying and rocking back and forth. There she was, in the middle of the negotiations for the international climate agreement, and then I got it: hers was the only sane response. In that moment I broke through my own denial about the threats posed by runaway climate change. I realized that it wasn't good enough for me to just read the scientific studies and the news reports—like that famous 2006 issue of *TIME* magazine that warned us to "Be Worried. Be Very Worried"—and depend on others to address our society's fossil-fuel addiction. I realized that even though I spent every day working on environmental issues, I had limited myself to working on forest issues. Yes, global warming was now affecting our forests, our water, our economy and even a stable climate, but someone else would deal with that. Wouldn't they?

Regardless of who we are, the realities of the climate era require us all to rethink how we spend our time and how we can engage in the energy debate. I realized I needed to stop relying on others to fix the problem and be willing to alter the issues I work on and how I work.

My shift to energy policy meant I wouldn't be focusing directly on the forest conservation work that had been so dear to my heart, and it is vital to do everything we can to protect what's left of our intact forests and to ensure that we create more ecologically responsible practices within the managed landscape; but for me, in that moment, the urgency of the impact of the carbon load in our atmosphere was moving me to start again on a long road of research, discovery and engagement. I began attending every scientific presentation on the impacts of global warming that I could. I immersed myself in the science, learning about both the physical effects of climate change and the moral implications. Every night in Bali, I would go back to my hotel room and cry. Then I would write a blog post, go to bed, get up and start again. In the blog posts I tried to share what I felt, express the urgency and move beyond keening for all we'd lost, and were continuing to lose, toward exploring what the hell we were supposed to do about it all.

I went to a panel on renewable energy. RSA Insurance Group, the largest insurance company in the world and based in the UK, said, "In one day, a small area of North Africa receives enough solar energy to feed human needs for energy for a year." In one day. Yet an hour later at the mayors' panel, the mayor of a town in Nairobi said, "We now have over a million people living in Nairobi slums, directly because of climate impacts today." Solutions are at hand but are not being applied, and the impact of our inaction is very real.

It will take all of us, doing what we can in our own lives, in our schools and at work, to make the changes we need to see in the world. There is no single action or silver bullet that will do the job. In fact, it will take a veritable ecosystem of activities, supporting each other, stronger as a result of our diversity, to make a shift as big as we need. The question for me at the time—and the question that should be on all our minds—is what's my role? What should I be doing at this critical moment in our history? Where or how, in whatever way, large or small, at home, in the office, in government, in our communities, can we help make a difference at this crucial juncture? That day in Bali I realized it was not okay for me to rely on others to try to save us from global warming, because fighting for forests without taking on climate change was like repainting the *Titanic* after hitting the iceberg.

—

WE ALL FACE CHALLENGES, big and small, on a daily basis—personal ones like illnesses and paying the bills; societal ones like the downturn in the economy that sees our hard-won savings diminish or vanish, or our nation's military policies that consume millions of dollars. Today we can't open a newspaper or turn on the TV without being bombarded with stories of melting glaciers, species extinction and toxic chemicals everywhere. But no matter how scary it sounds, for many of us the floods and firestorms are still happening somewhere else, to people we've never met, and they're just another image on TV. So what if the weather seems weirder and we all keep hearing that everything from tofu to tuna to water to the bottles we drink it out of are toxic?

When I was nursing Forrest the newspapers reported that if human breast milk had to be approved by the US Food and Drug Administration (FDA) it wouldn't be, because it's too polluted. We live so disconnected from nature and natural systems that it's almost impossible to believe or process this information warning us of impacts that are often invisible and seem unreal. We hear the news that 80 percent of the Amazon rainforest will be gone in forty years. We read the stories that say the majority of the earth's species are now under threat. Then we walk away from our computer to fill our kids' lunch boxes and take out the trash—and maybe the recycling and the compost, so we can do *something*—and live our regularly scheduled lives.

But our regularly scheduled lives are about to be interrupted, and we've got to act while we still have a chance to save those forests and animals so we can tell our children we did more than just pack their sandwiches in reusable containers. Change happens when there is enough of a public outcry, or the effects of a problem are so evident that decision makers are forced to act.

The 1987 Montreal protocol, which globally banned the harmful chemicals that were creating the hole in the ozone layer, happened in part because of successful global environmental campaigns, but it also passed because people were burning to death. Rates of skin cancer were skyrocketing, and in some countries like Australia parents were being warned to keep their children indoors. We could see the impacts in our daily lives.

This time we can't wait until we see the effects. In 2011, scientists discovered that the 2010 drought in the Amazon caused the death of billions of trees, and the forest that has long been considered the lungs of the planet may stop absorbing greenhouse gases and actually start creating them.[21]

The impacts we're already experiencing—from droughts in the Amazon and the Congo Basin to vulnerable islands in the South Pacific like Tebua Tarawa and Abanuea disappearing under sea rise—are the result of carbon trapped in our atmosphere twenty years ago. There's a time delay between the pollution we spew into the air and the impact it has on the earth. By the time many of us in the so-called developed world start seriously experiencing the effects of runaway climate change, it will be too late to stop it. So when the UN secretary-general declares the planet's current economic model a "global suicide pact," how do we figure out what we should be doing?[22]

CHANGE IS DIFFICULT, often painful, and so are real-world solutions, because they require compromises and co-operation. We don't want oil spills, but we also don't want wind farms. We don't want any logging, even though we still need wood for many things that we use every day. There are days I find myself under attack by the people whose values I share, and envying their moral high ground of "no."

I began to realize that it is simply not good enough to be clear about what you are against, you need to know what you support.

I can stand on a blockade or sit in a tree and say not one tree should fall and it's wrong to log—and as I do that we'll lose an acre of Canadian forest every sixty seconds. Or I can say that I value the protection of wilderness and I recognize that people have to work, and we need to redefine work and redefine industry in order to make it viable and protect nature, so what is the best way to do that?

Over the past few years, in negotiating with companies to make deals that have required compromise and often compassion on both sides, I've found that activists with little experience on the ground often attack the agreements. For myself, I always feel most comfortable taking a stance on an issue after I've immersed myself in the area under threat, whether walking through clear-cuts, visiting the tar sands or spending time in the boreal forest. I'm lucky to have had such opportunities. The quality of dialogue that comes through speaking from experience cannot be manufactured, as we all know. Once I've gained this experience, I realize that the path forward is almost always murky and never black and white. The tricky part is finding a way to advocate for the radical change necessary, while addressing the complexity of the problems and the economic and social impact, without compromising ecological values. Not an easy dance.

Throughout this journey, I've repeatedly tried to figure out how we, as a society, actually create social change and what we can and should do now and tomorrow. By offering some of my own battle stories, I hope to help throw light on your own journey.

Today we each have the responsibility and the capacity—as individuals, as groups, as members of organizations and our community—to hold the people in power to account, to expose them and to help make social change. Political careers can be destroyed with the click of a cellphone camera. A multi-million-dollar corporate ad campaign can be derailed with a YouTube video.

We have more tools and more communications opportunities as individuals than our governments had even two decades ago. On one of my first campaigns in the early nineties I was given a cellphone. It was as heavy as a brick and so big that it had its own briefcase. When I started this work, it was frequently about how many bodies you could get around your kitchen table. Today you can be sitting at your kitchen table and connecting to thousands, or hundreds of thousands, of people—and half the time I can't even find my cellphone because it's so damn small.

When I started getting involved in environmental issues, especially when we were fighting the big battles for the last of the old-growth forests, environmentalism was the purview of those with a soft spot for bears and big trees. Today's threats are no longer strictly *environmental* issues; they are economic issues, health issues, human rights issues. As I listen to my new colleagues at Greenpeace Africa talk about the hundreds of thousands of people dying from droughts and famines due to climate change, due to the pollution we have spewed into the atmosphere over the past hundred years or so, I realize that they are right—these issues are the moral challenge of our age.

That's why I had to take a leap off our cozy, quiet island (population 950), where everyone leaves the door unlocked and keys in the car and waves to every driver and cyclist and pedestrian on the street, and start a new life in this intense international hub in Amsterdam.

That's why I've written this book—because, regardless of our day-to-day responsibilities, we can all find ways to engage. If any of us feel we still have time on our hands at this critical moment in history, then we really are not doing enough. Becoming a martyr will result in your being ineffective (and unbearable), but you should give these challenges all you've got, before it's too late. I didn't always feel compelled to act, but the sense of urgency and opportunity has persuaded me to try. You don't have to commit your life and career to fighting these issues, but each of us can dedicate some ingenuity, some resources, some time. And we have to, because today we're all responsible not only for what we do but for what we don't do.

Our actions need to be commensurate with the true scale of today's challenges and today's opportunities. To "save the polar bears," as Quinn puts it, we ultimately have to shift development politics to ensure that countries like China, India and Brazil leap over the mistakes we made in North America and Europe, essentially bypassing the fossil-fuel era, while persuading developed countries to put a price on pollution that will stem the advance of new dirty energy infrastructure—like pipelines from the Canadian tar sands designed to keep the United States hooked on dirty oil. More often than not a cleaner and more sustainable path is possible if we can get greed out of the way and push our politicians to have some chutzpah.

For many politicians, all too often everything comes down to money and votes. We have the ability to control both. If we want politicians to act before the impact is so big that it's killing all of us, we need to show them they have the social licence to do the right thing and also that there will be political ramifications for not acting.

So as I sit at the café, canal boats drifting by, bicycles whizzing past me, I look at Quinn on my computer screen and tell him the only thing I can.

"No, honey. We haven't saved the polar bears yet, but we're working on it."

PART I **BLOC**

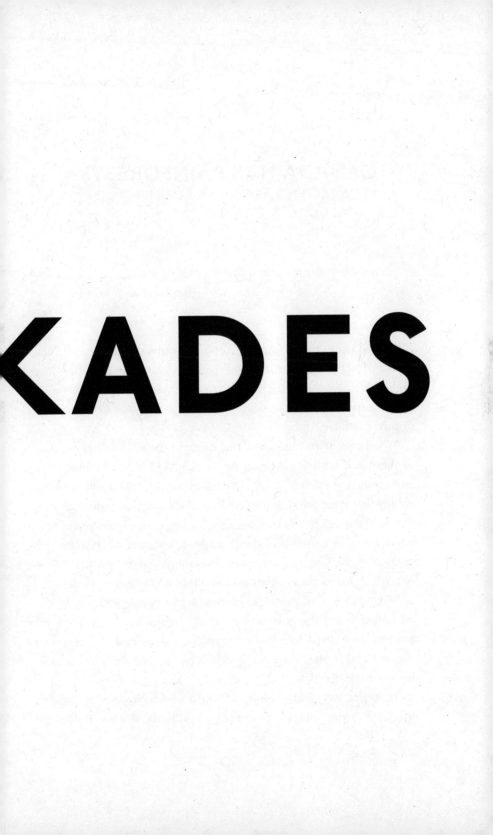

Chapter 1

CANADA HAS RAINFORESTS?
AWAKENING AS AN ENVIRONMENTALIST

In wildness is the preservation of the world.

HENRY DAVID THOREAU

I WAS BORN ON February 5, 1969, the same day a huge oil slick off the coast of Santa Barbara closed the city's harbour and, according to the *Los Angeles Times,* gave birth to the environmental movement. On January 28 there had been a blowout on Unocal Corporation's drilling platform Alpha.

"The blowout was the spark that brought the environmental issue to the nation's attention," said Arent Schuyler, lecturer emeritus in environmental studies at UC Santa Barbara. "People could see very vividly that their communities could bear the brunt of industrial accidents." The incident was credited with leading to the formation of new environmental groups and the passage of a variety of regional and national legislation, including the US National Environmental Policy Act, which led to the mandating of environmental impact studies.

"The spill caused many people to doubt the safety claims of the oil industry and the government," said Michael Paparian, state director of the Sierra Club. Environmental activism gained widespread support and in the two years after the oil spill, he said, Sierra Club membership doubled.

That was two years before the birth of Greenpeace. In writing this book during one of the next big oil spills, the *Deepwater Horizon* disaster in the Gulf of Mexico, I couldn't help wondering whether we would be able to harness this disaster for equally important changes.

I grew up in a conservative Jewish household in London, Ontario, a small city in Canada, built around a college and a university. Not only did we keep kosher and regularly attend synagogue services, but my parents were deeply committed to being part of the Jewish community. My dad, who owned a small advertising business, was involved with the local chapter of the B'nai B'rith, serving as president for many years. My mom, who worked alongside my dad and ran another company that made flags and pennants, had been president of Hadassah and B'nai B'rith. When I was in Grade 9, I was president of my United Synagogue Youth chapter. I had a close family and community, and though I didn't realize it then, my life was wonderful.

But when I was fourteen my dad died during a heart bypass operation. Less than two years later, my mom died of cancer. My oldest sister, Corinne, who was almost twenty-one, become our legal guardian a few months later. We continued to live in our family home, using life insurance policies to pay our bills. We'd hold family meetings to make key decisions on how to run the household. That was my first experience with working in a team and with negotiations.

My faith was shattered after my parents' death, and I turned away from the synagogue except in one area. I tried to honour my parents by going to the Or Shalom synagogue twice a day with my brother and sisters to say Kaddish, the mourner's prayer, but there often weren't enough men to form a *minyan,* the ten men necessary for public prayers to be said. Often there were only nine men, and despite the fact that my two sisters and I were there and had been bat mitzvahed, we still weren't allowed to say Kaddish. So that year I had my first exposure to campaigning and community decision making. A group of women and men in our synagogue had been lobbying to have women counted in the *minyan.* We joined the campaign, going door to door to talk to our neighbours. I believe that our story helped the cause, and we were able to convince the rabbi, cantor and synagogue board that change was necessary.

Despite this early campaign experience, when I graduated high school I saw my future in art and design. In 1989 I was studying

Fashion Arts Design at Ryerson in Toronto—cuts, patterns, styles, construction and composition. I finished my first year with honours. Canadian fashion maven Harry Rosen judged our final show and said I was "a bright light on Canada's fashion scene." I was thrilled, my life was set. Except . . .

I had grown up in a family with a strong social conscience. We were taught to think about our community, to volunteer, to give a part of our allowance to *tzedakah* (charity). And as I sashayed down the runway in one of my creations at the end-of-year show, I couldn't stop that niggling feeling that I was living in a pretty bubble and I was supposed to be doing something else.

I decided to take some time to think things through by backpacking around Europe for the summer with some friends. I was a typical twenty-year-old tourist, with a well-thumbed copy of *Let's Go Europe* in a backpack with the obligatory Canadian flag patch and just enough money from my part-time jobs as a cook at a vegan restaurant and a waitress at a not-so-vegan restaurant to afford to travel on a Eurail pass and stay in youth hostels. After I flew to England, saw the museums and visited the fashion districts in London, Edinburgh, Paris and Rome, I took the train to meet my sister Wendy in Athens. I've always been fascinated by art history, and I desperately wanted to see the Acropolis. I'd never imagined I'd have to see it through a thick cloud of smog.

That summer Greece had some of the worst air pollution of the modern era. The air in Athens was so thick, so toxic, that people were dying on the street. After we hiked up to the Acropolis, what struck me more than the magic of its history was how badly the walls were dissolving. One of the greatest landmarks of Western civilization was melting from the acid in the air.

When we got back to the hostel that night, I coughed up what seemed like a lungful of black goo. I stood in front of the mirror and ran a finger down my cheek, and it left a white line, showing a patch of my skin underneath the grime, as if I'd just emerged from a coal mine. I felt sick and filthy, and all I'd done was sightsee in one of the world's greatest cities.

Coming from Canada, I'd never experienced anything like this. Wendy and I both felt sick and depressed and decided to find some countryside, experience nature, go hiking for a few days. Since we both had Eurail passes, we randomly picked a place on the map and planned to explore the Harz mountains in Germany. We joked that we'd hike around in our lederhosen after drinking big steins of beer.

We took the train to the Harz mountains, dropped our stuff at the hostel, went out on our first day in nature and hiked for hours and hours and hours . . . through a standing dead forest. It was completely dead. Nothing alive. Finally we met an Austrian couple, asked what was wrong with the forest, and they showed us a plaque. Their translation: "This forest has been left standing as a testimony to the impacts of acid rain."

I was so horrified that when I returned home at the end of the summer, I dropped out of Ryerson's fashion programme and enrolled in environmental studies at the University of Toronto. It turned out that I loved academia. The lectures, the late nights buried in the stacks, surrounded by the surreal architecture of the Robarts Library with its mixture of organic design and concrete. I loved the afternoons spent debating issues with others in the programme who were clearly in the same throes of dawning ecological realization.

Coming to grips with the issues quickly led to trying to understand *why*, even when we know what we know about our impact on living systems, we don't change our ways.

FOR ME, environmental awareness has always been a bit like . . . toothpaste. Sometimes you squish too much out, but there is no way to get it back in the tube. There are so many times I've been kept up at night by the challenges facing our forests, our oceans, our atmosphere—and I'll lie awake, staring at the ceiling, wishing I could go back to a time when I didn't know. Once you have that environmental lens, you start to see everything through it whether you want to or not. You pick up your toothbrush and think, *Where did this plastic come from?* You look at your toothpaste and ask, *When the toothpaste is gone, am I just going to throw this metal in the garbage?* My trip to Europe smashed the toothpaste out of the tube for me, and it was the beginning of a dawning environmental awareness. I started to really notice the articles in the newspapers about species extinction, PCBs, toxins, acid rain, the hole in the ozone layer. It was as though these articles suddenly appeared from nowhere, and I had to confront the concerns expressed. As one of the grandfathers of the modern environmental movement, Aldo Leopold, poignantly wrote in *A Sand County Almanac*, "One of the penalties of an ecological education is that one lives alone in a world of wounds. . . . An ecologist must either harden his shell and make believe that the consequences of science are none of his business, or he must be the doctor who sees the marks of death in a community that believes itself well and does not want to be told otherwise."[1]

Slowly, throughout that year, it began to dawn on me that all these problems facing our planet aren't a bunch of disparate issues. We are living in a world in which we are divorced from the origins of what we use and create, and we blindly ignore where the cast-offs, the refuse and the garbage go. I remember standing by the garbage one day with a bunch of old batteries wondering, *Where do they go when we throw them away?* And it really hit me that, if everything is connected as an ecosystem, there is no "away."

I wanted to know how I could do my part before it was too late. With the drive, commitment and, I admit, the unbearable dogmatism of youth, I refused to get a car, I became vegetarian and (for a short period) I bought only used clothing. As part of my exploration of the issues and my place in relation to them, in 1991 I took an ecology class at the University of Toronto. One day my professor showed us slides of the Carmanah Valley in the Canadian temperate rainforest. I was stunned by the majesty of the forest, by the height of the Sitka spruce and the Douglas fir and the breadth of the old gnarled cedars clothed in rich green moss. I had heard of the Brazilian rainforests (between campaigns by stars like Sting and groups like the Rainforest Action Network [RAN] with their early attacks on companies like Burger King—who hadn't?), but I was shocked to discover that Canada had rainforests.

It seemed crazy to me, as a Canadian and now a self-identified environmentalist, that I knew so little about our forests. It seemed even crazier when I discovered that British Columbia held a quarter of the world's temperate rainforests, 70 percent of Canada's biodiversity, that some of the trees were over a thousand years old, and we were mowing them down like matchsticks.

So I stuffed my backpack, bought a plane ticket and, with a grand total of $200 in my pocket, flew to BC to visit the rainforests and see what I could do to help. The people who loved me, when they got over thinking I had lost my mind, thought it was "nice." The family consensus was "owls, bears, deer . . . saving the forests . . . that's such a nice thing for her to do on her break."

I knew no one in BC, so I stayed at the youth hostel near Jericho Beach, made my way down to the Western Canada Wilderness Committee (WCWC) office, walked in and said, "I want to volunteer in the rainforest. I cook. Sign me up!"

I was totally enamoured with the WCWC and that they were dedicated to raising awareness. I loved their strategy of building trails, doing scientific research and bringing politicians, journalists and people from all walks of life to see the thousand-year-old trees. The WCWC was doing research on marbled murrelets, a seabird they believed would be BC's answer to the spotted owl, an endangered species that would save a forest if its dependence on old-growth as habitat could be proven. After I'd spent days sitting in the office licking envelopes and doing any task given to me, the WCWC founder, the perpetually dishevelled Paul George, ambled out of his office and barked, "Is that girl still here? Somebody take her up to the camp."

Joe Foy, one of the WCWC leaders, was going up and offered to take me. He told me I could help cook and support the research teams. His truck arrived at the Upper Carmanah in the middle of a warm July night. There was no moon—you couldn't see a foot in front of you— and we didn't have flashlights. It was hot and dusty, and Joe said, "Just follow me." Fortunately he was wearing white runners, because they were all that kept me from losing sight of him and killing myself on the trail.

I followed Joe's runners but kept stumbling on sharp, jagged sticks that scraped my ankles and legs. The air felt hot, dusty and dry. Suddenly the air was cool and moist and smelled amazing. My first experience of the rainforest was in the dark.

I set up my tent in the dark, feeling around for a place to pitch it. When I woke up the next morning and crawled out, I discovered I was in the middle of a Sitka spruce grove in the Upper Carmanah, and some of the trees were over three hundred feet tall—the same height as a thirty-storey skyscraper—and six or seven hundred years old. At five foot eight, I didn't even reach up to the beginning of the root base on the tree next to me. Standing there staring up at these magnificent giants, I was struck by their size and the lush beauty and strength of this place. I felt an intense wave of awe. I also felt strangely peaceful and at home.

When I think back on it, I realize that this was the first time I really experienced a deep sense of spirituality. Until then I had equated spirituality with religion, and religion for me had, at best, been about history, heritage and community. It had been about requirements and, to a certain extent, morality and right and wrong. At its worst, it had been about rules that seemed out of date and arbitrary, restrictions that made me claustrophobic, and a sense of superiority and competition that I found offensive. I'll never forget that moment of crawling out of my tent and feeling so small and insignificant but amazingly alive. It was as if the earth was humming beneath my feet. I experienced nature with all my senses. I could see it in the ferns as high as my shoulders and the carpet of moss a foot deep. I could hear it in all the complex and varied sounds of the forest. I could smell the foliage and, as I was a city girl and an academic, this was the first time nature enveloped me. I don't think of myself as a spiritual person, but that depth of feeling, the awareness that I was a part of this living, breathing complex system would fuel my work for decades to come. My experience in this ancient rainforest valley on Vancouver Island that was threatened by imminent logging, my own recognition of how little I understood and appreciated the natural world and how complex and rich it is, drove me to try to understand its ecosystems and the impact we're having on them.

Most of us only ever appreciate nature in its component parts. We see the trees and their potential for timber; maybe we see the plants and their potential for medicine. We're starting to see other parts like water and carbon as having monetary value. But we fail to recognize inherent value, or, in fact, to see the whole. We fail to take into consideration the complexity of what we don't understand. And when we, as a society, don't understand something, we tend to undervalue it. We need trees for lumber and paper, so a monetary value is established. Will we have to wait until clean water is scarce for it to be counted in the balance sheets? A price on carbon might mean that we start associating a higher value with living systems that store carbon, like forests, but will we ever value biodiversity? Can we value what we don't truly understand?

Why does the marbled murrelet matter? Why should we care about the plight of the polar bears? Why should we pass environmental laws that will limit industry or cost jobs? We need to because the science of ecology tells us that affecting one component reverberates throughout the chain. We need to take a more pragmatic approach because if we continue to operate industry in a way that is simply unsustainable, jobs will dry up along with disappearing fish, forests and oil.

I remember how shocked I was when I found out that the health and size of the trees in BC's forests are dependent on how much salmon a bear eats. Scientists can look at the rings of trees and estimate the year's salmon runs because bears catch salmon in the river, eat them and then return to the woods and pee, releasing salmon- and marine-based nitrogen that contributes to the growth of the trees; during a particularly large salmon run, the rings will be thicker than in years with smaller runs. Logging right up to the streams leads to debris and siltation and less water flow, resulting in less salmon habitat and less food for the bears, which has a direct impact on the trees and the health of the forest as a whole.

The American biologist Walter Reid likens the different species on earth to the rivets in a plane. We don't actually know how many rivets can fail before the plane can no longer support us. As Edward O. Wilson wrote in *Biophilia*, "The one process now going on that will take millions of years to correct is the loss of genetic and species diversity by the destruction of natural habitats. This is the folly our descendants are least likely to forgive us."[2]

The majority of the world's intact forests are already gone, and so much of the remaining forests are threatened by industrial activity and climate change that we are facing the last of the wild.[3] With these last wild places goes a deep complexity and interconnectedness that supports life on earth.

I HIKED BACK OUT to the truck because we'd left most of our stuff there the night before, and I realized why the air had felt so different. As soon as I stepped out of the forest and into the clear-cut, I hit the dry heat like a wall. I'd read about how clear-cutting creates its own microclimate, but I hadn't imagined you could feel it. The actual look of the clear-cut was worse than I'd imagined. It was devastating: as far as the eye could see was a tattered landscape of massive stumps and endless piles of slash. I knew that some of these forests were being logged, but no one could have prepared me 'for the shock of what seemed like an endless sea of stumps and debris. Back then, logging companies were still burning the clear-cuts after they took all the trees, and what remained was a charred and devastated moonscape. It made the dead forest in Germany look vibrant.

According to the official government and forest industry propaganda, the clear-cut looked much worse than it was. The brochures and newspapers reassured anyone who cared to read them that those trees would grow back in a few years. But it wasn't long before I discovered that while trees would grow back, the diverse, lush rainforests would never return unless left alone for thousands of years, which wasn't in anyone's land-management plans. The government and logging industry in Canada and in many places around the world from Russia to the Amazon were involved in a massive conversion project, to transform complex ancient ecosystems into soulless industrial tree farms. This was the myth of the frontier in action. Settlers and resource extraction companies had steadily eaten their way through what they had assumed to be limitless resources. By the time I got to British Columbia, the lower forty-eight states had already lost all but 1 percent of their large tracts of original forest.[4] Two-thirds of the Canadian temperate rainforest had already been clear-cut or fragmented.[5]

In fact, it wasn't until 1997 that anyone really got a handle on the scale of the problem. Researchers at the World Resources Institute in Washington, DC, painstakingly mapped forests and crunched numbers to discover that only 22 percent of the world's original forests remained intact in areas large enough to sustain the web of life. Seventy percent of what did remain was found in just three countries: Canada, Brazil and Russia. Eighty-seven countries had lost all or almost all their intact forests. It turned out that Canada really was the "Amazon of the North" in more ways than one. The boreal and temperate rainforests of Canada were of crucial global importance.[6] For years these statistics gave me a deep sense of urgency as well as a recognition of the systemic nature of the problem that requires us to think outside of any one area-specific battle.

I SPENT THE SUMMER of 1991 in the Carmanah and Walbran Valleys, cooking, constructing trails, building boardwalks and helping researchers find evidence that the area was home to the marbled murrelet. When a documentary crew came out to film the conservation efforts, I was the sound girl and held the boom. That summer we camped beneath a canopy of nine-hundred-year-old trees, and often in the early morning or late afternoon, sore after the day's work, we would swim in a deep blue pool at the bottom of a steep waterfall. I thought I had found my calling. I would become a scientist, and my research would prove that we should protect more forests and change logging practices. While I knew it would be hard work, it seemed simple, clear and satisfying.

Late that summer, after countless hours of sitting perfectly still at dawn and dusk charting the calls of the murrelets and then searching the canopy in our targeting areas, we found a marbled murrelet nest on the branch of an ancient Sitka spruce. The nest proved that these forests were essential to the murrelets' survival. These amazing birds were flying twenty to forty miles a day back and forth from the ocean, where they feed, to nest in the old-growth forests. We were overjoyed that our scientific research might help save this forest. The scientists at the University of Victoria would write up our findings. The WCWC would lobby the government. We fully believed that we had saved the valley. It was a glorious summer, and I had completely fallen in love with that rainforest.

I went back to school and began debating whether to continue with environmental studies, teach, go into sciences or pursue an environmental law degree. Either way, I knew I wanted to help protect these forests. Back in Toronto, I organized fundraisers to raise money for more research and produced campus radio shows to heighten awareness. During the year, I heard from my colleagues that the government and industry had received the data. Practices would change. But I was warned that it looked like logging in some areas would continue.

The next summer I came back to the coast and contacted the researchers to see what I could bring to the camp. They told me they desperately needed a truck, some more supplies and volunteers. I convinced a few friends to come along, bought a used truck with the money I had raised and we headed back to the camp. After arriving on Vancouver Island, we got an early start and set off for the Walbran Valley to hike and swim in my favourite spot before going to the research camp. We drove for hours on the logging roads trying to find the trailhead. I was just about to give up and admit to my friends that we were horribly lost when things started to feel eerily familiar. We parked the truck at the end of a new road in a fresh clear-cut. It took me a couple of minutes to get my bearings, but I soon realized we were standing in the ancient Sitka grove that I had known so well from the summer before. I found the waterfall. It was now just a trickle of water beside a dusty logging road. In horror I realized we were not far from where we had found the nest. I took off at a run and seconds later sighted a couple of trees left standing in the middle of the carnage. In a pattern I would see repeated a hundred times in the years to come, the whole area had been cleared, leaving only a tiny patch of forest around the tree where we had found the nest. There were no murrelets.

I was furious.

This wasn't supposed to happen. We'd found the nests, we'd done our job, the forest was still supposed to be here.

This moment was seminal in my journey as an activist. Until that point I had faith that with the right research we could save these forests. That day I realized that science, in and of itself, was often too slow to effect social change, and having the facts on your side simply wasn't enough. This was crudely illustrated to me later when I met with one environment minister to argue for the protection of these rainforests and he bluntly replied, "What's in it for me?"

It was simply not enough to prove that the logging would have negative ecological consequences, or even that it would do irreversible harm to threatened species. We had to prove that protecting the forests would have benefits to the decision makers or that inaction would have negative consequences—real or perceived impacts on economic revenue, reputation or votes. Even though we could prove scientifically that this area was important, that information wasn't enough to save the forest. As I stood in the clear-cut, I felt fear, anger and a deep sense of loss. I heard a shriek, looked up and saw two eagles circling above and screaming. For years afterwards, that day, and those eagles, haunted my dreams. And throughout the coming years I learned that politics, short-term economics and greed usually trump science.

THE NEXT DAY a van pulled up to the Carmanah camp full of young backpackers bound for Tofino to join the local community blockading the logging road in Clayoquot Sound. After years of participating in failed land-use planning processes, letter-writing campaigns and government lobbying, many locals were fed up with the extensive logging taking place all around them and had decided to take a stand. Word was spreading up and down the island. Their campaign seemed so simple. So direct. The work I had planned to do seemed to pale in comparison to their direct action. Why build trails through a shrinking forest? Why conduct more studies that didn't seem to matter? They invited me to join them. I grabbed my backpack, said goodbye to my colleagues and jumped in the van.

I had never been to a protest in my life. Participating in logging blockades and potentially being arrested was not part of my life plan. I was mildly terrified, but I knew that the system had to change and what I had been doing so far was too slow.

When I arrived in Clayoquot Sound at the blockade camp on the Kennedy Lake Bridge I saw a sign posted that made me feel a bit more comfortable with what I was walking into:

> Our attitude is one of openness, friendliness and respect toward all beings we encounter.
> We will use no violence, verbal or physical, toward any being.
> We will not damage any property and will discourage others from doing so.
> We will strive for an atmosphere of calm and dignity.
> We will carry no weapons.
> We will not bring or use alcohol and drugs.

These people were serious and organized. It was not some dangerous, flaky hippie camp. The first person I met was a community doctor; then I met a schoolteacher, a kayak instructor, a restaurant owner. All of them had come together to raise awareness. To try to stop the logging of one of the largest intact rainforests left on Vancouver Island and one of the most beautiful places on earth, Clayoquot Sound.

Clayoquot Sound is sometimes called "the end of the road" because it really is: if you drive west across the Trans-Canada Highway, when your car drops off the First Street dock in Tofino and into the Pacific Ocean, you're in Clayoquot Sound. Next stop is Japan. This outer coast of Vancouver Island is an awe-inspiring place. Storms rage inland from the Pacific, dumping well over ten feet of rain each year—hence the rainforests. Clayoquot Sound itself is a labyrinth: islands, inlets and mountains surging from the sea. It is rugged, remote terrain (Tofino is known locally as "Tough City") and that's what had kept it fairly intact. Now that the old-growth forests that were easier to access and to log had been cleared, industrial logging had arrived in Tofino.

Actually the frontier had been arriving in fits and starts for some time. In 1984 the Nuu-chah-nulth First Nations had mounted the first logging blockade in Canada to protect Meares Island, 90 percent of which had been slated for logging. The Nuu-chah-nulth declared it a Tribal Park and won a court injunction to stop the logging. Over the following years, the Nuu-chah-nulth and non-native supporters fought a series of battles until 1993, when the BC government tried to settle the controversy with one of the biggest miscalculations in Canadian environmental history. The Clayoquot Sound Land Use Decision protected one-third of the area, allowing logging in the remaining two-thirds.

That summer I stayed in the background, trying to support the people blockading and learning everything I could. I cooked and carried water, volunteered to pick up supplies and registered for every training programme that the experienced locals had to offer. I didn't know anyone in Clayoquot. One of the backpackers in the van knew some of the people on the original *Sea Shepherd*—the anti-whaling boat run by Paul Watson, an early Greenpeacer—which was anchored in Ucluelet.

In less than two months I'd gone from being an academic who had never been to a protest to hanging out with protesters from the Friends of Clayoquot Sound (the Friends) and the proudly radical Sea Shepherd Conservation Society. I was living and breathing what later became known around the world as "the war in the woods."

This whole period was, for me, an exploration of how change is made, what my role was in it and what it could be. I wanted to figure out how I could help. If you read the newspapers at the time, it sounded as if the protesters were all a bunch of disgruntled hippies, but these were nurses and doctors and teachers and professors who had tried to follow the rules, who'd tried participating in process after process and study after study. They'd written letters to politicians and newspapers and lobbied governments. They'd done all the things you were supposed to do to change public policies. When the logging wouldn't stop, they finally tried civil disobedience in a very Gandhian way. They weren't putting sand in the gas tanks of logging machinery, or chaining themselves to the bridge; they were simply standing on the road, arms linked, peacefully placing themselves between the rainforest and the machinery.

One day someone came by the outdoor kitchen I was helping in to tell us that the main organizing group, the Friends, were having a strategy meeting in town and we were invited. I'd been living either on the old *Sea Shepherd* or out at the Kennedy Lake Bridge on the blockades site, and hadn't gone to one of their meetings before. I was curious about how these people organized themselves, what it looked like behind the scenes of the blockade and how decisions were made, so I hitched a ride to the office.

We arrived a half-hour later. In a dank basement office, I found a motley crew that seemed to have little in common except a shared love of the rainforest and a strong sense of purpose. There were the doctor and the kayak instructor I had met at the blockade, a grade-school teacher, a mom, an oyster farmer, students, hippies with dreadlocks and drums, and a woman who would become my friend, confidante and mentor, Valerie Langer—a curly-haired linguistics major in perfectly pressed jeans and shirt. Partway through the meeting, all I could think about was something I'd heard on CBC Radio once about how strange the people are in BC because it's west of the Rockies and all the nuts roll downhill.

The conversation veered like a car driven by a toddler. We'd circle around to an issue that seemed useful to address, and just when we were getting somewhere, someone would toss in a random philosophical thought or an offbeat idea and we would "lose the plot," as my Aussie friends like to say. Or worse, someone would go on an angry rant about a particular area that was being logged, and someone else would see this as an opportunity to let loose a tirade. About an hour into the meeting, just as I was thinking about the best way to escape, Valerie quietly stepped in. Without seeming as if she was taking over, she said, "Let's just pull this apart. What agenda items do we need to address today?" And "I haven't heard you talk much—what are you thinking?" Valerie's about five foot six, but for almost ten years I thought she was taller than I am because she has such presence, leadership and grace.

Valerie was so organized and inclusive that within an hour she'd walked us through all the things that needed to be discussed. Plans and decisions were made, and it still felt like a conversation. She was diplomacy in motion. She steered people away from anger and transformed a bunch of scattered ideas into a strategy. This was a woman I could learn from.

That night I started reflecting on the different roles people need to take to do this kind of work. When you think about environmental campaigns, you might picture people swinging off bridges, blockading roads, or the David Suzukis and Al Gores of the world who make the big speeches, but there are thousands of people behind the scenes who are incredibly good at facilitating meetings, or writing strategy plans, or cooking, or fundraising. They all contribute to this work, and they're all vital.

I went home at the end of the summer inspired by the people I had met but still puzzled by my place in all of it. I applied to do my master's in environmental studies at York University and took a job as a teaching assistant. Teaching students about the issues seemed like a safe and productive choice. But the more I talked to Valerie and others on the phone that year from my home base at the ivory tower, the more I felt as though I was running in front of a bulldozer. And the more research I did about the speed at which we were losing our forests in Canada and around the world, the faster the bulldozer seemed to be moving. I knew I couldn't save the whole world, but maybe I could have some impact on my tiny pocket of the world. I decided to write my thesis about Clayoquot Sound.

I started seriously researching how social change is made, how you campaign and what you need to do the job. I read the stories about Judi Bari and the Redwood Summer protests in California, and Lois Gibbs fighting against pollution in Love Canal. I learned about Petra Kelly taking the Green Party in Germany from scraps to becoming the world's first Green member of parliament. I started studying the speeches of Martin Luther King and the suffragettes and trying to understand successful social movements. Very early on, I began to see similarities between these movements and campaigns and which aspects of their campaigns were critical to success. While all the movements were, to a certain extent, fuelled by outrage and had clear "bad guys" or targeted decision makers to campaign against, they also painted a vision of the world they wanted to create: from a society in which all people were treated equally and could exercise their right to vote, to a world in which our kids could drink the water without fear of illness. These campaigns encouraged participation by proposing an alternative that was worth fighting for. In contrast, many of the environmental campaigns I was watching and participating in were fuelled by outrage but rarely, if ever, articulated a clear pathway forward.

Near the end of my school term, in May 1993, I got a call from Val. She was really upset. "The provincial government just made an announcement to allow logging in the majority of Clayoquot Sound. Most of us can't go back to the Kennedy Lake Bridge because of our bail conditions, and we need help." She tried to persuade me to ditch my studies and come back to assist in the protest. In order to avoid jail, most of the protesters had signed agreements not to go within one kilometre of the bridge. I made plans to rent a little cabin in Tofino, volunteer for the Friends, and work on my master's thesis. I packed three boxes of research books, spent the majority of my savings on my first laptop and headed back to BC.

Chapter 2

THE BLACK HOLE
SETTING UP CAMP IN CLAYOQUOT SOUND

*The best and brightest will go to the blockades this summer.
My heart will go with them.*

CLAYTON RUBY, CRIMINAL DEFENCE LAWYER AND
MEMBER OF THE ORDER OF CANADA

IN MAY 1993 I arrived in Clayoquot Sound and rented a cabin off
the main highway. I was trying to split my time between writing
my thesis and finding ways to help the Friends of Clayoquot Sound.
Neither plan was working very well. I couldn't concentrate on my
thesis because of the stress, intrigue and feeling of doom in the
community. Rumours flew around the Common Loaf Bakery about
logging crews seen throughout the Sound. There was a feeling of des-
peration and exhaustion in the Friends' office in a rented basement
room near the First Street dock. Tension ran high on the street, and
debates and arguments flared up everywhere, from the lineup at the
one bank to the aisles in the one grocery store.

Early that summer, the Friends had to vacate their little rented office
when the building was sold. We moved into Valerie's house, which was
six hundred square feet with two loft bedrooms under a sloping ceiling,
so you could stand up at only one end. But it was equipped with the
most high-tech communications device of the early '90s: a fax machine.

I started spending more and more time there trying to help. One
day, in frustration, I cornered Valerie and asked her outright, "What

does it mean to campaign? What do you mean when you say you're a campaigner? How do you 'campaign' to protect Clayoquot Sound? What am I supposed to be doing?"

Valerie is a no-nonsense, practical sort of woman, and she just looked at me unfazed and said, "Do you garden?"

The next day, while hoeing and pulling weeds, Valerie began to tell me stories about what she and others had done over the years to raise awareness and how it's all really about creating a dialogue. "You're creating a dialogue within the community. You're creating a dialogue with decision makers."

Valerie had come to Tofino in 1988 for a vacation and never left. As one of the spokespeople for the Friends, she participated in land-use planning processes, lobbied local and provincial governments, organized sit-ins, rallies and blockades and, on one memorable occasion, took the full bear carcass remains left by trophy hunters (skinned, de-pawed and beheaded) down to the legislative buildings in Victoria and demanded to see the minister of environment to ban trophy hunting. She talked about various projects she'd worked on, ideas she'd had and protests she'd participated in. She'd been arrested multiple times (once while sitting on a post cantilevered far out over the water from a logging bridge), and through her stories she began to paint a picture of all the diverse strategies and pieces that go into creating a campaign.

Valerie was practical, inspiring, full of ideas and fearless. There had been a hundred people on the blockade the previous year. Now the government had made a decision to allow logging in the majority of this rainforest, and it was a major news story. The more she talked, the more certain I became that we would have no problem raising awareness that summer. Valerie wasn't so sure. She told me about calling a reporter the year before about all the protests and his response was, "Yeah, yeah, protests. Call us when somebody dies." She told me how difficult it was to get press and that you need an outrageous idea or huge numbers of people.

Not long after that I sat in on one of the first strategy meetings to plan for the summer of '93. There were maybe six of us sitting around Val's living room. Someone said, "If we get two hundred people to come to Clayoquot Sound, we'd have a story." We started talking about how we could build interest without having someone die. It became clearer to us that for this stage in our work we needed to think like storytellers. We needed to create a narrative to frame our work, to engage people, to capture interest and focus attention.

So that was our goal. We were going to get two hundred people to come to Clayoquot Sound. We were dreaming big.

AS PART OF THEIR celebration of the province's 150th anniversary in 2008, the Royal British Columbia Museum named "Clayoquot Summer 1993" one of the most significant events in the province's history. It was the largest demonstration of peaceful civil disobedience in Canada's history,[1] and a sea change for environmental issues in Canada. The Clayoquot Sound Land Use Decision set aside only 33 percent of 650,000 acres of the world's largest intact lowland coastal temperate rainforest—an area with greater biomass, or organic matter, than any other ecosystem on earth. This was a place with thousand-year-old red cedars and 250-foot Douglas firs that provided habitat for species as diverse as the black bear, cougar, wolf, bald eagle, marbled murrelet, orca, grey whale and some of the rarest sharks in the world. The land the government chose to "protect" was the land the logging companies didn't want, in large part the high alpine reaches, the rock and ice. Adding insult to injury, the government designated some areas of the forest "scenic corridors" and others "special management zones." Over the years scenic corridors have proven to be thin strips of trees left along the water while the mountains are stripped clean, so tourists in cars and boats would see the environmental equivalent of a Hollywood facade. "Special management zones" appeared to be another term for "modified landscapes," a.k.a. clear-cuts.

The media touted the government's 1993 Clayoquot Sound Land Use Decision as a wonderful compromise. I'm not sure how industry could have seen this as anything other than both a clear-cut victory and a victory for clear-cutting. Before the great Clayoquot Sound compromise, the industry was allowed to cut almost 900,000 cubic metres (1,177,155 cubic yards) of rainforest a year. After the decision they were allowed to log 600,000 cubic metres (784,770 cubic yards) a year, which was still completely unsustainable, and if they'd logged their maximum, there would be no intact valleys left.

The Clayoquot Sound Land Use Decision became a flashpoint in Canada and around the world. In the fall, after the protest camp wound down and I joined Greenpeace, we did polling that showed that only 14 percent of Canadians supported the decision to allow logging in Clayoquot Sound. Our first ad in the *Globe and Mail*, Canada's largest newspaper, read: "Fourteen percent of Canadians support the logging in Clayoquot Sound. Seventeen percent still think Elvis is alive."

WE DESIGNED THE CAMP and the protest to be as inclusive as possible. There is a place for high-profile expert actions, like Greenpeace teams occupying deepwater oil rigs or scaling parliament buildings, but that summer our goal was to engage as many people as possible to show the government that they did not have support for the decision they'd made.

We realized that if we wanted people to protest with us, we had to educate them about the issues and give them reasons to want to come. We had access to really experienced activists, including community leaders who had blockaded in Clayoquot the year before, and others who came to us from campaigns in Northern California to protect the redwood forests. Some had experience from the Civil Rights protests in the southern US in the early sixties, and others had protested against the Vietnam War (there is, in fact, an interesting community of draft dodgers who live in remote areas on the west coast of Canada). We thought that we'd increase attendance if we set up training sessions on the rainforest, media skills and non-violent peaceful direct action from people who had been on blockades.

We arranged to hold a training session on tiny Clayoquot Island, which you can see from the Main Street dock in Tofino. My job was to help set up the training and deal with the logistics of how we'd feed people, get the right trainers and advertise the events. In the beginning I was worried that our plan was not enough. I had started to see multiple entry points to the issues and had a million ideas on how to engage. It was Valerie who kept me focused and who taught me that good organizing is built one task, one idea, one event at a time. Although "just dig in and start somewhere and focus your efforts" is a great lesson, I realize now that while it's true, single events are far more powerful if they're part of a larger strategy. At the time I don't think any of us understood how the blockades fitted into a wider political plan. We were simply desperate to create the biggest protests we could in order to convince government and industry that the logging was too controversial to continue.

We started by sending faxes to environmental groups across the province. We expected a hundred people to respond.

More than 250 showed up in Clayoquot Sound for our training.

They all had to be ferried back and forth to Clayoquot Island. Since we had expected fewer than a hundred people, things started to get a little crazy as more and more buses and cars pulled up. We arranged additional boats and supplies on the fly. The situation became pretty confusing pretty quickly. At some point on the first day, I found myself on the dock moving groups of people around like a traffic cop. "We need this boat to go there, and we need this person there, and if you're doing this training and you have this many people interested in it, you're going to have to take that space that we set up and . . ."

The training was a huge success. It motivated and empowered hundreds of people who then went back to their own communities and started spreading the word. That led to a flow of people into this remote rainforest wilderness and tiny tourist village, as well as a flood of calls from people interested in volunteering. We quickly realized that we could build on the interest and harness some of the attention in the big cities by replicating the training we'd held in the Sound, so we set up a free civil disobedience and rainforest ecology training workshop in the middle of Vancouver's iconic Stanley Park. For this training workshop, which was free to the public, we also invited news cameras, and that's how we started to seed the story that activists were organizing to blockade the logging and oppose the government decision. Hundreds of people came to the Stanley Park session, and several offered to organize busloads of people from their communities to support our protests that summer.

Back in Clayoquot Sound, our little steering committee made plans to set up a permanent protest camp that could offer training every day, engage volunteers and eventually coordinate actual logging blockades. After much discussion, we chose to locate the camp away from the logging roads and active logging for safety reasons, and instead set up the camp in a very public and open spot. Then someone suggested that if we were going to create a camp, we should put it in the middle of a clear-cut, where people would be reminded daily of why we were there. That's how the camp ended up in "the black hole": a horrible burned-out clear-cut on the side of the highway.

One day back at the office my friend Garth Lenz (an incredible photographer now known around the world for his powerful work documenting endangered places) suggested faxing every tree-planting company in the province to look for people willing to stand at the blockades. Garth and I stood over the fax machine, dialling the fax number for each tree-planting company, feeding the paper in, dialling again, feeding the paper again and sending a fax to every camp in BC, inviting all the planters to come and help us protect the rainforest. We wrote, "We promise fresh organic vegetarian food, training and an experience of a lifetime." That was it.

About that time I met Karen Mahon, a thirtyish woman with soft grey eyes the size of saucers. Her small stature belied the fact that she was one tough cookie and whip smart to boot. Karen was running Greenpeace's forests campaign. Prior to meeting her, my impression of Greenpeace, largely formed by the media, was that it was very radical and all about direct action related to nukes and whales. The thing that struck me about Karen was the level of sophisticated analysis that she brought to the issues and the way she thought about strategy. Until that point the Friends had spent most of their time discussing tactics or publicity. What Karen brought to the table was an understanding of the need for a strategy behind those tactics and how to truly leverage public awareness and power in order to engage decision makers. That was my introduction to what Greenpeace really is: a group of highly sophisticated thinkers with an enormous network around the world that does in-depth analysis of the issues and can work both inside and outside the system. Yes, Greenpeace has the climbers who swing off oil rigs and activists who chain themselves to logging trucks, but they also have some of the world's best campaign strategists and government lobbyists.

Karen was always looking to up the ante. Every time there was a good idea such as "Let's fax all the tree-planting camps in the province," she'd try to find a way to top it. "Great, let's also contact every other environmental group in BC and start building a coalition. This is not something a few of us are going to win on our own. And we don't need to."

When we had the idea of doing the civil disobedience training camp in the Sound, it was Karen who suggested we set up the session in Stanley Park where the media couldn't ignore it. She taught me that you can spend the same number of hours working on something small as you can working on something really big.

As I was to discover many times over the years, not all environmentalists agree on tactics and strategies. While we were teaching people the art of peaceful protest, Paul Watson arrived in Clayoquot Sound and declared that the best way to get the logging to stop was to spike the trees and start destroying property. One of the Friends' leaders, Mike Mullin, agreed with Watson's approach. Mike had been living in Clayoquot for close to twenty years. He'd participated in land-use planning, process after process, discussion after debate after study, and while everyone discussed, debated and studied, he'd seen the forest disappear all around him.

I was sleeping on Val's floor and the fax machine was on the desk above my head, so when faxes would come in at all hours of the night they'd fall down on me in my sleeping bag. One night the phone rang, and it was Mike. I could hear his voice echo through the fax phone, and he sounded really weird.

He said, "Val, I forgot to do this, but I needed to call and tell you that I'm resigning from the board of the Friends of Clayoquot Sound."

Valerie grabbed the phone. "Mike? Where are you?"

He said, "Well . . . this is my one call." And he hung up.

He'd just been arrested for trying to torch the Clayoquot River logging bridge. The bridge didn't completely burn down, but the security guard caught Mike.

I understood the frustration behind Mike's action, even though it went against the principles of the Friends. He was tired of watching the destruction occurring around him, in his home. The scale of the problem seemed to call for radical action. That said, the attempted bridge burning did not stop the logging. My experience is that in a world obsessed with property and consumer goods, destroying property is seen as violent and doesn't help draw people into the fight. Part of what drew me to the Friends was their commitment to ensure that all our work was peaceful and accessible, that while we often confront the problem by putting ourselves between the forest and the bulldozers, or on the drill ship, there was a commitment not to destroy property and to ensure safety. The bridge burning really brought this question—whether to push forward with Gandhian passive resistance or to employ more radical tactics—to the fore. It became a big issue of debate in the community, raising the stakes and pressure for us to prove that our strategy of peaceful direct action would have an impact.

AT THE END OF JUNE a small group of us finally arrived at the Black Hole with our pickup truck. We had shovels and big plans. We hung a banner declaring the camp in the clear-cut the "Clayoquot Peace Camp" and began to set up tents and a makeshift kitchen.

I was charged with staying at the front under the banner and dealing with anyone who came by—volunteers, police or loggers. I was nervous and felt a strange mix of defiance, pride and awkwardness.

The first vehicle to turn up with a crew to help us that summer was a dusty green van with two guys in it. They pulled up, and one of them got out. I am rarely shy or speechless, but the first time I saw Chris Hatch he took my breath away. He was tanned and muscular with sparkling green eyes and shoulder-length brown hair. We introduced ourselves, and he told me a funny story about trying to find the camp and being chased by a logging truck near the bridge. As we were laughing, our eyes met and I caught my breath again, covering it up with a cough. He asked what they could do to help, and all I could think to tell him was that back in the camp they needed help digging latrines. Years later Chris told me that after he got back in his van, his friend Peter turned to him and said, "You are going to marry that girl."

One morning, one of the earliest self-dubbed Raging Grannies, Jean McLaren, arrived at the blockade camp with bracelets jangling and eyes flashing. She was a maternal force of nature. That first morning, she sat on a stump in the middle of the road and serenely waited for the logging trucks to arrive. She treated the RCMP and the other protesters with equal respect, openness and humour. With a toss of her grey curls, she introduced herself as "Mother Earth" and explained to all of us that she was there to make sure everyone was respecting and taking care of one another.

That day was the beginning of a long journey where theory met action. I began to truly understand the power of knowledge, self-respect and wisdom, and just how blurry the lines are between environmental and social activism. I had studied social movements and feminist theory the previous year in university, and I was drawn to the idea that how we treat each other and how we function as "community" will be reflected in the outcomes we achieve and in how we treat the natural world. That said, good process, research, patience, respect, engagement and equity are time-consuming and difficult. I have often struggled with a sense of urgency and a need to just push an issue forward, take charge or even do it myself rather than take the time to plan and to empower a team of people to act together. I now understand that Jean was, in her own beautiful hippie-grandmother way, introducing me to principles of good process and relationship building that I would later find echoed in professional management trainings. That summer at the camp, Jean's patience, respect for all the players in the debate, and commitment to listening and engaging would play a big role in ensuring that we were successful in building a strong protest community that effectively communicated urgency on the issues through collective action and avoided violence.

Jean stayed at the camp for four months, getting up every morning to go to the blockade. She had trained with the women from Greenham

Common in England and she'd been part of the Civil Rights Movement in America. She taught us how to engage in non-violent protests and civil disobedience. She would do training sessions all day long, back to back. She must have trained thousands of people that summer. New people would come in and Jean would run full workshops on how to be a peacekeeper, how to engage in non-violent communication, how to peacefully calm violent situations, and the legal issues associated with civil disobedience.

As I welcomed more and more people to the blockades, I knew I wanted to be more involved in the blockades themselves. I called Greg McDade, executive director of the Sierra Legal Defense Fund, and told him who I was, that I was applying to law school to do a joint master's thesis at York, and that I was concerned about getting arrested on the blockades. He warned me that if I was arrested and came away with a criminal record, I would lose any chance of becoming a lawyer. But Greg and I had a great conversation about the role of law, and I realized that law, like academia, wasn't for me. It was too frustrating and too slow, and this direct action seemed so much more effective and satisfying. I wasn't planning to get arrested—we couldn't afford to have any more organizers arrested and banned from the area (as many, like Garth Lenz, had been the year before)—so I decided to pick up a bullhorn.

A few weeks later, after the crowds had started streaming in, a classic Volkswagen hippie van arrived with just one guy in it. That night at the campfire meeting someone came to me and said, "That new guy . . . Everything in his van still had the price tags on. Even his water bottle." We all shared the same uneasy feeling about him, but you can't kick someone out of a volunteer camp because he seems weird and all his stuff is new. We were debating how to deal with him the following night when a woman came up to us and said, "That van out there was my mother's. I'm sure of it because she cut up my old bedroom curtains to sew the little ones in the van's back windows."

I said, "Yeah, so?"

And she said, "A couple of days ago she had it listed for sale and the police bought it."

So a few of us, including Val, Chris and I, confronted our suspicious protester. He feebly denied the accusations for a couple of minutes and then, with a sheepish look, got into the van and drove away.

But while the police were interested enough to spy on us, we still couldn't get the media excited about covering another summer of blockades. Then we had the idea to send an anonymous fax to all the newspapers, TV and radio stations to build a sense that something secretive and exciting was happening. We figured out how to take the header off the fax machine so no one would know where our faxes were coming from. Our note read: "Clayoquot Blockades will start July 1st." That's all. That night, at the Friends office, we watched the news anchor on CBC national news hold up the fax and read it to his viewers. Cheers and high-fives broke out in the office. We had created a sense of drama. In the next few days, media speculation about who had sent the fax and what the blockades would be like were rampant in the local media. We had begun to create a narrative: a story people can follow.

I discovered a few key things that day, including the importance of playing into an existing dialogue. That's a central lesson for campaigns. If you come out of nowhere, and people have no context for your story and don't understand the issue, it's not going to make the news. But if you play into existing news, you're feeding the machine and giving the media what they need. The government's decision to allow the majority of the region to be logged had been covered extensively in the news. Our training sessions had built the story of the decision being controversial. The anonymous fax sparked more interest. We'd gone from a protest to a campaign. Thanks to the faxes, we were building a narrative through the media, and building the anticipation.

To develop a campaign you have to be creative. You have to come up with ideas like faxing tree planters or developing risky ads. We brainstormed as many ideas as we could and then tried to figure out which ones we had the resources for and what we could do. What ends up really working is marrying some of those wild ideas with a realistic assessment of your capacity and reach in order to prioritize what to do when. Having a group of people you trust and like to work with doesn't hurt, either. What ends up working in any campaign is, essentially, tossing a lot of spaghetti at the wall and seeing what sticks, and we kicked off the campaign with some pretty sticky spaghetti.

ON CANADA DAY, we launched the blockades with about a hundred people standing in front of the bridge, including a Canadian member of Parliament, Svend Robinson, and a member of the European Parliament, Paul Staes. Spirits were pretty high among the protesters at dawn, but as the logging trucks approached, people grew nervous. So I picked up the bullhorn and just started talking, asking people who did not want to risk arrest to get off the road, talking about why we were there, what was at stake. On instinct I led everyone in a song Jean McLaren had taught us by the campfire. "Growing inside me is the spirit rising. Spirit of the wilderness in my veins. Spirit of the people here beside me, standing on the road in the summer rain." Everyone calmed down and stood firm.

That first day, we shut down the logging completely. There were no arrests. Unfortunately it was not a sign of things to come. The next morning, we all regrouped on the road. The police arrived and arrested more than a dozen people who refused to move to let the logging trucks pass. I will never forget that day, watching Svend, tall, composed and dignified, led away by police. One after another, they were taken away. It was all remarkably civil. Even when one elderly woman, wearing a tan trench coat and carrying a cherry red leather handbag, turned to the officer who was leading her away and said, "Young man, you must be ashamed of yourself."

After that day's blockade was over, several people thanked me. The next day the Friends met and asked me formally to become the blockade coordinator. Inspired by the day, I said yes without hesitation. From then on I had a bullhorn in my hand pretty much the entire summer. All thoughts of my previous life and my academic commitments had disappeared for me until my thesis adviser called me. "Getting much writing done? Today you landed on my doorstep on the front page of the *Globe and Mail* with your fist in the air, standing under a blockade banner."

In our wildest dreams we'd hoped for two thousand people at the camp throughout the summer, but suddenly we had hundreds arriving every day. Buses started pulling up, and restaurants in Victoria donated vanloads of food. By the middle of the first week of July, we already had about five hundred people living in the middle of this remote clear-cut, hours from the closest urban centres, and more were showing up.

As people kept flowing in, others wanted to provide support, and we began seeing the funniest donations. One afternoon a Mack truck pulled up from Victoria, and the back of it was filled with muffin tops, but no muffin bottoms. We never knew what we were going to get, but somehow we managed to feed an average of five hundred people a day for four months, and we never ran out of food.

I was working the front gate of the Peace Camp one afternoon when a car pulled up containing a nurse from Saskatchewan with her eleven-year-old daughter. She'd seen us on the news and decided they needed to be part of history, so they had driven for days across the country. We realized this was getting so much bigger than we'd ever thought it would.

Within weeks the camp had become a social experiment—an eclectic community united by a common purpose. The Raging Grannies, my future husband, tree planters and the nurse from Saskatchewan were joined by business people from Victoria and professors from the University of British Columbia. The yuppies were showing up with their Gore-Tex jackets and the tents they'd just bought at Mountain Equipment Co-op. The hippies arrived with people and dogs rolling out of the back of their vans as if they were clown cars. It was an incredible cross-section of Canadians, figuring out how to live together, organize together and share shifts in the communal kitchen. One night I saw a business guy in his Oxford button-down shirt with his sleeves rolled up doing dishes in the camp washtub next to a heavily pierced man who made jewellery for a living and lived on the street in Victoria. As I walked by, they were debating the environmental policies of different political parties, and I remember thinking, *Where else would this happen?* Everyone was united by outrage over the logging and concern for the future of the forests, and they were overcoming their differences through a shared sense of purpose.

The code of non-violence really helped make sure everyone was comfortable together. The no-drugs-and-alcohol rule wasn't a big hit with everyone, but it was vital. We were in a stressful and at times dangerous situation, and we were committed to making the protest accessible to everyone. This was not a party, it was serious work and we wanted families and business people and people of all ages to come. We were risking our liberty. We were risking our safety. It was often fun, but it was also long, hard work, exhausting and sometimes frightening.

I believe that the non-violence code and the dignified behaviour of the protestors who viewers saw on the nightly news reinforced the accessibility of the protest to the average conscientious citizen. It's one thing when you see people chained to the underside of a truck with a U-lock, and it's a whole other thing when you see dozens of people of all ages—moms holding their kids' hands, business people, artists, students—standing silently and firmly in principle, with their chins ever so slightly tilted up in defiance, holding hands in front of a logging truck. I think those images of ordinary people doing extraordinary things together were in large part what skyrocketed the public attention and concern over Clayoquot Sound. When you turned on the TV and saw the blockades on the news, or opened the newspaper you could see someone like yourself or your aunt or your teacher in the photo.

MORE THAN TEN THOUSAND people arrived at the camp over a four-month period. As the crowds grew, one of my jobs was talking to the protesters each night. I had never been a spokesperson for anything before, and had never given a speech in my life. Every night I would talk around the campfire about why we were there and what we needed to do and what they could expect at the blockades. Sometimes there would be thirty people at the fire circle, but I remember one instance when there were more than seven hundred. I'd facilitate the circle, explain the legal implications of what we were doing, and get people to commit to the code of non-violence and safety. I'd explain what was going to happen the next day, ask who was coming and who was willing to risk arrest and block a road. If they didn't want to take the risk, that was fine. I'd try to get people united with a sense of purpose about what they were doing. And every day on the blockades when the situation intensified, or when there were arguments with the pro-logging groups who came to protest our actions, or the police arrived and the prospect of a first encounter with the law—or even the risk of arrest—spurred someone to cry, I would start talking to help crystallize the importance of the moment.

I found my voice in Clayoquot Sound, and along with thousands of others, I was inspired by the shared experience to remain committed to this work even after the camp closed.

I'd stand on the side of the road each day, advising the protesters to follow the code and working as a sort of liaison with the police, letting them know what we were up to, reassuring them that we wouldn't be violent. Every day I'd recite the non-violence code and remind people that we also had our own "peacekeepers" on site. If anyone saw someone getting out of hand—being verbally or physically abusive or threatening property—they should alert someone from our team to stop them. Other days I'd remind people of the best ways to get arrested. In case you're wondering, you never want to be carried on your front, always on your back, because otherwise you run the risk of your face dragging on the ground. If you have any necklaces or chains and you're going to be carried away, you should take them off and put them in your pocket to avoid losing or damaging them, or having them cut into you.

Sometimes I'd lead chants such as "We won't wait any longer. We are stronger than before." I was never just speaking to the protesters and the media. There were almost always counter-protesters there, too—loggers, their wives and community members (a coalition who called themselves "Share BC")—who tried to prevent us from disrupting the logging. One speech I gave was aimed right at the counter-protesters, facing their issues head-on. "Many people refer to this issue as a jobs versus environment issue. We are not here to block people from going to work. We are here because this is a means of public protest, because the democratic process has failed. While the membership in the International Woodworkers of America has decreased dramatically over the last ten years, only 3 percent of Vancouver Island has been saved. Three percent does not translate into eighteen thousand lost jobs. It is not a result of protection of our ecosystems that we are losing jobs, it's the result of mechanization."

Amazingly, halfway through the summer, a contingent of loggers did join the blockades, proudly holding a banner calling for sustainable logging. While they didn't oppose all logging, they were disgusted by the rate of logging and the practice of clear-cutting. They had started to realize that the industry was logging more and more, yet employing fewer people. They arrived unannounced on the blockades one morning and quietly yet courageously faced their fellow workers on the other side of the blockade. Once again our story rocketed through the national media, causing shock waves around the country and sending packs of reporters to the rainforest.

AS THE MEDIA started to focus more attention on the blockades, Karen Mahon, the Greenpeace Canada forest campaigner, began talking about how to seize the moment and expand the debate from the clear-cutting of Clayoquot Sound to the practice of clear-cutting everywhere. And she found a way to shine a spotlight on that larger issue after a late-night talk at Val's house in June. Valerie, Karen and I were lying around on Val's floor in sleeping bags, imagining what the summer was going to be like and how to make the biggest possible impact. Val said, "I want that band that sings 'Beds are Burning.' I want them in Clayoquot Sound."

Karen said, "You mean Midnight Oil? Their lead singer, Peter Garrett, is on Greenpeace's board."

Val said, "Yeah! Midnight Oil. Let's get them to come!"

Karen waited until three in the morning, because she knew Greenpeace International was having a board meeting in Amsterdam, and Peter Garrett was going to be there. I remember being half-asleep in my sleeping bag, listening to Karen on the phone in the bathroom whispering, "Is Peter Garrett there?"

She somehow got him to come, and along with Midnight Oil came more cameras than I had ever seen in my life—as well as MuchMusic and close to five thousand fans.

It was an insane time of working eighteen-hour days. We needed to build stages. Order portable toilets. Train hundreds of people in crowd control and peacekeeping. The day before the concert, Val and Karen and I fell into bed at around midnight but were woken up at two in the morning by the phone ringing. There was a traffic jam back through to Port Alberni (a town an hour and a half away). BC Ferries officials were scrambling to arrange extra sailings because so many people were trying to get across to Vancouver Island. I was told there were already close to a thousand people at the blockade site.

We hopped into our car to drive to the blockade, but the loggers and their wives had blockaded the road. We tried to negotiate with them, but they started rocking our car. It was all chaos and then the police came. As we watched, one defiant woman stood silently on the side of the road with her infant son on her hip, holding a sign that read, "Your party, our future."

When we finally got through the counter-protesters, we had to figure out how to bring Midnight Oil in with all their equipment. We realized it was going to be nearly impossible. We faced another difficulty. Many of the First Nations in British Columbia are still negotiating over treaties that are more than one hundred and fifty years overdue, which they needed to balance with their concerns about the logging. And while the First Nations chiefs would come to the concert and speak, they would not do so if the concert was at the blockade site itself. So with only a few hours left, we decided to keep the blockade at the bridge but move the concert to the clear-cut where we had our camp. Redirecting everything was a massive undertaking—we had to move flatbeds full of sound equipment, organize thousands of people, truck in the portable toilets and build an instant stage in the Black Hole.

On the morning of the concert, close to five thousand people showed up at the bridge at four-thirty. Even after we'd arranged to move the concert to avoid the loggers, Peter Garrett still wanted to appear at the blockade, so we crunched all six feet, six inches of him into Karen's Volkswagen Bug and snuck him to the blockade. I coordinated the blockade from the roof of Chris's van with a bullhorn. Somehow we managed to get the crowd in step. (Given the bleary eyes and party atmosphere, I had the sneaking suspicion that not all the people had been observing our no-drugs-and-alcohol policy.) Despite the chaos and the fact that most of them had been drawn there because of the rock band and not with the focused intention to blockade a logging road, once they arrived they were inspired by the sense of purpose that had brought the band out in the first place. By the time the police vans and logging trucks arrived, a serious calm had overtaken the crowd. The MacMillan Bloedel officials and the police took one look at the wave of humanity blocking the bridge and being recorded by dozens of news cameras, and they turned around and left. A cheer swept through the crowd.

The clear-cut where we had set up the concert was about two miles away from the blockade, so the next few hours were a blur of organizing to keep a team of people at the bridge to hold the blockade while moving thousands of others to the concert.

And when Karen jumped on the stage to introduce Midnight Oil, she also launched a new, far-reaching national campaign that would have reverberations throughout the industry for years to come. "Today we're not just calling for the protection of Clayoquot Sound," she said into the microphone. "We're calling for an end to clear-cut logging across Canada."

At the next morning's debriefing, as we read the headline "Greenpeace Calls for a Ban on Clear-cut Logging Across Canada," we were all a bit horrified at our success. We were barely succeeding at managing the campaign for Clayoquot Sound, and now Karen had launched a national campaign targeting the predominant logging practice of one of the country's most important industries. Today a call to end clear-cutting doesn't seem so radical, but back then it was extremely controversial. We started receiving nonstop calls to the Clayoquot Sound office and the Greenpeace office, from members of other concerned environmental groups: "You can't say you're against all clear-cutting—that's outrageous! We're going to get destroyed by the industry!"

But it was the right thing to do. Sometimes you need to leap. You need to take a chance. We had the attention of the nation, and the problems that led to the decision to log most of this rainforest were certainly not contained to this place. Karen created a conversation across the country with such questions as "What is a clear-cut? How do we define selective logging? Can the industry thrive by cutting less, but doing more with it?" I think that public moment, and the debate it generated, led to the creation of the first Forest Practices Code in BC—legislation that was a leap forward in regulating the industry.

The day of the Midnight Oil concert was truly amazing on a number of levels. Apart from sparking a new national debate, we had dramatically increased the attention our protests were getting. We had reached a younger audience drawn by the concert but engaged in the issues. People were so moved by the blockades and the speeches that they really wanted to support us. All day people kept coming up to us, thanking us and handing us money. They wanted to donate, and I just kept stuffing bills into my bag.

Crowd estimates ranged from three to five thousand on the day of the concert, but whatever the math, it was enough that we stopped the logging that day. Despite all the passion on both sides of the debate, there were no arrests and there was no violence.

The next day we asked if people would stay with us, wake up at 4:00 a.m. and blockade. Over half of them did.

At 5:00 a.m. a bunch of people had already started blockading the road. The police pulled up and went to the front, where everyone was blocking a truck. Then they looked around, talked to each other, talked into their radios and suddenly they all turned and walked toward me.

I was at the side of the road, sipping coffee, when one of the officers approached me. I wasn't alarmed, as I'd been acting as the police liaison, discussing how many people were going to be protesting each day, assuring them we'd behave. But he didn't want to talk about our plans for the day.

"I'm going to put you under arrest at this time."

I couldn't figure out what was going on. I was standing off to the side of the road, not blockading the trucks. Valerie asked what I'd done. The officer ignored her. I tried to remain calm.

"This is an unlawful arrest," I said. I handed Valerie my coffee cup. "I've always been at the side of the road. I haven't been impeding or obstructing logging operations."

He took me by the elbow and told me I was under arrest and had the right to remain silent. It's a right I didn't exercise. No one else had been arrested for participating in a blockade when they weren't actually blocking the roads or the trucks. I was led to another pair of officers and I repeated, "This is an unlawful arrest." The officer turned me around, told me to put my hands behind my back and marched me to a school bus parked between two police vans.

Two other officers followed. There were cameras everywhere, and as it hit me that I was really being arrested, I turned to one and shouted, "I am proud to be arrested in defence of Clayoquot Sound!" Other protesters cheered and applauded, some started to cry and one of the counter-protesters screamed triumphantly, "They got Tzeporah! They got Tzeporah!"

I stepped into the school bus they were using as a police vehicle and waited for them to round up the fifteen people who were actually blockading the road. Then the doors slammed shut behind us and we rode off to prison.

Chapter 3

SURFING THE BACKLASH
GOING TO JAIL

When they really start attacking you it means you have their attention. Surf the backlash. It's going to be a wild ride, but it will take us further than our budget ever could.

CHRIS HATCH

AT THE END OF Clayoquot Summer, I wrote in my journal, "Corporations have to follow 'environmental regulations' or they will be fined, and they call it 'the cost of doing business.' I'm mad that none of these men have ever gone to jail, but I've watched hundreds of people get dragged away for standing on a logging road because they wanted everyone to hold off and think about it all for a second. I'm mad enough to shake it all up and see if it will come unstuck."

It felt as if we'd done everything we could to unstick things in the summer of '93, and nothing was changing. We had worked night and day on the largest act of civil disobedience in Canada's history at that time, and the logging continued unabated. More than twelve thousand people visited the Peace Camp, nearly a thousand people were arrested on the blockades, and public opinion was in our favour, but the logging companies were still hauling off thousand-year-old trees every day.

The night of the first sentencings, Chris and I realized the only way to stop the logging was to stop the buyers—those who purchased pulp, paper and lumber. I talked with Karen, who was running the Greenpeace Canada forests campaign, and we came up with a plan to figure out who was paying MacMillan Bloedel (MacBlo) to cut down these ancient trees. Originally, for me the campaign was all about place: the pristine valleys, the majestic trees. I realized I'd achieved a new level of maturity around the issues when I started to understand the people. After that I started learning more about the products. We didn't know how to follow the money yet, but we could follow the products. We knew we couldn't get everyone to stop buying wood, but we could try to make buying products made from old-growth forests as politically and socially popular as investing in tobacco or butchering elephants for ivory.

We had no skills, no systems; we followed the trucks to see what mill they went to, then one of us would pretend to be a student, take the mill tour and casually ask where the wood was going. We'd hang out in local bars trying to overhear conversations that mentioned the names of customers.

These days, chain-of-custody research is less spying than science. Many organizations now have staff dedicated to examining shipping data, following mills and pulp flows in complex databases, tracking how the product travels from Canada to the United States, because 80 percent of Canadian timber and pulp is still exported there.

But back in the days of mill visits and barroom eavesdropping, after we collected the names of a couple of big-name customers (Scott Paper UK and *BBC Wildlife Magazine*) I would buy plane tickets, and a suit from the Value Village thrift store, and go to Europe to meet with the customers.

We quickly discovered that the companies were convinced that they were buying only second-growth forest that was selectively logged, and that they weren't buying from any clear-cuts.[1] It was up to us to show them that through their purchasing practices they were partially responsible for clear-cutting temperate rainforests. We were determined to ensure that the companies buying wood from Clayoquot Sound, at least, knew they were under scrutiny for their actions, and that we were prepared to let their customers know just how out of step they were with contemporary concerns and values.

But that day of the arrests at the Clayoquot blockade, the first task was to get out of jail.

Our first stop after being arrested was the tiny jail in Ucluelet, a small town southwest of Clayoquot Sound. While I was in the cell, an officer I'd been talking to for weeks came to the door. Ucluelet has a small RCMP detachment, so by now I knew the officers fairly well, as I'd been talking to them on the blockades every day.

Have you ever seen that cartoon where the sheepdog and the wolf punch in for work every morning and say hi before they start to chase each other? Each day was like that.

The officers would arrive every morning and we'd all say hi before slipping into our roles. I'd say, "Hi Frank."

And Frank, or whoever, would say, "Hey, Tzeporah."

And I'd say, "Don't worry, everything is under control. Everyone here has committed to remaining peaceful; X number have decided to block the road today."

And the officer would say something like "Okay, thanks. Looks like rain tonight. You guys get those ditches dug?"

It was all remarkably normal yet surreal at the same time. After I was arrested, it wasn't a surprise when one of the officers came to my cell and told me he was sorry, and that he and others had been against my being arrested. But once he started talking, it was clear he wasn't *that* sorry.

"You're a bright woman," he said, "and I hope this is a lesson to you that you have to switch tracks. You don't want to be on the wrong side."

"How do you define the wrong side?"

"You know exactly what I'm talking about. You can't get in the way of progress."

"I just don't think this kind of devastation is progress."

His compassion shifted to anger. "You're inspiring people so that they want to get arrested, and it won't change anything."

"I'm sorry," I said, "I didn't realize inspiration was a criminal offence now. And I think we will be able to make change."

And he said, "You know, Tzeporah, you're a bit big for your britches, and you'd just better remember that the flame that burns brightest is the flame that burns out the quickest."

"The flame that burns brightest is the flame that burns out the quickest." It wasn't a threat, but not long afterwards it seemed like a pretty accurate prophecy.

When I've met young environmentalists over the years, one of the first things they ask is how to avoid burnout. But when I was in my mid-twenties I never imagined burnout was possible. Once I became an activist, I barely imagined a life beyond the cause was possible either. One of the other challenges was wrapping my head around the idea of being on the wrong side of the law. I wasn't afraid of challenging rules, but I'd always challenged them the "right way." My sister Wendy was now a lawyer. Breaking the law—and advocating for other people to break the law—rocked me to my soul.

I spent a lot of sleepless nights thinking about the law, but also thinking about my heroes like Martin Luther King and Petra Kelly and Gandhi and how unjust laws were changed. In 1969 the Canadian Council of Christians and Jews wrote, "Law and order, though vital for society, can often be used to cover injustice. It is no longer sufficient merely to advocate obedience to law. The attainment of justice is first; without it, law is merely a façade. Law is the product of an evolving process and as such it should reflect issues important to society. As values and perceptions change, the law must be recast to reflect new realities."[2] That quotation fuelled me as I faced being on the "wrong" side of the law for the first time.

Throughout history, social conflict has proven necessary to attain dramatic social change. At one time blacks were treated as slaves and women were considered their husbands' property. For many people who stood on the road in Clayoquot Sound, viewing nature as a commodity that humans had the right to exploit also seemed backward. Before millions of people were given the right to vote—whether in North America, England, or elsewhere in the democratic world—there were passionate demonstrations: thousands of women were jailed for picketing polling stations and chaining themselves to legislatures during the suffrage movement; later, in the United States, protests took place at lunch counters and on buses in the South during the Civil Rights Movement. For many in Canada, the catalyst to reevaluating our relationship with nature was the summer of 1993 in Clayoquot, when going to jail seemed like the only way to fight for justice.

THE OTHER PRISONERS and I were brought from Ucluelet to the Nanaimo Correctional Centre, and the officers walked us through the prison. That was scary, because there were a lot of drunk and angry men in that jail who started catcalling, threatening us.

While the guards were processing us, they asked us to strip down, and that was when I realized . . . I'd just started my period.

So I went over to the guard and said, "Umm . . . I have my . . . I need . . ."

He turned various shades of red and with a panicked voice said, "I'll put you in the infirmary. Wait here, it will all be okay."

I knew it would be okay. It had happened every month for years and wasn't that scary.

He put me in the infirmary, where there was a TV. I wasn't locked up, and no one else was there. So I flicked on the TV, and the first thing I saw was myself. I hadn't slept in days, and there I was watching myself being arrested on national TV.

After a half-hour the guard came back and gave me my prison garb and a complete selection of what must have been every possible kind of pad, tampon and liner in the Nanaimo drugstore. I put on my prison outfit and went to where belongings were catalogued. As I emptied all my pockets and dumped out my bag, I discovered I had almost $5,000 in small bills that people had shoved at me as donations. As the intake officer counted the money, he looked at me as though I'd done some kind of drug deal. "It was a concert, on the blockade, I spoke and people just kinda gave me money . . ." I trailed off when I realized I was only making the situation worse.

The guards had separated the protesters from the locals because of the potential for violence, so it was a relief when I got to the special section where they were holding all the Clayoquot prisoners. Our cells were together, and we got to eat together. That was when I grew to admire Betty Krawczyk, a feisty, white-haired former Civil Rights protester with a Southern accent. She went on to become one of BC's best-known activists, serving more time in jail for protecting trees than anyone else in Canada.

Betty had been in jail for ten days, having been arrested on the first day. Many protestors were vegetarian and wouldn't eat the prison food, so Betty persuaded the guards to let her cook. Along with many others she had refused to sign the bail conditions that required protestors to agree not to go back to the area. Like her, I wasn't prepared to sign such a bail order, which I believed was a total violation of our right to lawful assembly, so I was expecting to settle in for the long haul. That day one of the officers I knew quite well came to see me and apologized. He didn't think what was happening to us was right. I asked him what I was doing in jail, then. And he said, "They want you off the road."

They?

"It's not our fault," he said. "Our orders come from above. Just so you know, the police are working with MacMillan Bloedel to build the case against you."

This did not sound good.

The next day, we all received our prison request forms to ask for toothpaste or other small items we needed. At the bottom of the form was a category that read "Other." So in that space I requested a press conference. A half-hour later, I was brought in to speak with one of the higher-ups, and he was totally flustered.

"I see you've requested a press conference. I don't think that's going to be possible."

I said, "I'm allowed visitors, right? How about CBC with a camera crew?"

He said that wasn't standard protocol, but he smiled and said he'd try to figure it out. And I think he might have figured it out too, if I'd stayed in jail much longer.

A little later that day, a guard came to tell me I had a visitor. I went to the visitor room, and there was my oldest sister, Corinne, trying so hard not to cry. She and her husband, Jeff, had been in BC to visit me on the blockades, and were on their way home to Toronto when they had heard what happened, cancelled their flight and booked a trip to Nanaimo. We talked, and I told her it was all going to be okay.

Corinne had been told she could buy me things from the prison canteen and offered to get me whatever I wanted. I was a strict vegetarian at the time, and all they had that I could eat in the canteen were chocolate bars. I asked if she could buy me thirty. She looked at me as if I was crazy, and I said, "Well, I'm in here with thirty other protestors and we do everything together." So I went back to the tank with thirty chocolate bars.

Chris came to see me that day too. He told me later that he'd arrived just in time to see my sister tear a strip off the prison guard who was refusing to let her see me. "Are all Berman girls this fierce?" I laughed to think of Corinne as fierce until I remembered her catching me smoking when I was fifteen.

The next morning I was half asleep when a guard came to my cell to wake me with some totally unexpected news. My lawyer had arrived. I sat up quickly, startled. I didn't have a lawyer. I definitely had no money to pay a lawyer. I didn't have enough money of my own to reimburse Corinne for the chocolate bars.

I went to the room where prisoners meet their lawyers, and in walked this guy in an Armani suit. "I'm a senior criminal attorney in British Columbia, and I want to represent you. I'm pulling together a legal team."

I said the first thing that came to my mind: "I don't have any money."

He smiled. "Yeah, we figured."

The next day, he went to court and fought the bail requirements, pro bono. The provincial government fought back. But he won, and I didn't have to sign bail conditions to stay clear of Clayoquot Sound. After three days in jail I was released without charges or parole and went right back to the blockades.

Once I was back at the camp, I discovered that Wendy and Karen had tried to figure out the best way to get me out of jail and decided to call the most famous criminal defence lawyer in Canada to represent me. They phoned Clayton Ruby in Toronto, and he told them he'd seen my arrest on the news and was happy to help. He called one of the top lawyers in BC, and that's why David Martin flew to Nanaimo that night.

The bad news—and the truly shocking news for both David and me—was that after I had returned to the blockades, I wasn't charged with blockading the road as everyone else had been. BC's Crown attorneys invented a whole new crime for me: "aiding and abetting" every single person arrested on the blockades. Throughout the summer I was re-charged every couple of weeks with additional charges reflecting new arrests on the blockades. By the end of the summer, I had been charged with 857 criminal counts of aiding and abetting. There was a point when I was standing at the blockades being taunted once again by loggers and their wives yelling at me to "get a job" when I realized, *This is my job.* There was nothing else I wanted to do. I felt that there was nothing else I could do. A couple of days later, Karen offered me a full-time job at Greenpeace Canada.

AT THE BEGINNING of August we organized a mass protest day for Clayoquot Sound. We had advertised it as "Mass Protest: If you've ever thought about standing up for the forest, come on this day." People started flooding in.

It was 5:00 a.m., and I was standing on top of Chris's van with a bullhorn looking out over five or six hundred people gathered on the logging road. I was collecting my thoughts, trying to remember all the advice Jean McLaren had given me about maintaining calm and safety when Chris tugged my shirt and I looked down.

"What? I'm about to make a speech."

"I just wanted to introduce you to my parents."

This couldn't be happening. *Not now!* I thought. I was the new girlfriend. I was also this loudmouth woman who was organizing logging blockades and hollering into a bullhorn and I hadn't showered in days. His dad was a professor at UBC. His mom was an editor. They ran a literary press together. They had just returned from a sabbatical in Germany, and I'd never met them. They'd decided to come and see what Chris had gotten himself into and, of course, they'd arrived on the day of the mass protest.

I could see the dust rising from the police cars and logging trucks coming down the road toward us, and feel the panic and anger starting to roll through the crowd. A combination of training and instinct took over, and I started speaking through the bullhorn. "If you are on the road you are risking arrest! Supporting those making this decision is just as important and there are many other ways that you can protest and take a stand. If you don't want to risk arrest, please move to the side of the road now."

Very few people moved.

"To maintain calm, please sit down."

Like a wave down the road, hundreds of people sat down.

"Wow, that was cool," Chris whispered to me.

The crowd was so quiet that you could hear the crunch of the gravel under the tires of the approaching trucks. Someone started chanting, then hundreds of voices joined in, as if we'd rehearsed it. "If we all sit on the road, they can't arrest us all."

That chant made national news coverage—and became the defining moment of the protests—because it turned out that, actually, they could arrest us all.

The police had brought in all the buses from the local schools, and they hauled off anyone who stayed on the road.

Chris's father, and other professors from UBC and Simon Fraser University, were so outraged by what they were witnessing that they too sat down in the middle of the road.

And then the police started arresting the children.

It took a long time to arrest 309 people. *Seven hours*.[3] Teachers, business people, mothers, grandmothers, children, Chris's dad and the other professors, even some loggers who wanted more responsible logging practices—they were all taken to the buses. It was a zoo.

One beautiful woman in her forties, Sally Sunshine, from a small local island, turned to the TV cameras as she was being arrested and with her vibrant blue eyes flashing she channelled all her hippieness and said, "Join us." Over the coming months I would meet hundreds of people who saw that news coverage of Sally and got in their cars or on a bus and headed to Tofino.

Chris and I raced from the blockade to the jail cell in Ucluelet, trying to negotiate the release of his dad, the other professors and hundreds of others, trying to figure out where they were taking the children. When we finally got back to the blockade camp five hours later, exhausted, we drove past Chris's mother, and Chris shouted out the window, "Hey, lady, wasn't your husband arrested today?"

She did not laugh.

Instead of getting upset at Chris and me, his parents organized a whole faction of professors and teachers to protest the injustices they'd seen that day. They even published a book: *Clayoquot and Dissent*. That wouldn't be the last time they stood up to support us when we got in too deep on one issue or another; that day I didn't just meet my future in-laws, I met my safety net.

BACK IN VANCOUVER, I was regularly seeing lawyers and trying to raise money for the legal strategy for all the people who'd been charged, and we were also trying to create new tactics with Greenpeace.

Meanwhile, there were almost a thousand people being processed through the legal system, and we were working with a group in Victoria organizing legal support for them.

The trials were heart-wrenching. Before that first sentencing, no one had gone to jail except grannies like Betty who'd refused to sign the bail conditions. No one imagined jail terms were even possible. Now the shortest jail term anyone was getting was forty-five days. Most people had taken just a few hours off work, or from school, or hired a babysitter for the afternoon so they could attend their trial. As everyone was led away that first day, it felt as if all hope was gone. Everyone was going to jail. The logging was continuing. We had lost.

After facing a reporters' scrum, I left the courthouse and went to the little office we'd set up in Victoria, the Clayoquot legal defence fund office, to try to figure out how to make sure everyone's families were cared for and contacted, kids were picked up, relatives and friends were found to look after them—to make sure people had support.

That first sentencing pretty much incited mass panic because there were another eight-hundred-plus people scheduled for trials, and suddenly it looked as though we were all going to jail. The phones in the office started ringing off the hook. The next few months were some of the longest in my life, with all of us running around, trying to figure out how to deal with the situation. I couldn't help wondering if the government was right and if any of this was my fault, if anyone really was in jail because of something I'd said or done.

I was cited in one of the trials against the protestors as saying, "MacMillan Bloedel has obtained a legal court order, an injunction on this area, saying that no one can physically impede or obstruct the logging operations in this area. What this means is that if we stay on the road, if we are arrested and pulled off the road, then we are in contempt of court. We're not in contempt of the court. We're in contempt of the forest practices that are happening at Clayoquot Sound." The Crown counsel used this as evidence of my misleading the public and "aiding and abetting"—my own charge—criminal offences.

I began to wonder if I was guilty of aiding and abetting, if people were going to jail because of me. The only thing that helped me shake the guilt was when I started getting calls and notes from people saying they felt empowered, that the experience had a dramatic influence on their lives and they were signing their names with their arrestee number. They had all made personal and difficult choices that could not be attributed to any one person's influence.

That September, having just started to understand the importance of raising awareness in the marketplace, Karen and I invited executive directors from Greenpeace offices in key markets to come to Clayoquot Sound and take a stand. It was one of the smartest things we ever did. The protest garnered media attention and slowed down the logging for a day, but the big impact was within Greenpeace. After being arrested in Clayoquot Sound, while chained to a cement barrel with Chris, the executive directors of Greenpeace in Germany, the UK, the Netherlands and other countries went back to their offices horrified at the logging and steaming mad at the Canadian government. Within a week there were teams in every country and the markets campaign took off.

With my trial looming, Greenpeace asked me to fly to Europe to dog BC's premier, Mike Harcourt, who was going there to try and counter the negative reputation our campaign was giving wood products from Canada. By this time the campaign against clear-cutting in BC had really hit the international radar and we were seeing it in *TIME* magazine, the *International Herald Tribune* and *Der Spiegel.* Everyone was starting to question Canada.

Once I was back in Canada, my lawyers wanted to see me to figure out our strategy. The government appointed one of their best Crown counsels to prosecute my case. I'd never heard of him, but I remember David Martin's face when we got word of whom he was going up against. He said, "Now we're really going to have to work to keep you out of jail."

After that, David Martin wanted me to brace for anywhere between six months and two years in jail. The Crown was requesting six years. That wasn't sounding impossible, either. Then he told me there was an "off the record" offer on the table. If I could promise no protests—by anyone—during the upcoming Commonwealth Games, which were being held in BC that summer, all charges against me would be dropped.

I sat there stunned. This was the kind of backroom deal that I didn't think happened in real life. I could have my freedom as long as I guaranteed that the government would have no protests at their party.

I was horrified, wondering whether our justice system was working for the people of Canada or the logging companies, because this certainly wasn't about democracy, law or justice. The Crown was charging me with aiding and abetting, and now it was trying to get me to make a dirty deal to quell public dissent.

It also made me realize that governments clearly don't understand anything about social movements. Did they really think one person could speak to every activist out there and say, "Hey, I'm going to get off scot-free if you guys just make sure you're silent during this moment on the world stage." Who can do that? Who would?

That was when the last vestiges of my naïveté about the judicial system fell away. I was facing six years in jail, and I already knew no one was organizing serious protests at the Commonwealth Games. I couldn't help thinking, *All I have to do for my get-out-of-jail-free card is tell them I'll try to stop protests that aren't happening.* But the idea that they thought they could threaten and control one person, and then one person could command a movement, just pissed me off. It was the same concept behind charging me with aiding and abetting.

You can't aid and abet a movement, and you can't aid and abet civil disobedience. It's a personal, difficult choice. They had missed the whole point of what was happening. And nearly a thousand people had put their freedom on the line. The fact that the government thought I could control thousands of people and tell them where to protest and not protest was a signal that they really didn't have a clue what was going on. They didn't understand the will of the people or the concern out there, or the organizing system behind the movement.

Not surprisingly, I said no.

But I really wished I could have said no publicly because the whole offer was so hideous.

MEANWHILE, MY PROFILE was so high after the Harcourt trip, the arrest and the blockades that in 1994 I couldn't walk into a restaurant in Victoria without people swivelling around to look at me. Feeling that everyone knew me, and had an opinion about me, left me jittery and nervous in public. I would cringe when I saw the light dawn in their eyes or hear the whispers, "Isn't that that tree girl from the news?" When I got back from Europe, I'd lost about fifteen pounds (it's not easy travelling through Germany as a strict vegetarian when you don't speak the language and don't have time for anything other than fast food). I was a total wreck and, thanks to all the attention, I was also turning into a diva.

To paraphrase Spider-Man, "With great profile comes great responsibility." And pressure. If you're strong-minded and stay healthy, you know you're actually representing hundreds, if not thousands, of people, and it's not about you, but it's hard to hold on to that because everybody likes to have a hero or a villain, and everybody likes to have one focal point, especially the media. I was not doing well at juggling ego and profile.

One day Chris and Karen sat me down in the Greenpeace office, and Karen said, "This is an intervention."

And I said, "Okay . . . what do you mean?"

Karen was blunt. "You're turning into an asshole."

They said my expectations of how I should be treated had shifted, and it had happened in a way I hadn't even noticed. I had become more demanding and more authoritarian. "You have got to keep your eye on the prize," she said. "This isn't about you. You are just a tool in the same way Greenpeace and its brand are a tool. You, us, Greenpeace, it's all a means to an end and that's why we do this work." And of course I knew that intellectually. But my closest friends telling me that they found me unbearable was a huge wake-up call. Thank God they did it, because since then, every time I see myself acting the prima donna, expecting a certain level of support, thinking about the work as though it's about me, I take a step back.

When you're in a position of leadership, especially in front of a movement or major campaign, it's too easy to puff yourself up and conflate yourself with the image in your press clippings. But obviously none of this work happens without thousands of hands, and several leaders working in tandem and calling on their strategic and tactical knowledge and skills—some, like Karen, who had long experience in the field.

That said, I had become the public face of the fight, and I was getting so many death threats that my friend Sue Danne at the Greenpeace office was assigned to listen to my voice mail before I got in every morning. She'd save the threats on a separate tape for the police and keep the rest of my messages. Normally, the police would take the tapes every few days and say, "Well, what can you do?" until we received a letter composed of cut-out letters from newspapers and a picture of me with a red swastika across my face. The hate mail came in a typed envelope which looked totally normal, but said something like, "You Jew bitch trying to destroy British Columbia. I'm watching you, and you won't last long. You should die." As a young Jewish woman, you can't see your own face like that without being disturbed. That hit in a way that all the crazy-ass voice mail messages hadn't. I started to shake, thinking, *What do I do now?* It wasn't that hard to reach me. It wasn't as if I had a security crew. I wasn't a pop star or a premier. I frequently walked home from our office to our dingy apartment on the corner of Commercial Drive and Eleventh at eleven o'clock at night. One night not long after that I was in the middle of writing a report on clear-cutting when I received a call. The gruff voice on the other end said, "I'm a logger from Horsefly, BC."

And I knew I couldn't take it.

"I saw you on TV," he said.

I was scared, I was tired, I wasn't sure I could handle another person screaming at me because he thought he'd lost his job as a result of the protests. Just as I was about to hang up, he said, "I want to thank you for everything you've been doing."

And my first thought was *He's not going to yell?*

"I've been a faller for twenty years. I've lived beside the Fraser for thirty-three years, beside the largest salmon spawning bed in BC. The salmon aren't coming back this year. Two years ago I was laid off because there wasn't anything left to cut up here. They've clear-cut the forest, my job and now the salmon. I don't really know why I'm calling you except to thank you. I can't do much out here. I started speaking out last year, and they came and shot at my cabin at night. I went up to the Yukon for a year. Now I'm home, but I'm scared. I wrote down the changes I've seen in the river and the mountain range over the past thirty-three years, and if it could help you, I'll send it."

I didn't know what to say. I could barely speak. "Yes," I said. "Thank you. It would help. I'm preparing a report right now on the effects of clear-cutting on salmon. Could you fax it to me?"

He went quiet for a moment. "You mean through the phone line? I don't know. I'm at a payphone and we don't have any electricity in the cabin. Could I mail it to you from town?"

"That would be great," I said. "That would be great."

A few days later, Chris and I were on the ferry going to Victoria to meet with the government, and I'd barely slept the night before, preparing for the meetings. I went up on deck to get some coffee with Chris. We were standing in line, and a woman I'd never seen before came up and threw her arms around me. "Oh my God! You've changed my life! Clayoquot was life changing for me!" I remember trying to untangle myself and thinking how tired I was and how much I just wanted to get a coffee. "Thanks," I said. "Nice to meet you."

But now everyone was looking at me. A burly guy in a plaid shirt and ball cap was getting his coffee as I was about to get mine, and said, "It really is you." He looked at me, leaned in really close, and spat directly into my face as hard as he could. He started yelling that I didn't care about people, I only cared about trees. I'd been taking this kind of thing for months, and I normally have a thick skin, but my nerves were shot. I burst into tears. Chris grabbed me and took me downstairs to the car, where I tried to get it together.

At this point much of our research focused on how unsustainable the forest industry was as a whole. British Columbia was exporting raw logs, or minimally processed wood, which meant that our rich forests were providing fewer jobs per tree cut than almost any place in the world. There are a lot more jobs in what we do with the wood than there are in cutting down the trees. There were times when I met with loggers or mill workers and we stuck to the conversation long enough until they admitted that, yes, their jobs were disappearing far before the environmental campaigns kicked in, but their communities were dependent on these logging companies. They were of course desperately worried and they needed someone else to blame; the senior logging executives were only too happy to fan those flames and let the workers battle the environmental campaigns.

We docked in Swartz Bay near Victoria and drove to an office we were borrowing for the day. I needed to do some press calls and print documents for a meeting. When we arrived there was already a line of people waiting to talk to me and a camera crew in the lobby. Reuters was waiting on line one. Someone said, "You can use that office." I stepped inside, closed the door and began shaking. Chris came in and asked if I was okay. He told me I had to get it together, and I told him I couldn't. I couldn't stop crying.

For almost a year I'd been willing to deal with anything that came my way. But in that moment I couldn't handle any of it. The pace was exhausting, but almost more exhausting was the pressure of the constant interviews and having to carry into every room the weight of both my new reputation and Greenpeace's—knowing that government and industry would parse and analyze whatever I said. I was supposed to be speaking on behalf of thousands of supporters and volunteers. I remember Jack Munro, the Harley-driving head of the International Woodworkers of America (IWA), calling me "a menace to society" and I kept thinking, *Who is this woman you're talking about?*

I felt that I'd lost myself in the media image of me. I was in over my head both personally and professionally. I was being looked to all the time as an expert, but through the Clayoquot campaign I'd always been flying by the seat of my pants. And it was tough to fathom that I couldn't go anywhere without people hugging me or spitting at me.

Chris said, "What do you need? What do you want to do?" I couldn't answer him, because it hadn't been about me for so long. It had always been about what I needed to do next for this issue and what was the smartest next move. But as for what I wanted and needed? I had no idea.

I'm not sure what happened the rest of that day, but Chris took care of me. He cancelled everything, and said, "We're going away." He booked tickets to Guatemala.

Before that I wouldn't agree to leave the office before nine or ten at night, ever. I hadn't had a day off in at least a year. Guatemala, even once I got my wits back, sounded okay, but there was one thing I had to do first. Greenpeace International was holding a meeting in California in a week with all the forest campaigners from all over the world. They held these strategy meetings only once a year, and I didn't want to miss my first one. I'd heard from friends that this was an especially important event. You'd meet the Brazilian forest campaigner, and the Japanese forest campaigner, and you'd share stories and discuss strategies. Besides, it was going to be on a ranch in California; it would be fun. I told Chris, "I'll meet you down there after the meeting."

He said, "Whatever. You'd better just come to Guatemala."

We went home to our apartment, the first place we'd ever had together, which we shared with a roommate, Peter, and packed for our trips. He went to Guatemala and I flew to California. The meeting was incredible. I learned an enormous amount, and I realized how much more there was to learn. It was all going exactly according to plan until the moment in a meeting midway through the conference when the man who ran the ranch came in with a fax for me. He was as white as the sheet of paper he was holding. He handed it to me, and I saw the words scrawled in black marker: "Apartment has burned down. Police say it's arson. Please call Peter."

I wondered if I should go back to Vancouver, but I knew Chris was already in Guatemala waiting for me. I called Peter and said, "If you can salvage anything, great. I'll call Chris's parents and ask them to pick it up. In the meantime, find another apartment, and maybe for your own safety it should be without us."

CHRIS AND I spent a month in Guatemala. The only rule we had was that we weren't allowed to talk about any of what we'd left behind. I didn't think we could pull it off because we'd never talked about anything else, ever. But we didn't talk about it, and it was absolutely fabulous. We immersed ourselves in the culture and wandered wherever we felt like wandering. We visited Mayan ruins. We went hiking in the rainforest. We went to Belize and lay around for a week on a white sand beach. It was beautiful and rejuvenating.

I think if Chris hadn't done that, and if I hadn't gone, I wouldn't have lasted very long in the movement. There was still this nagging feeling that I could go back and do my PhD, become an assistant professor and make a real salary. Wouldn't that be easier, and saner? Go home. Go to Toronto. Be close to my family. Go back to academia. But I didn't go back because I felt a strong sense of purpose and urgency in the work I was doing.

When I returned to Vancouver and Greenpeace, I also understood that it doesn't all just collapse if you aren't there. That was a good lesson, because when you're in the middle of a campaign you have this feeling that if you're not there it's all going to fall apart. It was great to acknowledge that no one is irreplaceable. I started thinking about how to bring in new campaigners, as well as training and capacity building. I learned to pace myself and recognized that you must have a life outside the movement. Those are things no one had told me.

Or I hadn't listened. Someone had tried.

The founders of Hollyhock (a retreat centre similar to Esalen in California and the Omega Institute in New York) based on Cortes Island, an isolated community near northern Vancouver Island, wanted to support some of BC's activists in their work to protect the rainforests. Their invitation read, "We were following what you were doing in Clayoquot Sound. We would like to support you and others in the environmental community. So we're inviting you and ten other leaders to come for a week of rest and relaxation, to relax in our hot tubs, have massages, do yoga. Rest and renew."

Rest and renew? I didn't have time to rest or renew. We were in the middle of fighting to save Clayoquot Sound and trying to figure out where they were going to log next. I was working twenty hours a day and spending nights in a sleeping bag under my desk. One day I'd scrawled a note in my journal: "I'm running so hard, I've forgotten how to breathe." I looked at this invitation and thought, *Are these people crazy? We don't have time to go meditate in some hippie island hot tubs.*

I found out later that some of the older activists did go. They had the experience to know that this was their life and that the work required rest and relaxation for the long haul. My plan was that once we won Clayoquot Sound I would go back to my real life. I hadn't yet realized that this *was* my life.

ACCORDING TO the *Oxford English Dictionary*, the term "show trial" was coined in the 1930s to describe Joseph Stalin's trials of his enemies. Show trials usually refer to court proceedings where the verdict is a foregone conclusion, so it's not quite fair to call what I went through a show trial—but it was a trial that was more about the show than it was about justice. And I almost missed the show.

The day before my trial, Karen went into labour. It was a home birth, and I was supposed to be with her in Vancouver as her coach. When you're in labour the world ceases to exist outside the breathing and crying. We were doing it all with her, in and out of the tub, and we were trying to birth this baby. Next, my sister was standing beside me in a suit, saying I had to go.

I said, "I'm staying here with Karen for this baby."

Corinne said, "Your trial starts tomorrow morning. It's eight o'clock at night and we have to catch the last ferry. You have to come with us to Victoria."

I refused.

She and Chris dragged me out of Karen's house and shoved me in the back of Chris's van, drove me to Victoria and tossed me onto a bed. I hadn't slept in over twenty-four hours. When I woke up, they handed me a coffee and a suit. I walked with them from the B&B, totally disoriented, and suddenly heard loud noises and some chanting. I was still focused on Karen. I was on my cell talking to other friends who were by her side, trying to get news of the baby. But as we approached the courthouse, the noise grew louder and louder, and finally we saw hundreds of people. When they saw me they went silent, then started clapping. Many held signs that said, "Save Tzeporah!"

I had no idea they'd be there and no idea what to say. I was very moved as I walked through the applauding crowd to get to the courthouse. As soon as I walked in, David Martin asked if I'd practiced my testimony. I said, "No. But I'll go to the bathroom and write something down."

My lawyer was not impressed with my lack of preparation. On the first night of the trial, my sisters and I sat in his fancy hotel suite, and he read me the riot act. David Martin is a terrifying man when he is angry. He was calm, but too calm, with steely eyes and a grim expression. "I don't think you understand. I. Do. Not. Lose. I am one of the best criminal attorneys in this province. I'm doing this free, and you are not focused. I don't lose and we are going to lose—unless you focus."

Then Karen called and said she was fine. She'd finally had the baby. Aedan Magee Mahon had arrived in the world, and everyone was healthy.

So I started focusing on keeping myself out of jail. Karen had already done her part to help me. Just before the trial started, while she was days away from giving birth, she'd worked with Chris to line up an open letter to BC's attorney general that was published in the *Globe and Mail* and other newspapers. It demanded that the Crown review and drop the charges against me. It was a little overwhelming to read the letter and see that some of Canada's most famous citizens, some of my heroes, had signed it. The people demanding my release included the writers Margaret Atwood, June Callwood, William Deverell, Jane Jacobs, Farley Mowat and Michael Ondaatje;

the musician Bruce Cockburn; the filmmaker Norman Jewison; and the American activist/politician Robert Kennedy Jr. The attorney general ignored the letter and signatures, but the increased media and public interest in my trial likely didn't go unnoticed by the judge.

That night, and in the nights to come, David, Chris, my sisters and I would sit for hours going over and over the trial and my testimony. In the end we needn't have bothered. What we didn't know when we were preparing was that the Crown's high-powered attorney, a formidable adversary for David, would just sit back for the whole trial and not say a word, deferring to a junior lawyer.

At one point the Crown lawyer showed a video of me singing a protest song and said, solemnly, "Your Honour, Tzeporah can be seen singing a song obviously supporting those arrested."

I turned to David and whispered, "I'm going to jail for singing?"

As I sat in the seat reserved for the accused, listening to everyone talk about me without addressing me, often without looking at me, referring to me as Tzeporah while referring to every man in the proceedings as "Mister" followed by his last name, I felt strangely disembodied. In case that wasn't insulting enough, the Crown used analogies to gang rape in their argument that I was encouraging the protesters to commit their crime, or trying to stop the clear-cutting of our ancient forests.

I began imagining that I was already stuffed and mounted on the courtroom wall. I started scrawling notes in my journal about what I wanted to say to the judge in my final testimony:

> At one time women were considered property of their husbands, blacks were considered property of their owners. Should trees have standing? Environmental rights in this country are in their early formative years. While I am not asking the court, my lord, to give trees standing, what I am saying is that given that the natural environment which sustains all of us does not have standing in this court and that all of us, without exception, do need to drink water and breathe air, my actions, my speeches, which I believed I had a constitutional right to make, should be judged within this context.

I didn't get to give this speech to the judge. I didn't get to speak at all. In retrospect, the turning point in the trial was likely when the Crown prosecutor showed a video clip of me talking to a child on the road and argued that I was even encouraging children to break the law. I remembered that day vividly and asked my lawyer to insist the tape be replayed with the audio turned up. The second time it was played, we could hear that I had, in fact, been telling the child and his parents that I thought they should get off the road and not risk arrest. By the fifth day of the trial, after legal arguments from my lawyer (that my sister Wendy had helped develop) that there was no legal basis for the charge of aiding and abetting, the judge harshly noted that he would have loved to put me in jail but that there was no legal reason to do so. I was free.

THE SUMMER OF PROTESTS in Clayoquot Sound in 1993 had a huge impact on Canadian environmental politics and the future of the forest industry, and a direct impact on thousands of lives. In Clayoquot many of us learned about the importance of seeing past an individual's career or clothing and finding common ground. We learned about the importance and difficulties of working in a coalition and of the inevitable backlash that you have to surf whenever you really challenge the status quo.

The government and industry condemned the protests by calling environmentalists "hysterical" and worse. They'd said the same thing before about people who warned that the cod stocks in Atlantic Canada were being depleted at a dangerous rate . . . right before the stocks collapsed. For years Dupont dismissed environmentalists as "hysterical" for claiming chloroflurocarbons (CFCs) were eating away at the ozone layer. In fact, every new campaign that challenges the status quo goes through this same first phase of attacks and criticism. I find it's not unusual, years later, to be congratulated by some of the same politicians who once condemned us. Change can be threatening, and we were calling for not only significant change in our laws and industrial activities but in what we deem valuable and what we do not.

One remarkable thing about working on these issues was the realization that our society is designed to protect the right to make money before protecting living systems that support us. Standing at the blockades, I discovered that our challenge was to reverse the burden of proof. Why wasn't the burden of proof on corporations—and the governments supporting them—to show that their practices were ecologically and environmentally responsible—especially when they were dealing with public land and public health?

The summer of 1993 was an important moment in Canada because, for the first time, regular citizens had a voice loud enough to break through convention and ask hard questions about the full cost of industrial activity. The protest and resulting trial sparked important debates that had unimagined consequences across the country. Years later I would meet industry executives who told me of changed practices, or government officials who talked about areas they had protected in order to avoid "another Clayoquot Sound." Over the years, I have been contacted by hundreds of students and professors writing papers about the conflicts in Clayoquot Sound, many of them concluding that the summer of 1993 was when Canada began to see the forest for the trees.

I would like to say that this was a turning point for Canada that led to fundamental changes in an economy built on harvesting natural resources and shipping them out as quickly as possible. Unfortunately, while the events had a big impact on changing forest practices and protecting many places around the country, what we see today playing out in the oil fields of Alberta is simply another chapter in our frontier approach—and unfortunately our logging practices are still far from sustainable. We have run out of cod, we are forced to access more and more remote forests that are increasingly expensive to log in a global economy fed with fast-growing plantations from the south. And now we have turned to the Alberta tar sands. Many of the same people with whom I stood on the road in Clayoquot and later worked with to create the markets campaign are now in the fight to stop the tar sands. Their resolve stems from Clayoquot: not only did it create real change in policies and protected areas, it also transformed people's lives and perspectives.

It certainly transformed mine. The experience of being part of one of the largest outpourings of public dissent on environmental issues in Canada changed me forever and inspired my commitment. I began to understand how to channel the anger and despair that I felt from experiencing firsthand a familiar place being destroyed. It was a process of understanding what makes up the anatomy of a campaign, how social change is made, and what I actually could do every day. It was a journey of understanding how environmental issues are seen and analyzed from different perspectives—whether it meant learning from First Nations who live in the region, or learning from the local community—and then marrying that understanding and experience with research and knowledge of the economic and political systems that drive decision making about land use and industrial development. In meeting after meeting with First Nations, industry heads or forestry workers that summer, we didn't always agree with what we heard, but every conversation helped me to better understand what was required to find resolutions.

At the time, building a coalition or, as we now refer to it in strategy sessions, "putting up a big tent and inviting our allies in," was in fact frowned upon by some in Greenpeace. Building a coalition remains one of the most difficult things we do. Many organizations depend on their brands to fundraise and, therefore, to survive. Sharing the work means sharing the glory. It also means negotiating positions and policies, sharing information and letting go of control. Difficult steps, but essential. There is, of course, strength in numbers, but more than that, there are frequently better ideas and more diverse strategies. Working with other environmental groups, First Nations and unions forced us to think about what we were *for* instead of just what we were against. It led to soul-searching and some compromises but ultimately also to fairly strong alliances that could craft solutions.

Reflecting on the legacy of Clayoquot Sound makes me realize too that it was the beginning of really understanding that the issue wasn't about right or left, or whether you were a hippie or a business person; it was about whether you shared values. Finding common ground with unions and First Nations, and watching the business person and the hippie wash dishes together—those were the moments that gave me the courage to reach out and have conversations with the CEOs of logging companies. Every day for four months I saw people defying all the labels that were put on them.

The shared sense of purpose, inclusiveness and commitment to a wide engagement that we tried to mirror in all our work had an impact far beyond that moment and place. Two decades later I still bump into people and find that their lives were dramatically changed by Clayoquot Sound. Some who were there for only three days have written to me and said it changed what they were studying, what they did for a living and how they saw the world. One protester, a nurse, Marlene Cummings, went back to Ontario after the experience and realized she wanted to devote more time to this type of work. Several years and university degrees later, she moved to Vancouver to direct forest and climate work with ForestEthics. I've heard hundreds of these stories.

For me, Clayoquot Summer was an education in activism and real-world politics. It's also where I discovered what I wanted to do and whom I was going to do it with. By the end of the summer I had decided that I would try to finish my graduate degree from afar, but I was not going into science or law. I would continue trying to figure out what campaigning was and how we could build on the experiences in Clayoquot Sound to protect more old-growth forests and ensure more sustainable logging practices.

Chapter 4

THE MORAL HIGH GROUND
WORKING WITH FIRST NATIONS

You, Tzeporah Berman . . . the blood of our children's future suicides will be on your hands.
CHIEF SIMON LUCAS OF THE HESQUIAHT FIRST NATION

IT WAS 1994, the year after all the protests, and MacMillan Bloedel was still logging Clayoquot as quickly as they could. In my new role as a Greenpeace forest campaigner, I requested one of the Greenpeace ships come to Clayoquot Sound to oppose logging in Bulson Creek. Many First Nations leaders didn't want us to oppose the logging company because it offered them jobs and money—and they needed jobs and money. Of course, this is a simplification of complex and often heart-wrenching circumstances. The First Nations are trying to resolve disputes that are hundreds of years old while working to lift their communities out of poverty. First Nations leaders had protested the Clayoquot Sound Land Use Decision, some even going so far as to fly to Washington to meet with Robert Kennedy and the Natural Resources Defense Council (NRDC) to coordinate efforts and to make their views known. And at this particular moment in the campaign, the chiefs did not want Greenpeace upsetting their discussions with the company.

A notice arrived at the Greenpeace ship. The Nuu-chah-nulth warned that unless I came to a meeting with all the chiefs to be held in Port Alberni that afternoon, they would issue a formal warning of their intention to mount their war canoes and physically force Greenpeace to leave Clayoquot Sound. The senior management team at Greenpeace was freaking out. Imagine the front-page story: "First Nations War Canoes Chase Greenpeace Out of Rainforest."

All I heard from everyone was "You've got to go to this meeting."

I was twenty-four and terrified. I had not only my job but Greenpeace's reputation in Canada and potentially beyond in my hands.

I hopped into a rental car, drove several hours down the winding island highway to Port Alberni and walked into the meeting room. There were thirteen chiefs and First Nations leaders—all men—waiting for me. And they were mad. I'd heard the phrase "steam coming out of the ears" before, but that was the first time I truly understood it. They had been carefully building a truce with the logging companies, and the Greenpeace ship and the controversy we were creating over continued logging were causing divisions in their community and infuriating the corporate leaders.

As soon as I sat down, they started yelling at me. Each chief appropriately took the time to speak, each standing up in turn, and they all yelled. They were venting years of frustration and anger at being sidelined by all parties and watching their communities suffer. Behind their rage I could sense their fear that they would now also lose whatever the company was offering their communities. After the first chief finished, I tried to explain why we were opposing the logging and how together we could help ensure more options for them than they had now. But it was not yet my turn. "You are here to listen," a chief I didn't know thundered at me. After the first hour I was holding back tears. After the second hour I was sobbing openly. After three hours I asked if I could leave the room for a moment so I could get myself together and use the bathroom, and someone replied, "You will sit here until we have been heard!"

A big guy with a mane of snow-white hair—Chief Simon Lucas of the Hesquiaht—stood up and said, "You, Tzeporah Berman—if you stand in the way of our progress, the blood of our children's future suicides will be on your hands."

When it was finally over, I returned to my rental car and headed back up the highway. I was so shaken that I could barely drive, so I stopped at a pay phone to call Chris and Valerie and tell them what had happened. "It was horrible. I don't know what to do," I said.

They told me to come back to the ship, that we would figure it out together.

I got in the car and drove toward Clayoquot Sound in the dark. Just after the turnoff between Tofino and Ucluelet, I noticed a red pickup speeding in my direction. I made eye contact with the driver. I recognized him as one of the loggers who opposed the blockade and could tell that he recognized me. He got a nasty look in his eyes and veered his truck straight at my car. He was playing chicken. He was coming at me head-on.

I swerved my car off the road. The car flipped and did a full roll, somehow ending up back on the wheels. I hunched over the steering wheel in the dark trying to control my breathing and deciding what to do. I was scared and alone at the side of the highway. The logger who came at me was gone. Tentatively I tried to start the car. The engine sputtered, then caught and I inched back onto the highway.

I finally got back to the ship at ten o'clock, bruised, exhausted. And in a few hours the Nuu-chah-nulth were going to take out the war canoes. I was sure, as sure as I'd ever been of anything in my life, that I'd just destroyed Greenpeace.

IT WAS A WHOLE LOT easier to say "not one tree shall fall" before meeting with the chiefs whose people have lived in and on and with these forests for thousands of years. And here I was, a frizzy-haired Jewish girl from downtown Toronto, shouting, "Not one tree shall fall!"

The first thing I ever wrote in my journal in Clayoquot, when I started coming to terms with First Nations issues, was "I've quickly realized that the moral high ground that I'm standing on is eroding faster than the clear-cut hillside." The First Nations coastal peoples had the highest suicide rates and the highest poverty rates and the highest unemployment rates in the country.

After meeting those chiefs, after hearing their stories, I knew it was time to get beyond simply being against logging and try to figure out what I was for. It's so much easier to be against than for because no real-world solution is ever going to be as pure as "stop all logging now and forever." But if you're going to campaign effectively, and protest, blockade, and do direct actions with positive results, you have to be willing to talk to all the players and work out solutions. Otherwise, that's not campaigning, it's just complaining.

After that meeting with the chiefs, during the time I campaigned on Clayoquot Sound and later on behalf of saving what we would call the Great Bear Rainforest, I worked closely with many First Nations leaders and developed lasting, deep relationships. The work was fraught with difficulties and layers of complications. I learned the hard way that there is no one right answer for balancing indigenous rights with ecological risk and economic impact.

At one of our first meetings a very, very knowledgeable chief, Moses Martin of the Tla-o-qui-aht, said to me, "You have to understand you're concerned about the trees and the wildlife, and many of us share those concerns, but we're also carrying into this meeting the highest suicide rates in Canada, we have the highest unemployment rates in Canada, and our people are struggling so hard to survive that our culture and language are dying." The reality for the Nuu-chah-nulth people, which includes the Tla-o-qui-aht and the Hesquiaht, is that they never did cede their territories, which they have lived in for so long. They make up 40 percent of the regional population of British Columbia, but live on only 0.4 percent of the land base. They have a 70 percent unemployment rate.[1] The reality of the temperate coastal rainforest was that it was continuing to be clear-cut, which was devastating the region—and one of Canada's prime ecological assets, but the logging provided urgently needed jobs in their eyes. In Clayoquot Sound it wasn't just the First Nations who made the so-called moral high ground a quicksand. The woman with the boy on her hip and the sign that read "Your party, our future" kept showing up in my dreams. Seeing her was also the beginning of trying to redefine what I called success.

I came to see that it wasn't "my side" killing the logging towns, it was the increasing mechanization of the logging companies. The data showed that these communities were slowly losing jobs even though there was more logging every year, and that in Canada we were getting fewer jobs per tree cut than almost any jurisdiction in the world. I learned from talking to Herb Hammond, who a couple of years before had written a seminal book on eco-forestry called *Seeing the Forest Among the Trees,* that if Canada ensured selective logging we could create more jobs per tree cut. We needed to think beyond creating unlogged parks and start looking at possible systemic changes to the way economic development happens. Yes, we had to protect more forests, but we could also create more jobs. This did not have to be an either/or proposition.

First Nations have been living here for thousands of years. They were decimated by the conquering Europeans and their children were appallingly kidnapped from their families by government decrees to "Christianize" them and assimilate them so as to control their lands. The children were forced into residential schools, often hundreds of miles from home. Now the governments and our own organizations were saying, "Now it's a park and you can't do your own logging there even though your grandfather lived there and his great-grandfather lived there." Is that a victory? If we protected the rainforest and the logging towns became ghost towns and the First Nations were kept from living in their ancestral homelands because we'd created a park in a sea of clear-cuts, was that a success? If we backed down and agreed that the logging should continue because these communities needed to put food on their tables, would they still have jobs there in five or ten years when the old-growth binge ended or moved farther north to find and exploit more old-growth? The resource development model that was designed to access bountiful natural resources as quickly as possible and export them out of the country even faster came at the tail end of my generation. These issues played in the media and in the local communities like Clayoquot as though it was simply about jobs versus trees. You either cared about people or you cared about nature.

That summer as I stood on the blockades facing the loggers' wives with their kids on their hips, and as I sat across the table from weary First Nations chiefs still waiting for justice and respect that was hundreds of years overdue, I began to seriously think through and research what a "solution" could look like. The fact was that the clear-cut logging being proposed would not provide jobs for long. Mill towns were shutting down all over the province because in a country as cold as Canada we simply can't grow trees as quickly as we can log them. We needed a long-term economic diversification plan to support the remote communities. In the meantime, we had to be willing to support some logging and figure out how to increase jobs and economic revenue from every one of the old-growth giants that fell. To many in the environmental community, that position was and is heresy.

AFTER THE DISASTROUS meeting and the game of chicken on the highway, Valerie calmed me down. She said, "I know there's a compromise here. Moses and I have known each other for a very long time. I'll give him a call."

Val called Chief Moses Martin of the Tal-o-qui-aht over the radio. By this time, I think he was feeling terrible about what had happened to me. He agreed to bring the chiefs together once everyone had cooled down a bit and suggested we meet again the next morning. He said he could get them to hold off on sending the war canoes and putting out the press release. So the next morning, we got in the Zodiac just as the sun was coming up. I was an absolute wreck and Val was driving. We were zooming across the waves of Clayoquot Sound, and suddenly Val started humming the theme from *The Lone Ranger* and yelled, "Who would have thought it? The dyke and the Jew racing off to save the day and broker peace with the Indians!" Then she went back to the *Lone Ranger* theme. I laughed so hard that I nearly fell out of the boat. Val's humour and fearlessness grounded me. This was her home. She had been doing this work a lot longer than I had. If she was collected enough to crack jokes, everything was going to be okay.

This time when we met, everyone was calmer. We agreed to quietly pull the ship back from that particular blockade, but said Greenpeace wasn't leaving Clayoquot Sound. We agreed that the following week we would sit down in meetings to fully understand the chiefs' concerns around their lack of control over the lands. They explained that the provincial government was offering to make an agreement with them, but only if they supported the logging. We realized the government was using them to block us—and it wouldn't be the first time the British Columbia government had played this card. So we reached a quiet compromise to make room for calmer discussions.

Eventually, after months of discussion and trust building, our coalition of environmental groups[2] reached an agreement with the Nuu-chah-nulth that there would be no logging in pristine areas by anyone—including First Nations. In fact, we found that our map of pristine rainforest areas that were the most important for the protection of water and biodiversity were the exact areas the First Nations considered their most important spiritual areas, or *Eehmiss,* and that was part of the reason that they had been reticent to reveal such locations on the maps. We also committed to lobbying for the Nuu-chah-nulth to have increased control over their traditional territories equally with ecological protection, and promised we would not oppose selective logging in areas outside the pristine valleys. We had begun crafting a solution that First Nations leadership could support and that seriously threatened the government and industry plans for the region—and I made my first enemies within the environmental movement.

THE FIRST TIME your friends call you a sellout, it hurts like hell. Those who hold extreme radical positions within any movement—including the environmental movement—like to "play" issues as though there's always a clear and obvious case of radical politics versus compromise solutions, strong positions versus incrementalism or "weak" positions. From my perspective, I came to see that those same "radicals" who believe you should never support any logging also romanticize First Nations; they feel strongly that social justice requires that we must support First Nations no matter what. Similarly, if certain First Nations agree with industrial logging, social justice "radicals" argue that we need to support the First Nations who are "correct," as though anyone has the right to define which leaders are true to their heritage and which are tools of the state. The fact is that support for First Nations and strong environmental positions often do not go hand in hand.

After spending long nights discussing the issues with Val, Karen, Chris and others, I realized that the challenge in dealing with First Nations, and other local communities, was trying to find a balance and, hopefully, some common ground. This balancing act has been incredibly difficult at times, for myself as for the wider environmental community. Most environmentalists understand the need for our society to redress past injustices, recognize traditional territories and do what we can to support the survival of indigenous cultures and First Nations communities' right to self-determination. But like all communities, First Nations groups are diverse. Sometimes the leadership has strong environmental values, and other times it does not. And the Nuu-chah-nulth, like other First Nations, rightly want to be treated as a government, as a nation.

I realized early on in my work that we should indeed be treating First Nations as governments and nations, and thus like any government they had to be held accountable for their decisions, especially for decisions that would cause irreversible damage to ecosystems. That controversial position led to many confrontations with First Nations leaders who expected that if they were supporting the logging companies we wouldn't oppose them on social justice grounds. Finding common ground with the First Nations leadership was a constant challenge. Many initially didn't want to see any logging, but they had other concerns. They felt that Greenpeace was trying to prevent economic development in their communities, which explained why they were angry with us in our first meeting. We endured months of gruelling discussions until finally reaching an agreement to support what became known as the Interim Measures Agreement (IMA) with the BC government, a sort of pre-treaty to final resolution of land claims disputes, and by publicly calling for them to have increased decision making around their economic development.

WE SHOWED OUR SUPPORT for the chiefs and the IMA in a quite dramatic way. After several months of working with Robert Kennedy, Liz Barratt-Brown and other lawyers at the National Resources Defense Council on their IMA, the chiefs reached out to several environmentalists—Adriane Carr from the Western Canada Wilderness Committee (and later deputy leader of the Green Party of Canada), Vicky Husband from the Sierra Club, and me—to tell us that they had an important meeting coming up at the Legislative Assembly in Victoria. They wanted to know if we would join them. They said they were not going to tell the government we were coming. They did not want us to speak, they just wanted us to stand behind them in the room.

The doors opened and we all filed in and stood behind the chiefs' chairs. The chiefs said, "Our friends here have just come to observe the meetings. They're here in support of our request for an interim measures agreement." The government negotiators went slack-jawed and I think several broke a sweat. The meeting was a massive success and a turning point in talks about Clayoquot Sound. Afterwards, the government agreed to a whole new decision-making regime in Clayoquot Sound called the Central Region Board, on which First Nations had 51 percent of the decision-making power. The government also created a science panel to review the logging practices in the region.

A few years later, the Nuu-chah-nulth created Isaak, a company that was initially 50 percent run by MacBlo and 50 percent owned by the Nuu-chah-nulth. Isaak's mandate was to do only selective logging and eco-forestry, and to not log any of the pristine valleys. Today First Nations fully own Isaak, and while we still don't have a permanent resolution to the land-use disputes in the region, the pristine valleys are standing intact.

LATER THAT SAME YEAR Greenpeace received a call from some of the hereditary chiefs of the Nuxalk First Nation in Bella Coola, located in a coastal valley north of Vancouver Island. They were concerned about the salmon disappearing, the scarcity of animals in their traps, not being able to find their medicines in the forests because of all the clear-cut logging. They wanted to meet and see if, just maybe, we could work together. Chris was now working with Greenpeace too, and he and I took a ten-seater plane to Bella Coola, flying over the

Fraser River, which was stacked with log booms. We watched as the city vanished behind the snow-covered Coast Mountain range. Every so often we'd pass one of the mountains, and the lush landscape would disappear, scarred by jagged, zigzagging roads and clear-cuts. There was a moment when I was holding the camera and my hands went limp because I didn't want to capture this picture, I wanted to erase it.

When Chris and I arrived, we found ourselves booked into a crappy little hotel, where I proceeded to have the weirdest dreams and the absolute worst sleep of my life. The next day I was feeling like a complete wreck. Chris was moody, and it turned out that he had slept terribly as well. So we sat down at the meeting with the chiefs, and Chief Lawrence Pootlass, who must have been almost seventy, greeted us by asking, "Sleep well?"

I said, "No, I woke up feeling like I'd been run over by a truck."

And he said, "Yeah, they built that hotel right on top of our graveyard." Then he laughed.

I asked why he had booked us there.

He said, "Just checking." Then he laughed again. That was our first test.

Bella Coola was torn in half over whether to log. Chief Pootlass's brother was the elected chief, and he was cutting deals with the logging company Interfor (International Forest Products, based in Vancouver). Lawrence and Ed Moody (known as K'watsinas), hereditary chiefs, and the whole hereditary council were against all the logging. It was a nightmare.

We did some research and knew that we wanted to help them stop Interfor from going into some of the areas that held major significance for the Nuxalk. There were so few intact areas left that we decided to send a message to Interfor and build awareness of this area outside of Clayoquot Sound. This was the first time there was any major anti-logging activity on the BC coast outside of Clayoquot Sound.

We arranged to bring the Greenpeace ship *Arctic Sunrise* to Bella Coola. The chiefs were hoping we could help save an area called the Tallheo Hot Springs, which Interfor had already marked with yellow tape for immediate logging. Honestly, we really weren't sure what we would do when we got there, but we knew showing up in this remote logging town on the coast with a big Greenpeace ship would get Interfor's attention; after that, we would make it up as we went along.

Bella Coola inlet is stunningly beautiful, with high mountains and crystal-clear water. Blankets of dark forest cover the mountains, scarred intermittently by logging roads. We went all the way up the inlet on the ship. The chiefs were waiting on the dock at Bella Coola with drummers in ceremonial dress, and half the community came out to welcome the ship. I wasn't sure what the proper protocol was for such an important occasion. I looked up at Lawrence as our boat pulled close to the dock and mouthed, "What do I do now?"

And he said, "You and the captain come up onto the dock. You bring your chiefs, we've got our chiefs. Come on, get up here."

The chiefs presented us with a stunning eagle feather headdress and a beautifully carved paddle. We were given a welcoming ceremony and were then introduced to William Tallheo, a regal elder with salt-and-pepper hair who must have been ninety years old, whose family name had been given to the local hot springs. That night we agreed to take a number of people on the *Arctic Sunrise* from the community to the Tallheo Hot Springs, where some of the chiefs wanted to perform a protection ceremony. We'd brought some cameras and we were going to record ourselves taking down all Interfor's logging and flagging tape.

It was about an hour and a half by boat, and the trip was breathtaking: glacial mountains, rushing rivers, deep inlets, thick green forest. Only the scars of the old logging roads and the bare strips riddled with landslides marred the trip. When we arrived at the hot springs, William Tallheo was sitting on a chair on the deck of our ship. I noticed tears running down his face. When I approached him he said, "I was born here. I haven't been here since I was a child."

I asked, "Why?" It wasn't that far away.

He said, "Because we don't have any boats."

I was suddenly hit by the level of poverty in the community and how important it was that we were bringing this boatload of fifty or sixty elders out to the hot springs.

We had a beautiful protection ceremony. As it was ending, we noticed a company boat full of Interfor employees heading toward us. They were shocked to see us there and clearly didn't know how to react. Chief Ed Moody stood out front and bellowed across the water, "This is our land and we are claiming it back! You can't log here!" Interfor didn't come any closer. We took down the logging tape, had a wonderful lunch on board and headed back to town. We were so inspired that the next day we jointly went to Interfor's office and surrounded it with drummers and singers. We stopped the logging of the hot springs that year, but debates within the Bella Coola community raged on. Greenpeace and many other environmental groups worked for years off and on with the Nuxalk, and they continued to protest at home and abroad.

ONE OF THE MOST frustrating aspects of watching the Canadian government deal with First Nations is seeing the lip service paid to "consultation," the disrespect for traditional structures and hereditary leadership and the cynical buy-offs by both government and industry.

In many cases, desperate communities find themselves forced to choose between standing up to government and industry, or accepting short-term payouts for new schools and new housing and other facilities they desperately need. I was frequently in awe of their courage in standing up and saying, "No, it's not right and we won't support the logging." I've watched chiefs and communities do that, time and time again, only to be stuck later with even more insulting offers, and left with no remaining forests. And I've talked to elders in communities where logging had already happened—where they'd been fighting logging and either agreed to it or it happened without their consent—and they'd seen the boom-and-bust cycle. They'd suddenly get the infrastructure, the jobs and the money, but most of it would last less than a generation. Then the companies moved out and the communities were left with a devastated landscape and the memory of a couple of years of living high on the hog. It's binge economics: a short-term cash infusion followed by starvation.

Ecotrust Canada, a non-profit that works to develop the conservation economy, published an atlas in the late '90s that charted forest loss up the coast of North America from California to Alaska and simultaneously tracked the loss of indigenous languages. You can see that as the forest cover disappeared, so did the languages and culture. That's how intimately the communities have been tied to the land, and that's a deeply serious cost of unchecked logging.

It is always difficult when social issues butt up against what are categorized as "environmental issues." I think that for the environmental community—many of whom come from the left—it's a challenge working with First Nations issues on forestry and land use. Our society has traditionally dealt with First Nations by ignoring or romanticizing them. People on the left especially have a tendency to accept as dogma that because First Nations culture and history are closer to nature, they are always right about how to deal with nature. But to say that any one community—First Nations or otherwise—has a single opinion and only one ideal is ridiculous and itself patronizing. There are diverse interests in every community.

In the forest debates in the '90s, the tendency was to sideline First Nations. Environmentalists did it by either calling an occasional meeting and holding a token consultation, or logging companies did it by throwing a cheque at a band council and refusing to negotiate beyond that. Some of the strongest ecologists and environmentalists I know, who are traditionally left on social politics, were so racked by white liberal guilt that they were prepared to step back and say that if First Nations wanted to clear-cut forests that was okay. But that's not right either.

Yes, we have to respect, engage and learn from First Nations communities and individuals, and if we respect them we must treat them as nations. They have their right to decision making over their traditional territories, and everyone has a democratic right to protest if we believe an agreement—First Nations or otherwise—has made a wrong decision. All of us have to be accountable for our effect on the planet. I recognize the United States as a separate nation from mine, but that doesn't mean I don't have an opinion on deepwater oil drilling being allowed again in the Gulf of Mexico.

PART II **BOY**

Chapter 5

THE WATERBED EFFECT
BEGINNING THE MARKETS CAMPAIGN

If you think you're too small to make a difference,
you haven't been in bed with a mosquito.

AFRICAN PROVERB

THE BLOCKADES IN Clayoquot Sound were, in many ways, a huge success. They raised the profile of the issues nationally and internationally. The experience gave birth to a new awareness and inspired thousands. Environmentalists were in discussions with First Nations, and government was scrambling to create a more rigorous process for overseeing the forests, but there was still little willingness to reduce the logging or protect what was left of the old-growth valleys. And the logging continued unabated

We had tried to create political change at Clayoquot Sound. Local groups had participated in government land-use decision-making processes for decades while watching government after government ignore all the recommendations and hand the forest over to the logging companies on a silver platter. We stood on the road. We went to jail. The polls showed the numbers were on our side. And the government refused to change. We ultimately realized that the companies held all the cards, and if we couldn't make government change, we'd make it an irrelevant player in the debate. That was, of course, a huge failure of democracy and in many ways a problematic approach for a movement that inherently distrusts major corporations, but we needed industry clout in order for the government to listen. In addition, Clayoquot Sound was the tip of the iceberg and the logging was rampant across the west coast and the country—most of it feeding the export markets.

After my trial, Greenpeace International hired me to help build a new international forests campaign. I had tried implementing solutions through academia and science, creating public campaigns and coordinating massive protests, building coalitions with First Nations and lobbying government. It was time to follow the money and research who was buying the wood and paper that came from these trees.

In early 1994 the Greenpeace office in the UK discovered that Scott Paper was buying products from MacBlo harvested in Clayoquot Sound. They were making toilet paper out of old-growth rainforest. At our first meeting in London with Scott Paper, we laid out what we'd learned about the source of their paper. Their response, which would later be echoed by many of the companies we met with that year, was "Oh no, our paper is not made out of clear-cut old-growth rainforest. Ours comes from sustainable harvesting. And we never buy old-growth." The government and industries' PR machines were in full swing. Whether it was denial or the result of outright lies they were being fed, many of the international customers we met with insisted we were wrong about the source of their products—until we showed them the pictures and chain-of-custody research. Then all hell would break loose. Many company officials were privately shocked to hear they were making toilet paper, magazines or newspapers out of rare ecosystems that were the result of ten thousand years of post-glacial activity. That some of the trees were a thousand years old. That the forests were home to black bears and wolves and numerous species that don't live anywhere else on earth. By the second meeting, Scott Paper and others moved on to another line of argument. "All the products we buy are logged according to strict laws. This really isn't our issue. Talk to your government. The Canadian government has to regulate and control and oversee."

In the case of Scott Paper, Greenpeace's response was simple. "The government has been intransigent on this issue. These issues are your problem too as long as you buy these products. You have a choice." And that's when we showed Scott Paper the ads we had mocked up showing a cute little puppy that looked exactly like the one in their ads, falling down stairs with soft toilet paper rolls. In this ad, however, there was a cartoon speech bubble coming from the puppy's mouth that said, "I destroyed the rainforest to make toilet paper."

Then the UK campaigner said, "We'll have fleets of people going through the supermarkets, putting these on all the toilet paper on all the shelves of every store, because we believe your customers have a right to know where your paper comes from. You choose. You have thirty days."

As the VP tried to catch his breath, we left the meeting.

Scott Paper was the first company to cancel its contract for rainforest pulp from MacBlo. The contract was worth several million dollars. This was the beginning of the "markets campaign" to stop the logging in Clayoquot Sound.

ONCE WE'D WON the battle with Scott Paper, our approach became more polished. We started a coalition the Clayoquot Rainforest Coalition: Rainforest Action Network, Greenpeace, the Pacific Environment and Resources Center and the National Resources Defense Council—to run the first markets campaign in the United States and Canada on Clayoquot Sound.

Liz Barratt-Brown at the NRDC began meetings with the *New York Times, TIME* magazine and other buyers. Chris, who was working with RAN, organized our first big public American campaign. He was targeting Pacific Bell because their phone books were made from rainforests. We put stickers on telephone booths (remember telephone booths?) that said, "Let your fingers do the chopping." At Pacific Bell's annual general meeting that year we had a six-foot-tall phone in front of the building that rang every sixty seconds because at that time an acre of rainforest was being destroyed every sixty seconds. It rang so loudly that it completely disrupted their meeting. My friend Mark Evans was chained inside the phone, so it was impossible for the police to remove it. Two people scaled a building next to the San Francisco Bay bridge and hung a massive banner on the side. The banner read, "Let your fingers do the chopping. Pacific Bell Stop Destroying Rainforests." Inside the building, United Church representatives (who became shareholders in order to intervene at the AGM) were making an ecumenical case for why Pacific Bell needed to do the right thing.

The next day Linda Coady from MacBlo called me at the Greenpeace office in San Francisco. "This has got to stop," she said. "We just can't do our business. Our customers are going crazy and now this Pacific Bell thing . . . what do we have to do?"

I said, "You have to stop logging Clayoquot Sound."

She said, "Fine. We'll shut down the whole division. We need to talk."

I was speechless.

I did a little happy dance around the office. Had we actually stopped the logging in Clayoquot Sound?[1] An agreement of this magnitude had never happened in British Columbia before. We'd saved places, but never against a company that had already spent millions of dollars building road networks. Yes, we had literally stopped the bulldozers, caused them to back up and leave the region. I called my friends at RAN who had played such an enormous role in creating the campaign and said, "We did it! We won! They're pulling out of Clayoquot Sound!" Chris got Atossa Soltani, the director of the programme, and Randy Hayes, the founder of RAN, on the phone. It was Randy who stopped me in my tracks.

"That's great. MacBlo is pulling out of Clayoquot. But what's Pacific Bell going to be making its Yellow Pages out of?"

I didn't know and didn't care. They were pulling out of Clayoquot Sound! We'd won.

But RAN hadn't. They had of course been campaigning against Pacific Bell using *any* old-growth in the Yellow Pages, not just Clayoquot's old-growth forest. We'd saved one forest without any real plan for saving all the trees. We'd been so excited about forming the US coalition that we'd never taken the time to agree on what we were trying to achieve.

After several screaming matches, and some long meetings into the wee hours of the morning, the other groups reluctantly but generously agreed to stop the public campaign against Pacific Bell in order to save the now-iconic Clayoquot Sound. Meanwhile, they would continue pressuring Pacific Bell to shift their purchasing practices, using the threat of another campaign.

While we were able to achieve a resolution on a path forward, that experience created a much larger conversation about the power of the markets-based campaign work and forced us to ask an important question: Is it enough to save one small place if the big corporations can just buy from somewhere else?

IN ADDITION TO following the money, we started following the government. We made Freedom of Information requests and found out the best-managed part of British Columbia's forests bureaucracy was its marketing arm. The government was spending millions of dollars a year on PR to convince the marketplace that BC forest products were green. At the time, I think the collective budgets of all the environmental programmes challenging the province might have hit $100,000 maximum. It was a total David and Goliath battle. All we could do was try to track what they were doing, and use the moments they were creating—by organizing meetings with customers or releasing reports or advertising initiatives—for our campaign. If you use their moments, they create the platform, but you create the controversy, and the conversation becomes yours. It's PR judo: using your opponents' strength against them.

I went straight for my PR judo black belt when someone leaked the news that the premier of BC, Mike Harcourt, was going to be stumping for the forest industry trade across Europe. Harcourt is arguably one of the greenest premiers Canada has ever had—and he certainly has shown that with his work since he left office, advocating globally for sustainable cities. However, at the time he had made the disastrous decision to allow the logging in Clayoquot Sound.

Greenpeace decided that if he was going to be in Europe, we should go everywhere he did, making sure customers, media and the public heard the other side of the story. So I went to Europe, and it was one of the scariest things I'd ever agreed to do. Still just twenty-four years old, and it was my job to embarrass and upstage the premier of BC. I didn't realize until I got off the plane in Hamburg that the German research department for Greenpeace had booked me on the same plane as the premier. Once I realized the premier was disembarking with me, I wasn't quite sure what to do. Then I saw a line of about a dozen people in the waiting area all standing silently, glaring at him with their arms crossed. They were wearing T-shirts with his face on them, and underneath, in German and English, the words "Mr. Clear-cut." The premier and his press crew had to walk by this welcome-to-Germany line. After they had passed, I too walked by them and finally reached the end of the line, where I turned and whispered, "I'm Tzeporah."

They steered me to the car and immediately handed me papers. "This is your itinerary, you're doing a speech here, we're doing a protest here . . ." When we arrived at our hotel, the head of the German team turned to me and said, "By the way, you're staying in the same hotel as the premier, you're booked on all the same planes, and we are going to seven cities in the next eleven days."

I walked into the hotel lobby with my bag, totally jet-lagged, and there was Harcourt and all his press crew. They didn't realize I was there until someone spotted me, and a moment later the whole lobby went quiet—like in a classic Western showdown. The premier turned around and looked at me. I walked up to him and said, "Hi." He looked flustered, and that's when I realized what a brilliant move this was because he was completely thrown off his game.

The next day Harcourt was scheduled for a debate at the University of Hamburg, and he thought he'd be debating some environmentalists or Greenpeace Germany, whom I expect he assumed he could debate under the table. But Greenpeace Germany had a surprise for him—it was going to be me. However, he had a surprise in store for me, too. When I got to the debate, it wasn't the premier on the stage, it was George Watts, a pro-logging chief from one of Vancouver Island's First Nations.

In Germany, First Nations are romanticized at least as much as big trees, if not more, so this was one of the smartest things the provincial government could have done. The moment Watts called Greenpeace "eco-imperialists trying to destroy First Nations' potential for economic security," he owned all the headlines. It was a nightmare for Greenpeace Germany, and the German head strategist and their team leader were demanding that I "get [them] an Indian." I was not going to call our First Nations colleagues and put them in that position. We were up late that night strategizing. What were we going to do? What were they going to do?

We finally decided to stick to our ecological message, tell the truth and be as clear as we could, as loud as we could. The Germans put together a truck with sixteen people playing the Canadian national anthem on chainsaws, over super-high-decibel loudspeakers, and they drove it wherever we went each night so that it was outside every one of Premier Harcourt's meetings. As soon as the truck pulled in, they locked the driver to the steering wheel so the police couldn't remove it.

Now I was riding through Europe with the chainsaw truck, doing interviews, meeting customers and debating the premier. If the premier was meeting at the Canadian consulate in Zurich, there was the chainsaw truck. Meanwhile, the Canadian media were sending stories back home. Every night, I'd do interviews for several hours before going to bed, get up at four in the morning and sit down with the team to figure out what the day was going to look like. I'd never worked that hard in my life, but with such lukewarm success. We were successful in raising awareness in Europe, but the "eco-imperialist" tag hurt us. And back home Canadians were circling the wagons around Premier Harcourt. At the time, the majority did not like the logging, but Canadians are polite people and they really did not like the personal attack on Harcourt, or Greenpeace airing Canada's dirty laundry abroad. We didn't attack or vilify a Canadian public figure again in our campaign.

On the premier's next trip to Europe, Greenpeace UK upstaged him with one of the most inventive actions I've ever heard of. In the middle of the opening ceremonies for British Columbia House—BC's posh trading hall near Trafalgar Square in the centre of London—Mounties in full regalia walked in and stood beside the other Mounties in their red serge. Then the dignitaries started arriving, and that's when *our* Mounties reached into their pockets and pulled out banners that read "Greenpeace." They put the sashes across their chests and started reading declarations to the incoming VIPs. "We declare today that BC House is open and as a nation we are disgraced by the logging that is going on . . ." The British prime minister and the premier were arriving and had to walk past them. Then, just as the Greenpeace Mounties were being arrested, a banner rolled down Nelson's Column right across the square that read, "God Save Canada's Rainforest."

OVER THE YEARS we became better at doing chain-of-custody research. We scoured shipping data, reviewed databases, made cold calls to pulp mills and read government and industry reports. We discovered that the *New York Times, TIME* magazine and the *LA Times* were all using rainforest pulp. In fact, we discovered that more than half the trees logged in Canada every year were used to make pulp and paper, and were ending up in catalogues, newspapers and junk mail. While some of the products wound up in Europe and Asia, the vast majority of everything logged in Canada was heading to the United States.[2]

At that point we began to realize that because 90 percent of the old-growth forests in the United States had already been destroyed, the products from Canadian old-growth forests were everywhere in the American marketplace.[3] We decided to take a bold broad-sweep approach. Our coalition mailed a letter to five hundred of the largest consumers of wood and paper products in North America, informing them that their products might be "tainted" with ancient rainforest destruction and that they needed to take immediate action. Nothing gets a quicker response than threatening a major corporation's brand. Within days we were receiving responses from hundreds of companies. The first round of responses came from companies that had checked their sources and wanted to assure us that they were not buying from the region. The second round came from those that were buying old-growth pulp and paper and wanted to know what to do. The silence from major brands that did not respond helped us to figure out who might be buying and who might be most vulnerable to media and public pressure. We began making calls and setting up meetings.

We contacted Home Depot, Staples, Office Depot and Office Max. Sometimes the companies would agree to work with us. More often than not, the companies would say, "That's not our problem. We're only buying legal products and that's the problem of the government." So we would organize protests in front of their stores, place controversial advertisements in major newspapers, release reports showing the chain of custody of what they were buying and where and organize tours through the rainforest and the clear-cuts.

When they saw what we were up to, the chiefs from Bella Coola had the idea that they should join us in the marketplace to "take back [their] wood," which they deemed stolen property. What followed was a series of hilarious yet deadly serious protests in the United States at Home Depot stores, and in Europe, where the First Nations elders and chiefs would walk into a Do It Yourself store dressed in full traditional regalia, pick up lumber and start walking out. Security would stop them and the police would come to arrest them, and the chiefs would turn to the TV cameras and say, "This is ours, this is our rainforest and it was stolen." Greenpeace Germany would have been thrilled.

As a result of the controversy our work had created, Larry Pedersen, British Columbia's chief forester, and company officials were asked to come to Hamburg to meet with German paper buyers. To make the most of the moment, we commissioned a sixty-foot-tall inflatable bear that we named Sparky. Every time we found out about a meeting we would inflate the bear in front of the building and then hold a press conference with Sparky there. At one particular meeting in Hamburg, two unusual things happened, adding up to one pretty magical day.

The first was that Chief Ed Moody and several others from the Nuxalk came to protest with us. When the industry representatives arrived to go to their meeting, they had to pass by First Nations wearing full regalia, standing outside, protesting alongside the Greenpeace activists. While they were in the meeting we started to inflate Sparky, but we soon realized we'd screwed up and Sparky was positioned backwards. Instead of facing the street as he was supposed to, our bear had his butt to the media, the TV cameras and the photographers.

It wasn't until much later when we saw a story in *Der Spiegel* that we realized what had happened inside the building. The German paper buyers talked about being in the meeting, looking out the boardroom window and getting the evil eye from our sixty-foot-tall bear.

A couple of weeks later I went to a meeting with *BBC Wildlife Magazine* and again faced off with the chief forester of BC, who had been asked to come and debate the issues with me. The irony was that *BBC Wildlife* had just done an extensive feature on the importance of the white Kermode bear (also known as the spirit bear) in BC's rainforests. I walked into their meeting and told them they were printing their magazine on the habitat of the Kermode bear. They were furious because they had been told that their paper came from "sustainably managed and harvested forests." They cancelled their contract.

BUT IT WAS A MEETING with the Belgian paper industry that was the real tipping point. On the Harcourt tour, we were always on the defensive. We had some distinct wins, but most of the time we were completely out-resourced. Harcourt's camp defined us as "eco-imperialists holding the economy hostage." They were doing big glossy ads and full-court tours. But we were breaking through, because we had the data and the images, and the images didn't lie.

We'd been meeting with customers and providing information in the marketplace for a couple of years when I got a call from Greenpeace Belgium saying the Belgian paper industry would like to meet with us, the forest ministry and the government. So one day in Brussels, Larry Pedersen, the chief forester of British Columbia, Linda Coady from MacBlo, Bill Dumont of Western Forest Products and I all gave presentations to the Belgian paper industry. The Belgians were frustrated at the contradictions. The government and industry claimed that BC had some of the strongest laws in the world and the forest practices were sustainable. I showed images of clear-cut logging, explained how it was a massive conversion of a complex and old ecosystem into a simplified tree farm and backed it up with signed declarations of hundreds of scientists calling for the region to be protected.

The Belgians cut right to the chase. "Are you saying that what she's saying is not true?"

Looking uncomfortable, Ric Slaco of International Forest Products replied, "Well no, it's true but—"

"I don't want to hear 'but.' Is it true? Are you logging thousand-year-old trees and turning them into paper? Is it old-growth rainforest or not? Have you really only protected less than 10 percent of it? Could we all at least agree on some simple facts?"

Industry and government were forced to agree on the facts. Then the guys in the Belgian paper industry announced that they were taking a break and they'd be back with their answer shortly. Before any of us could catch our breath, they left the room.

The chief forester looked at one of the industry leaders. "What do they mean, their answer?"

Half an hour later the Belgian paper industry rep walked back in and read a prepared statement: "We, the Belgian paper industry, are recommending to all of our members as of this date to no longer purchase from British Columbia."

The room erupted.

People were yelling, "You can't do this!"

The contracts were worth millions and millions of dollars.

But he was very clear. They did not want to keep buying BC pulp as long as the controversy continued.

We replayed that meeting in Canada with the German Publishing Association. Again we had the chief forester, the minister of forests and all the company representatives, and this time both Valerie and I were there.

I had to leave the meeting every few hours because I was breastfeeding my first child, Forrest. So I was sitting in the meeting with a huge tableful of men, and every couple of hours I'd have to run out into the hallway, where Sue Danne, my best friend and assistant, was pacing with my baby up and down the lobby in one of the big hotels in Vancouver. Then I'd go running into the bathroom, nurse and run back into the meeting. Mid-afternoon, shortly after I had returned from nursing, Sue came into the meeting and gestured to me. I thought, *Oh no, the baby must need me again. But I just nursed him!* When I left the meeting she told me, "No, no, Chris just called—look at this." She handed me a note that said Home Depot had just made a public announcement that they were going to phase out using any endangered products, including British Columbia's rainforests.

This was pre-iPhone and BlackBerry, so no one else knew yet. I walked back into the meeting and announced to the German publishing industry reps, the minister of forests, the chief forester and all the logging companies that the largest lumber consumer in the world had just walked away from old-growth lumber. Then I turned to the German publishing industry rep and said, "So as you can see, a number of customers who hold strong environmental values are very concerned about what's happening in British Columbia. You really need to make your decision about whether or not you want to continue to recommend these controversial products in Germany."

The government and industry reps in the room went white, and the German publishing industry asked for a break, just like the Belgians. And just like the Belgians they came back in and announced that they were finished with BC until our logging became more environmentally responsible. I leaned over to Valerie and passed her a note that said, "I've dreamed about meetings like these."

She burst out laughing. Ten years later she still has that note stuck above her desk, because it felt as if that was the moment when the power shifted. The government and industry could no longer call us crazy and hysterical, or refuse to address our concerns. It's one thing to fight or ignore a bunch of hippies blockading a logging road; it's quite another thing when those activists are backed by some of the largest corporations in the world.

AS SOON AS we started seeing some success in the markets campaign, customers began to ask us, "If I can't buy that, what can I buy?" Of course, this is the same thing all of us now think when we need to buy paper or lumber or even a can of tuna. Environmental campaigns arc great at telling people what *not* to do, but not so good at being clear on what to do.

Our initial conversations with companies like the *New York Times* and Home Depot took us into the boardrooms of some of the largest consumers of wood and paper products in the world. We'd tell them not to buy from Clayoquot Sound, and they'd look at sourcing from another endangered forest that didn't have anyone campaigning to save it. When we balked at their response, they asked us where they should buy from, where they shouldn't and which companies were doing the right thing. Here we had been trying to run a campaign to save BC's rainforests and now, through our networks and the groups we'd been working with, like RAN, the NRDC and Greenpeace International, we started realizing we could have a positive or negative impact on logging elsewhere in the world. But if we said, "Don't buy wood," did that mean we were advocating for more steel? What about mining? What about the environmental impacts of cement? Is wood ultimately sustainable? Where should companies source their pulp, paper and lumber?

Suddenly we were being asked where logging should happen and how. That's a very complicated question and one we hadn't spent much time exploring. Giving a considered answer not only means that on one level you're agreeing to the idea of mass consumption but also says okay to *some* logging because you can't just say, "Only buy recycled; or don't buy lumber." And we realized we couldn't just say, "Don't buy from Clayoquot Sound" because some of the companies we had convinced not to buy red cedar from BC then switched to mahogany from Brazil. We were saving our forests only at the expense of someone else's.

We dubbed this reaction "the waterbed effect," in which a company's good deeds in one area—like their decision to not buy from the BC rainforest—meant they'd increase the demand and therefore the damage done in another area of the world, like the Amazon. Similar to the way that when you sit on a waterbed, the water doesn't vanish, it just moves. In order to address the waterbed effect, we began to create comprehensive criteria and rules about which forests were endangered.

WE STARTED HAVING conversations about certification and how to define and differentiate between logging practices so we could determine what ecologically responsible logging looked like. We had to move beyond simply opposing logging to figuring out how to create a classification for kosher wood.

That shift led to epic debates about what logging was good, or at least acceptable. Greenpeace International hired BC forester Herb Hammond to meet with us, and together we produced the *Guide to Ecologically Responsible Forest Practices*, which became the basis for our negotiations in the process that led to the foundation of the Forest Stewardship Council (FSC). The FSC is now the preeminent international certification body and is supported by First Nations, industry and environmentalists around the world. How do you get a green stamp of approval on a product and know Greenpeace isn't going to crash your board meetings? That's where FSC certification comes in. Of course, soon after the FSC standards were created, industry leaped in with its own certification systems, the Sustainable Forestry Initiative (SFI), Canadian Standards Association (CSA) and others. It became a veritable battle of the acronyms, unfortunately and intentionally confusing consumers even more. At the time of writing, though, it seems that the FSC will prevail. Certified lands are growing quickly, and companies all over the world have realized that if they're going to the bother of becoming certified, or stating a preference for certified product, they might as well choose the system supported by the majority of environmental groups and indigenous peoples. The FSC also has tougher standards for protecting biological diversity, endangered species, indigenous peoples' and workers' rights, and forests of high conservation value than any supposedly comparable system. But then again, what can you expect from the other systems that were funded by the logging industry? It's a bit like asking Wall Street to regulate the stock market.

One of the biggest challenges in creating the standards was that if we were going to sign off on logging operations, the criteria couldn't simply be about doing the right kind of logging. Even if companies practised the best selective logging and never created another clear-cut, we still didn't want them logging places like Clayoquot Sound. We believed that some areas shouldn't be touched because they are rare, or extremely important for biodiversity. That realization led to the Wye River process, so named because the first meeting was held at Wye River near Chesapeake Bay. We brought together conservation biologists and environmental groups from all over, including the World Resources Institute (WRI), Conservation International, the NRDC and Greenpeace. We defined endangered forests and criteria for forests so important that they should never have any industrial incursion at all. These were complex conversations, and the process went on for several months as we tried to reach some agreement. Once we did, we mapped those values with Global Forest Watch.

In 1997 the WRI produced a report titled *The Last Frontier Forests*. It showed that half of the world's forest cover was gone, much of it impacted and degraded in the past thirty years. Only 22 percent of the planet's forests were still in areas large enough to sustain themselves long term and be able to generate and maintain the biodiversity on which we all rely.

It showed that seventy-six countries had already lost all their frontier forests, and that the remaining frontier forests store more carbon—433 billion tons—than will be released from fossil-fuel burning and cement manufacturing over the next sixty-nine years at current global emission rates. The greatest threat to these forests? Commercial logging. Over a quarter of the world's remaining intact forests are found in Canada. And Canada was still logging about one hectare of forest a minute. This work by the WRI put into perspective the challenge that we faced.

In 2002 Columbia University produced two studies called *Human Footprint* and *Last of the Wild*, which refined the WRI's findings. These studies showed that 50 to 90 percent of the earth's terrestrial species inhabit the world's forests and that many of them are threatened by extinction due to habitat loss. Again, logging was cited as one of the primary factors. We were making headway, the companies were starting to listen, but ultimately it was too slow. The logging was happening too quickly, not just in our backyard but all over the world. We needed to figure out how to up our game.

Chapter 6

GETTING OUT OF DODGE
LEARNING HOW TO CAMPAIGN

The way Greenpeace works on all levels from confrontation to cooperation with governments and corporations is an inspiration. The mix of pragmatism and passion really gets things done and effects real change in the world. I believe that Greenpeace is one of the most precious assets the global community possesses as a critical part in reversing the current fatal trajectory of our planet.

RHODES SCHOLAR AND FORMER SECRETARY-GENERAL
OF CIVICUS KUMI NAIDOO ON HIS APPOINTMENT AS
EXECUTIVE DIRECTOR OF GREENPEACE INTERNATIONAL

I GOT OFF THE redeye flight to Amsterdam with my suitcase, boarded the train and then hopped a tram from Central Station. I was disoriented and totally haggard as I arrived at one of the oldest, most beautiful historic sites in Amsterdam. At eight storeys, this marble building is one of the tallest in the area, and has an impressive clock tower in front. Tourists take pictures of it because it's so spectacular. I stood outside staring up at this huge clock tower thinking, *This can't be the right place.* Then I noticed the word "Greenpeace" embossed on the glass front door.

The Greenpeace office in Vancouver consisted of four dingy rooms on the second floor of a nondescript building on Commercial Drive, a Vancouver neighbourhood known for lefties, lesbians and lattes.

The rooms were covered with posters of campaigns and there were frequently babies and dogs everywhere. We had a staff of a dozen (eleven women, one man—Chris) and three dogs.

In Amsterdam the upraised marble reception area of the Greenpeace office had three receptionists seated at a high, high desk with their little headphones on, all saying, "Good afternoon, Greenpeace. Could you hold, please" in at least three different languages.

I stood there, trying to take this in, until one of them removed her headset and looked at me. "Can I help you?" she asked, in the kind of impeccable English you almost only hear from Scandinavians.

"Hi, I'm the new forest campaigner. I'm starting today and—"

She asked my name and sent me toward the annex.

I climbed the stairs in the centre of the building, and people in suits whizzed past me. I thought, *What the hell have I gotten myself into? I've gone from sitting in the middle of a clear-cut, eating out of a tin can to . . . this?*

I arrived at the annex attic to the sound of folk music on the radio. I passed through a beaded curtain to discover my old friend and new boss, Patrick Anderson. He had a long brown ponytail, his bare feet were on the desk, and he'd just gotten back from Indonesia, so he was wearing a sarong. He was on a conference call. He winked at me and I breathed a sigh of relief. The forest office felt like a little oasis in the middle of this imposing corporate complex. It was going to be okay.

I'D NEVER PLANNED on becoming an environmental campaigner. I didn't have any formal training and I knew I had a lot to learn. So when Greenpeace International offered me a campaigner position at head office, I jumped at the chance to learn from some of the best in the world.

I also had my own agenda. After the Clayoquot campaign, Greenpeace International decided that Canada was "over" for them. My Greenpeace colleagues really felt they'd devoted enough time, money and resources to the campaign in Clayoquot Sound. They had other countries on which they needed to focus their energy and resources, which was fair enough. But I felt strongly that we had to find a way to build on the momentum we had created. The fact is that long-lasting change is a slow burn, and all too often environmental groups move on to the "next big thing" before really capitalizing on the dialogue that they had created. So when I talked to people at head office, they'd tell me that Canada was finished as a priority—it was now time to work on the Amazon, or Indonesia.

But I knew it wasn't. It couldn't be. Canada was still logging faster than almost any place in the world and was being described as the "Brazil of the North"—a reference to the deforestation of the Amazon—for good reason. A 1993 comparison of Canada with Brazil showed that in Brazil one acre of forest was cut or burned every nine seconds, and in Canada the rate is one hectare every 60 seconds. Canada was logging about 1 million hectares (2.5 million acres) per year, 90 percent of it in old-growth or "primary" forests.[1] And so far we'd only helped save a small region of Vancouver Island. I hoped that once I got inside I could make sure Canada was not over for Greenpeace International. I was helping to coordinate the international team on forests and, while I was doing that, I continued trying to interest all the different countries in how we'd had success in Clayoquot, but we also had momentum that we could potentially use to protect millions of acres if we continued to expend our efforts on Canada.

The Greenpeace complex has its own pub in the basement, and on any given day there were people from twenty or thirty countries in there, depending on which of the ships were docked in the harbour. Every chance I had I was downstairs in the Greenpeace Bar, having a beer and trying to bend the ear of Greenpeace International's executive director. Or the team from Germany would be in town and I'd make sure I went to the pub that night. That was my internal campaign. Patrick's help made it possible for me—and the Vancouver office—to sell Greenpeace on a return to Canada.

MY FIRST FORMAL assignment in my new job was to work with Greenpeace UK on the international overfishing campaign. I'd had experience on the markets campaign, and they were looking for ways to make their issue real to people. I sat in a strategy meeting with some of my heroes, John Sauven and Chris Rose, the guys who created the *Brent Spar* campaign, in which Greenpeace occupied an oil-storage rig off the coast of Scotland and stopped Shell from disposing of their waste at sea. These guys had worked for Greenpeace for over a decade.

We brainstormed on the fisheries campaign and tried to figure out how to handle the unsexiest task in the world: getting people worried about sand eels. I'd gone from talking about majestic thousand-year-old trees to ugly, tiny sand eels. But the ugly fish needed help: massive trawling was turning them into fish oil which goes into everything in the UK from margarine to McVitie's biscuits. Sand eels may not be sexy, but they are a critical link in the food chain and were being wiped out. The trawlers were basically strip-mining or clear-cutting the oceans. These massive nets would take everything, and they'd take so much they'd leave ecological devastation in their wake.

So our campaign was about the ecological integrity of the oceans, but the focus was on the massive overharvesting of the sand eels and trying to persuade huge companies, like Unilever, to take a more sustainable approach to fishing. We finally came up with a strategy, which was identical to what we had done on forests. We traced what the sand eels were going into—which was everything—and we searched for the spirit bear of the sand eel campaign: puffins.

The British love puffins. They're beautiful, adorable birds—penguins in slightly less formal wear. They were directly threatened by the overharvesting because they eat sand eels to survive.

We organized a massive protest featuring 150 people dressed like puffins marching in front of the McVitie's biscuit factory. It was huge news, with great front-page photos. The sand eel campaign was a real lesson in how to popularize an issue and make a direct connection with customers. Nobody cared who Unilever was or what they did, but everyone in England has a connection to their biscuits—they have them with tea at four o'clock every day.

Companies like Unilever can't afford to have their brands tarnished. There is just too much biscuit competition out there. No company wants the public questioning its practices. And no government wants its public thinking it's doing something horrible to puffins.

HELPING TO DESIGN the eel/puffin/biscuit campaign clarified something that had been hovering in my consciousness since the blockades in Clayoquot Sound. In the end, the driving forces behind most decisions that government or industry make come down to money or votes. I have met both corporate decision makers and government officials who are truly motivated by their own values and a drive to do the right thing. I've met exceptions to the money-or-votes rule—like the folks at Williams Sonoma who approached ForestEthics because they really wanted to figure out how to have green purchasing practices (and later saw that they could get good press and save money by doing it); or Barry Penner, the minister of the environment for BC, who stayed on a politically poisonous file because he truly loved the forests and rivers of the province and wanted to protect them. But all these good people and millions more still have to meet a bottom line or get a policy past the party strategists.

Over the years whenever I've been frustrated and stuck I've often realized that I've fallen back on that old activist fallacy of "if I could just explain the problem and the consequences, surely they will agree with me." No, they won't. In my experience, campaigning to make positive change on environmental issues is not about education. Of course you need to get your facts straight, but I'll always remember that environment minister who asked, "What's in it for me?" when we were lobbying to protect Clayoquot Sound. Now when I am planning a campaign, every step of the way I ask myself how our plans will affect money or votes. If I were X decision maker (Barack Obama, the CEO of BP, the prime minister), what would convince me there was a benefit to doing what they want me to do?

LATER THAT YEAR I was seconded to the genetic engineering campaign, which was starting to take off. For that campaign we sent a Greenpeace action team to one of the first fields of genetically engineered crops: a Monsanto-run factory farm in Illinois. We select-ively dusted the entire crop with flour; what wasn't dusted made a huge X. We had someone fly over by helicopter to take the photo, and the picture went around the world. It featured people in hazmat suits standing in a field with a big X across it. In our press materi-als we framed the contaminated and genetically engineered crops as "Frankenfoods." The brainstorming to frame that campaign and the experience of launching it were formative experiences for me in understanding how to frame an issue and drive a debate.

We used other images, like a strawberry turning into a fish. For the genetic engineering campaign we asked European companies to say they didn't want the European Union importing what we'd christened "Gen X" soybeans from the United States. Once again we were using the marketplace to generate pressure on the North American companies.

After our trip on the *Arctic Sunrise*, the genetic-engineering cam-paign gave me additional experiences onboard a Greenpeace ship. The MV *Greenpeace* docked in New Orleans to draw attention to the practices of Monsanto in creating both genetically engineered crops and the chemical herbicides and pesticides on which these crops depended. There were people from all over the world on our ship. We would sit up late at night analyzing what we could do, and scouting the facility in New Orleans that was producing and ship-ping genetically engineered soybeans. Eventually we brought the ship right up to the front of the facility so they couldn't ship out the soybeans. Simultaneously, vanloads of activists in white Tyvek suits with "Greenpeace" emblazoned on them pulled up to the front of the facility, walked inside and chained themselves to the machinery. It was incredibly exciting, and it gave me invaluable knowledge about Greenpeace actions and how to coordinate a Greenpeace ship.

At the same time we had action and protests trying to get Europe to disallow the sale of the modified soybeans. President Bill Clinton was in the middle of the Monica Lewinsky scandal, and he was going to England to meet Prime Minister Tony Blair. In London, Greenpeace drove a truck to the front of the Parliament buildings and dumped four tons of genetically modified soybeans. Then they hung up a huge banner that read, "Tony Don't Swallow Bill's Seed."

This event was one of many times I was reminded of the value of humour in campaigning. Sometimes in our earnestness and urgency we forget that we're talking to real people with busy lives, and if we're too damn serious we're not only boring, we're insufferable. These issues are hard to engage with, they make you feel guilty, they make you feel helpless—but humour helps people connect and care.

The day the Greenpeace newspaper ad that compared people who wanted to cut Clayoquot to true believers in Elvis came out (remember—14 percent of Canadians support the Clayoquot Land Use Decision; 17 percent still think Elvis is alive), I got calls from several journalists and one person in the Prime Minister's Office to say the ad was brilliant. That one reference to Elvis captured people's attention; it made them laugh and want to show that ad to someone else. The ad had a huge impact on whether decision makers were thinking about our point. Using humour in our ads, banner slogans or campaigns often captures people's attention and gives them an access point to the issue that doesn't make them feel badly.

Similarly, after ForestEthics ran a campaign that prompted Staples to dramatically increase the amount of recycled paper they carried, and stop buying from key endangered forests, we issued an ad that said, "We've been calling Staples names for years. We never thought 'treehugger' would be one of them." That ad not only captured a lot of attention, but it also showed that we were willing to give kudos where kudos were due, which was a rare thing for an environmental group to do. In 2008, Staples announced that FSC paper would become "the standard offering for black and white high-speed copy and print jobs."[2]

IT WAS THROUGH my work at Greenpeace that I learned the concept of a critical pathway: identifying where you are and where you want to get to in order to understand what you need to do. The key to figuring out the critical pathway for an issue is power mapping: understanding who can make the decision that you want to see made in the world. You need to know who or what influences that person and what he already knows about the issue. You also need to look at what real-world events or timelines are going to impact any decisions on those issues: election dates, global events, policy conventions.

It has amazed me over the years how many people start campaigning on an issue without any strategy in place. They know what they want to accomplish, but they don't know how to get there, and they're not clear on who can ultimately make the necessary decisions to achieve their goal.

Here's a little outline for whatever you might want to sink your teeth into, whether it's a change in the recycling policy of your school or office, or a campaign to end offshore oil drilling. You need to be really clear on your ultimate goal, set some clear objectives, and understand who holds the power to make the change you want and what influences them. Then you have to brainstorm events, compile reports and use other tactics that will help capture their attention and meet your objectives. You then marry those ideas with a clear and realistic sense of your resources: how many people you have, what your skills are and how much money you have. That's it. That's the formula I learned during my first year at Greenpeace International, and it has served me well.

GOAL SETTING: WHAT DO YOU REALLY WANT?

Goal setting in itself is often a surprising challenge. Recently at Greenpeace International I found myself the arbiter of a debate between national offices regarding the appropriate response to the *Deepwater Horizon* oil spill in the Gulf of Mexico. Several offices wanted to immediately launch a boycott of BP. It may feel good to boycott BP, or protest at gas stations, but ultimately what are you asking of BP? It's our national governments that need to regulate the oil industry and reduce our dependence on fossil fuels. So by boycotting BP, we're not putting pressure on the right decision maker, and we're offering consumers a false choice. Is it really that much better to fill up at Exxon? The goal of the work in this case was to leverage the concern and interest in the spill to highlight the threat and risks of all oil drilling and push for a legislative response by governments. What you decide to do at any given moment needs to be driven by a clear goal and some even clearer time-bound objectives. In strategic planning lingo, good objectives are often referred to as SMART: strategic, measurable, achievable, realistic and timely. Your goal can be wide and far-reaching, as ours was in the oil work, to set a clear direction. Your objectives, however, need to identify milestones that can help you decide which tactics to employ when. In the early forests-markets work, we focused on having two big-brand companies cancel contracts and make public statements supporting the protection of the rainforest. This achievement in itself wasn't going to protect the rainforest, but it was a step along the way to building our power base.

POWER DYNAMICS.

As I worked on the international campaigns I realized that regardless of what issue you're dealing with, you have to analyze the power dynamics of the people you're trying to influence. You must figure out what the public and decision makers know about the issue in order to determine what you want to say about it. Then you need to find inventive ways to say it that will capture media attention. It doesn't matter if you are working on soybeans, ancient trees, elegant puffins or ugly eels. Critical to understanding power dynamics is figuring out who can make the change you want to see in the world and who (or what) influences them. In Clayoquot Sound it was ultimately the provincial government that could create the right laws and policies to protect the region. We found out the hard way that they were not influenced by civil society (at the time the ruling party held fifty-one out of sixty-eight seats and was not facing an election for another three years), but they were influenced by customers of BC forest products.

Both the goal setting and power mapping are simply about taking the time and harnessing the intellectual capital and research necessary to understand where you are and where you want to be. There is a beauty and creative energy in the throwing-spaghetti-on-the-wall phase—and you have to make room for that, too, because you will never totally control the issue. But at Greenpeace, if you put forward a plan without power mapping, critical analysis and critical pathway, you don't get approval for your plan or the money to do it. This formula is not unlike the corporate world, where you need a solid business plan to get financing. You need to be able to show how your efforts will help bring you to the goal line.

A critical pathway means identifying each stage/event/move and also predicting what response it will receive in order to avoid being surprised by the effect of your actions, or the response to your actions. For example, if we released a report that outlined Staples' connection to logging old-growth forests, Staples would likely deny it and release an unrelated environmental initiative. What would we do? Good campaigning is about combining that analysis with your own capacity and skills to figure out what you need to do.

Karen Mahon had explained the concept of the critical pathway to me, but until working with Greenpeace International, I'd had a far more organic and chaotic approach to campaigning. "That sounds like a great idea. Let's do that! They'll hate it!" My approach was completely different from doing a power analysis, in which you understand how you want to move the issue, and determine who can accomplish what needs to get done before talking about tactics or events.

It was also vital to learn how to navigate organizational politics and lobby for a cause within Greenpeace. Patrick Anderson became a mentor for that. An intense, lovable Australian, who was really involved in the formulation of the rainforest protection movement out of Australia in the '80s, Patrick is a pure "back to the forest" hippie who made his way through Greenpeace but maintained a real connection to the land and to people. He taught me how to manoeuvre through the machine while keeping the connection to place. Patrick had worked with grassroots groups in Australia and Indonesia, and he could gracefully operate in both worlds. He also had a knowledge of global forest issues that was invaluable to me. Patrick understood the kind of grassroots and community-based activism I had experienced at Clayoquot Sound that I knew was so essential to truly building social movements. He was also a master of the kind of sophisticated and professional, big-organization campaigning that Greenpeace did.

When I started working in Greenpeace, there was less of an understanding and appreciation of community organizing and coalitions and social movements than there is today. It was much more insular. Greenpeace was built on individual or small-group heroic acts. That history, combined with the need for brand protection that came from the fundraising department, seemed to coalesce into an organization that was more likely to carve out its own space and identity than build coalitions. Back in the '90s I would say, "I'd like us to work with the local community and help support them, and if we do it in a coalition with them it will make us stronger." People would stare at me blankly. Today there is a different culture at Greenpeace due in large part to the success of coalition building in the forests work, the campaigns against toxins run by Greenpeace US, and the cultural shift brought on by new offices in China, India, South Africa and other countries that have a strong community-outreach bent. There is also a growing recognition that we need to participate in, and potentially help catalyze, grassroots work and the development of larger social movements if we're going to have the power we need to make systematic change on energy policy. Back then there was a sense that meeting with the local community was a waste of time, and that we should go directly to a government and say, "Greenpeace says this."

While with Greenpeace International, besides building the next phase of Canadian rainforest campaigning and cutting my campaigning teeth on sand eels and genetic engineering, I worked to develop forest policy for campaigns around the world. There are policy experts who are consulted at various stages to develop ideas, but a lot of the decisions are just hammered out by very passionate, experienced people. When we were discussing First Nations' and indigenous peoples' policies, we nearly came to blows. Some people, especially from our Alaskan office, weren't interested in lying down and playing dead while the First Nations in their region—who owned the pulp mills—clear-cut the forests. The fight over acceptable logging that led to the creation of the FSC was another epic battle. How do you define ecologically responsible logging?

It took us a long time to realize that we were not only dealing with cultural differences between countries from the Northern and Southern Hemispheres but also with major ecological differences between how quickly forests grow and what size of an opening (the area of a forest that is logged) is ecologically acceptable in the different hemispheres. How do you define principles that could be applied by a company that sources globally and from both tropical and temperate forests? In some respects our debates reflected a microcosm of society and we were learning about the issues as we debated them. These debates served us well in the years to come as we talked through the issues with governments and major corporations. I have realized only this year, being back at Greenpeace for the first time in a decade, how far this work has spread.

Chapter 7

REDEFINING PROTECTION POLITICS
TRANSFORMING THE MID-COAST TIMBER
SUPPLY AREA INTO THE GREAT BEAR RAINFOREST

We would never buy paper made from dead bears, otter,
salmon and birds, from ruined native cultures, from de-
stroyed species and destroyed lives, from ancient forests
reduced to stumps and mud; but that's what we're buying
when we buy paper made from old-growth clear-cut trees.

MARGARET ATWOOD[1]

BUT BEFORE I could become a useful strategist, I knew I had to get my feet wet, which is why, back in the winter of 1995, I found myself chained to a log barge in Vancouver Harbour.

While the Clayoquot markets campaign was capturing the attention of decision makers and media, it was also providing government and industry with considerable ammunition in their attempts to drive a wedge between us and the unions and some First Nations peoples. The last thing government or industry wants is an effective alliance between unlikely allies to strengthen the call for change. As a result, in the early days of the markets campaign in Canada we were building alliances with workers to show that we weren't against jobs. After several meetings we found common ground with the Pulp, Paper and Woodworkers of Canada (PPWC) and agreed to co-operate to raise awareness about how British Columbia was creating fewer jobs per tree than almost any other jurisdiction in the world. We took out a full-page ad on the back cover of a truck-logger magazine that said, "Greenpeace wants your job." And underneath, in big letters, "To be there in ten years." Even with this ad, as well as releasing reports and lobbying government officials, we couldn't seem to catch any media attention or get any traction. We decided to do an action that would give us a media moment to talk about the issues.

So that's why I'd chained myself to the barge.

I was pretty excited because I'd done a lot of actions by this point, but I'd always been the campaigner, the spokesperson, the organizer. This time I decided that since everyone on a team really has to try every job, it was time for me to attempt some serious civil disobedience.

We had contacted a couple of friends and some folks who worked for Greenpeace and asked them to go to the docks, meet the media and support the action. Then we went to Jericho Beach in Vancouver and boarded the Zodiacs. It was a cold, wet day. There were four people in each action team and we were all wearing the signature white Tyvek suits with "Greenpeace" on the back. Just as we came into Vancouver Harbour, one of the boat motors conked out. So we tootled around the harbour, hoping the harbour police didn't see us with the Greenpeace suits on, and tried to get the motor started. Meanwhile, back on the docks, one of the old-time Greenpeacers, Janos Mate, saw that it was way past time for the action. The media were getting frustrated, talking about leaving, and the log barge was almost loaded and preparing to depart.

Janos panicked, stripped off his pants, jumped into the icy cold water, swam over to the log barge and climbed up on the logs as they were loading the barge. Naturally, they stopped loading. Then Janos realized he didn't have a placard. So he jumped back into the water, swam to the dock, got a placard, swam back to the barge and climbed onto the logs. The rest of us didn't know any of this, because we were in the Zodiacs.

As the media took footage of Janos in his underwear, we got the motor started and raced toward the log barge in our Zodiacs, pulled ourselves up, clambered onboard, chained ourselves to the logs and stood there triumphantly. Then we looked over at the end of the log barge, and I couldn't figure out what I was seeing . . . but it sure looked like a guy in wet underwear.

The harbour police arrived and arrested us all for criminal trespass. That night while we were in jail we heard the police laughing their heads off. Then an officer came in, wiping away tears, and said, "We just taped it. Do you want to see the news?" He put us in a holding room that had a television, popped the tape in and the announcer came on. "Today a lone Greenpeace activist in his underwear protested raw logs." There was a picture of Janos freezing in his underwear with his little placard.

Luckily people are right when they say you'll laugh when you look back on it, but it definitely wasn't funny that night in jail, or during the weeks that followed in which the underwear protest became infamous.

A COUPLE OF WEEKS after the underwear fiasco, we had a visit in our office from Ian McAllister and his dad, Peter. They arrived in our office very excited about the potential of expanding our markets campaign from Clayoquot to the mainland coast.

Peter said, "Hey, love what you've done in Clayoquot, but the rainforest on the central coast is twenty times as big, and it's disappearing really fast." Peter is an ex-pat American environmentalist who had tracked barges full of big trees to the central coast and was shocked to discover . . . paradise. He founded the Raincoast Conservation Society. His son, Ian, now lives on the central coast and runs Pacific Wild, an organization dedicated to protecting the central coast through conservation biology and outreach projects.

I'll never forget when I sat down with Ian and Peter. They had us put a map of BC on the wall and point out the places we'd campaigned, then asked us what we wanted to do next. Did we want to run a campaign to save the Johnson Valley on Princess Royal Island, the home of the beautiful, white spirit bear? Should we run a campaign on King Island near Bella Coola? Every one of those campaigns would take three to five years to resolve. They showed us a map of the whole west coast of Canada and pointed out that of the original 359 intact rainforest valleys on the coast,[2] only 69 were left, and all these valleys were slated to be roaded and logged within the next five to ten years. This area is the northern end of the narrow strip of temperate rainforests that extend from California's redwoods through the red cedars of Canada and into Alaska. It's a rugged area of mountain fjords mostly accessible only by boat.

The McAllisters explained that we could fight for one or two valleys, but while waiting we'd lose most of the entire coast. Chris, Karen and I took a big green marker and drew a circle around everything that was left. It was an area that went from halfway up British Columbia to Alaska. At the time the area was known as the "mid-coast timber supply area."

Several months later Valerie, Karen, Ian and I were in San Francisco trying to meet with US groups. We were sitting around at dinner one night at a cheap Italian restaurant with a bottle of great wine, writing potential names for the land: "raincoast . . . wilderness . . . great rainforest . . . great bear . . ." Having learned the lessons of how much more attractive puffins were than sand eels, I knew we needed a name that was iconic and created an image in people's minds. We needed a name that immediately defined the area. We wanted the next Amazon. We wanted people to hear the name and be mad as hell that anybody could turn it into toilet paper.

Ian is a scientist, he knew the area best and he kept insisting, "It's got to have 'bear' in it. This is the last stronghold for large mammals, for grizzly bears and Kermode bears—the spirit bear." Ian made it clear that this wasn't just about saving the forest but about creating a conversation about how to interact with some of the most important wilderness areas left on the planet. We agreed to use the spirit bear as the icon in the campaign. We named it the Great Bear Rainforest.

Coming up with this name was, perhaps, the most successful single action in any campaign I've ever worked on. The mid-coast timber supply area sounded like an aisle at Home Depot. The Great Bear Rainforest was definitely something that people wanted to protect.

We decided to campaign simultaneously for all sixty-nine watersheds—hundreds and hundreds of valleys. We were called "crazy" and "unrealistic"—and that was by the people on our side. When we launched the campaign several colleagues said we were ruining the environmental movement because we were asking for so much. There had been campaigns for individual valleys: the Stein, the Carmanah, the Walbran. Then we fought for Clayoquot Sound, which opened up a new level: instead of focusing on a valley, it was about a whole sound and several intact watersheds. The Great Bear would be orders of magnitude bigger. We were trying to protect every intact forest valley left on the west coast of Canada. All at once.

We started sketching out our vision. We needed to identify the world we wanted in ten or twenty years. What was the eventual solution? We identified benchmarks along the way, and made sure that each of them continued this momentum, this sense that history was shifting, because the momentum was catching the attention of decision makers in the logging industry. This momentum was the reason they were talking to us at all.

A number of groups in British Columbia were working to protect the area (like the Valhalla Wilderness Society), but they weren't getting enough traction. We were able to build on their work and take it to the next level because we had bigger organizations like Rainforest Action Network, the National Resources Defense Council and Greenpeace.

When we launched the Great Bear campaign, we called for customers to stop buying products from Interfor, Western Forest Products and MacMillan Bloedel—the three largest logging companies in British Columbia (essentially a boycott, but for legal reasons many felt we couldn't use this term). BC premier Glen Clark responded by calling us enemies of the state. The logging companies ran full-page ads calling us "eco-terrorists" and the *Province* newspaper ran a full front page with only this headline in huge type: "Greenpeace—will they wreck British Columbia?" Our board was scared. A lot of people were cancelling Greenpeace memberships, and we were getting death threats at the office every day, which was pretty terrifying.

But a couple of seasoned campaigners told us, "This is the moment. First they're going to ignore you; we've been through that. Then they're going to ridicule you. And then, eventually, you'll win." So we just tried to turn the attention around and keep it going.

—

EARLY IN THE CAMPAIGN we worked with Greenpeace to coordinate blockades in the Great Bear Rainforest. We aimed to do something so controversial that the media would have to cover it, and the
logging in the region would be exposed. We brought two Greenpeace
ships up to the rainforest with a helicopter, *Tweety*, onboard, and we
used the helicopter to figure out where they were logging. We spent
months touring up and down the coast, evaluating the logging, and
trying to figure out where the active logging would be starting next.

Most of the people in the region were from the logging companies
or small First Nations communities. The whole country and some of
the world knew about Clayoquot Sound because of our campaigns,
but here was a region that was so much bigger, with so many critical
ecosystems and thousand-year-old trees, and no one knew the logging
was happening. It was so far away from Vancouver that we couldn't
easily get press there. This wasn't like Tofino on the west coast of
Vancouver Island, accessible by a highway, where people could see
the trees for themselves, so we really needed a huge controversy to
kick open the door. We needed to bring the forest to the people.

We knew the loggers knew we were on the coast, because we tuned
in to their radio traffic. They were trying to figure out where we
were, and we were trying to figure out where they were. For months
it was a kind of cloak-and-dagger, cat-and-mouse game, which was
scary. We had a satellite phone that cost thousands of dollars to run,
when it worked, and we were in the middle of nowhere, surrounded
mostly by people who hated us with a passion. If we had needed to
get someone off the ship, we couldn't fly them out because we were
banned from the local airlines. Campbell River and Port Hardy had
signs up when you entered the towns: "Greenpeace-free zone." We
would pull into small towns to get gas and buy food and be refused.
Sometimes some of us would go to town in unmarked Zodiacs,
leaving our Greenpeace T-shirts at home, and pretend we were yach-
ters so we could buy supplies.

We finally decided to target Roderick Island for a blockade because
it was spirit bear territory and the logging there was devastating: huge
clear-cuts and, just beyond the carnage, some of the biggest, oldest
trees I had ever seen. Roderick Island is the territory of the Kitasoo

First Nations, so we called the band office, requested a meeting and headed toward Klemtu. We had to walk through the village to get to the band office, and people came out of their houses and stared at us, wondering what we were doing there. We sat down in the band office with eight others, mostly men, and they definitely had a preconceived notion of who Greenpeace was. Before we could even start the conversation, they yelled at us for an hour about the seal hunt and about how we didn't respect First Nations' rights.

Then, once we actually started talking, I asked, "Are you happy with what's happening on your land?"

That was the point when the conversation completely changed.

One of the chiefs said, "This is our lifeblood. You think we are happy? We're not. Our history is not as loggers, we are fisher people, we are gatherers. The only logging we ever did was for our canoes, and now we are watching as landscapes are devastated. But it's the only money that's flowing into our communities. It's the reason we have a new school."

They couldn't align with us without taking the risk that their government support would dry up, but we definitely did not feel good about going ahead if they were going to publicly oppose our activities. Eventually we reached an agreement. They wouldn't support us, but they also wouldn't oppose us or object to our presence on their land.

Then we went back to the ship and organized the blockade.

AT 2:00 A.M. we anchored the Greenpeace ship in a remote inlet on the east side of Roderick Island, and a team of people hiked quietly across the island into the active logging area. We hid in the slash until the loggers came in and started their equipment. At a sign from the action coordinator we ran out, and designated people waved to the workers to kill the engines. We explained to them who we were and what we were doing while our videographers got footage of the rest of us climbing onto the grapple yarders and chaining ourselves to the equipment. The next few days were a blur of trying to organize media who were flying in, operating twenty-four-hour security shifts, filtering water from streams, hiking food in from the ship and negotiating with the logging company. We'd pack beta tapes on a floatplane that flew them to CBC Vancouver so we could try to show people what was happening at the blockades.

One afternoon we saw the dust rising off the roads below (our warning sign that someone was coming) and raced to chain ourselves to the equipment. As the dust cleared we saw there were a *lot* of trucks. The first person to get out of the truck had a video camera. This wasn't a routine visit. A photographer got out and then a bunch of the company guys we knew from Western Forest Products appeared. I thought for sure this was it: they were finally going to arrest us. I assumed the police would get out of the other cars.

Then Chief Percy Starr of the Kitasoo stepped out of one of the cars. You couldn't miss Percy—he has white, flowing hair, and he is a very majestic elder. My brain started racing. *Oh . . . it's the company . . . it's Percy . . .*

That's when I noticed they were all wearing new ball caps. And the ball caps read: WESTERN FOREST PRODUCTS. KITASOO FIRST NATIONS. WORKING TOGETHER FOR A SUSTAINABLE FUTURE. They had matching sweatshirts too. Before Percy said anything, I knew: we were in big trouble.

Percy said, "Tzeporah Berman, I need to talk to you."

"Sure, Percy." We sat down on a couple of stumps.

Then the camera started rolling, and Percy attacked Greenpeace for intruding in their territory and their business. On camera Percy called us "eco-imperialists."

I sat there shocked. What could I say to that? In the meeting just days before we had shared perspectives and found common ground, and the First Nations had seemed fine with our plans.

Then the company representatives and their cameras left, and I knew without any doubt that the tape was going to the CBC. It was 2:00 p.m., and this was going to be on the news by 6:00. I had to figure out what to do. I had to call my bosses and tell them what was going on.

Meanwhile, the camp was going crazy. Here were fourteen activists who had been living and breathing this issue, chained to machinery in a very tense situation, and a First Nations chief had just told them that they were terrible people. Many of them had an idealized notion of First Nations, and until a few minutes before they thought they were on the side of the angels. Suddenly they were *not* on the side of the angels?

A minor civil war erupted between people on one side saying, "We gotta get out of here!" and the other side saying, "It doesn't matter if they're First Nations! If they're going to log, I'm staying!"

I pictured how I could easily end up with a bunch of renegade Greenpeace staffers chaining themselves to the logging gear no matter what we decided. So I had to facilitate a discussion, figure out which decision to make, and then get them to follow it. I had the ship's crew patch their phone in to the radio so I could talk with our team in the Greenpeace office in Vancouver and the ship's captain. The action coordinator in Vancouver said, "I just scouted the Western Forest Products building in Vancouver, and it's looking good for an easy lock-down. Why don't we just move the whole protest to their corporate headquarters?" Western Forests Products was trying to put the First Nations between us, but since our fight was with the logging company, we had to take it back to the logging company.

When you've been protecting a forest, it's always very difficult to voluntarily walk away knowing that they're going to rev up the machines as soon as you go. But we packed our stuff and took down our tents, bundled up our equipment and raced back to Vancouver, chartering floatplanes so we could make the trip at top speed. We arrived at about 11:00 p.m. and stayed up all night organizing. The next morning, at about eight o'clock, we blockaded the corporate headquarters of Western Forest Products. Within minutes there were cameras and police everywhere. Within an hour all the activists had been arrested, and I was doing wrap-up interviews and lining up legal support. After we'd spent fourteen days blockading in the wilderness, the whole experience felt surreal, fast and somewhat anti-climactic. It's one thing to be chained to a grapple yarder in the middle of a remote rainforest and a whole other thing to be arrested while chained to a potted plant in a nondescript lobby. This time, the company had gotten the upper hand, put us on the defensive and defused a blockade that had been building into a major national story.

—

ONE OF OUR BIGGEST challenges at the time was trying to get national and international interest. The MacBlo agreement in Clayoquot Sound had resulted in media, customers and the public thinking that the issues were resolved: BC was green, and companies were all starting to do the right thing for the rainforest. But the truth was that BC was still logging an acre of rainforest every sixty seconds.

We couldn't physically bring many people to these remote areas, so our strategic plan was based on the need to bring the forest to the people. We did public slide shows and events and developed materials for our meetings with customers. We also knew we needed to create conflict to get media interest and spread the word that Canada's old-growth rainforests were still being clear-cut. The blockades and corporate headquarters arrest had helped, but we needed to build more pressure before the government and industry would take us seriously.

Most of the pressure came from customer meetings, public events and protests targeting customers in Europe, the United States and Japan. We met with hundreds of companies, such as *TIME* and *BBC Wildlife Magazine*, in London and New York. In 1998, as a result of our meetings with them, the German Publishing Association and the Belgium Paper Association cancelled their contracts with Canadian companies who were logging in the rainforest. At the time we estimated that we cost the industry at least $30 million—and that included only the contracts we knew had been cancelled.

Needless to say, they weren't very happy with us.

I WASN'T GOING TO be able to continue working on the Great Bear campaign from Canada. I was now living in San Francisco with Chris, who was working for RAN. In 1999, I had begun coordinating the market campaign for Greenpeace in the United States, and at one point I went back to Vancouver to discuss strategy with several environmental groups, taking our six-month-old son, Forrest, with me. Once the meeting in Vancouver was over, my friend Sue Danne offered to drive me to the US border crossing. This was just before the World Trade Organization meeting, which turned into the infamous "Battle in Seattle."

It was dark, and suddenly, in front of the car, as clear as day, I saw a brick wall across the highway. I yelled "Stop the car!" I was sure Sue was hurtling toward a wall. She stopped, then looked at me as if I'd gone crazy and asked what was going on. That's when I realized the wall was a hallucination.

I thought, *Oh my God. I have got to get more sleep. What's wrong with me?*

Then we pulled up to the border. The guard scanned my passport and asked who I worked for.

I said, "Greenpeace." I had a work permit for the US, but it had expired and I hadn't received the new paperwork before I'd gone to Canada, so I was trying to re-enter as a visitor. I knew it was wrong, and a bit risky, but I had a new baby, was tired and just wanted to get home. In the end it seemed that whether my work permit was being renewed or whether I was trying to enter as a visitor didn't interest him. He asked me to come inside and questioned me for hours as I held Forrest and stared at the gun magazines on his desk and the girlie calendar on the wall. He repeatedly asked if I was going to protest at the WTO. And every time I said no he told me I was lying. At midnight he stamped my passport REFUSED ENTRY FOR FRAUD and impounded Sue's car. Sue and I were left standing on the Canadian side of the border with a crying baby.

My mother-in-law picked us up. I contacted our lawyers, and they said that because my work permit had in fact been renewed we should be able to sort things out in a few days. When the days turned into weeks, people started calling to ask if I could help with the Great Bear negotiations, and I began working on the deal. After a month, Forrest and I were still camped out at my in-laws' place and Chris was flying home to visit every weekend.

As it became clear that this was going to take a lot longer to work out, Sue and I rented a place on Bowen Island. Sue was working half-time for me as my executive assistant and half-time as my nanny. Chris was missing us, but he was working his dream job as campaign director at RAN—an incredible group of people, a fantastic organization. He was doing meaningful work and he loved it. Besides, every time I talked to the lawyers they were sure I'd be allowed back in the

United States "next month." But it got to the point where every time a plane flew overhead Forrest would point up and yell, "Da-da!"

Meanwhile, I had started some of the most intense, high-pressure negotiations that I've ever been in. The logging companies were furious about the markets campaign, and they couldn't believe they were being forced to the table with us. Our community of environmentalists had mixed feelings about negotiating with the "enemy." In fact, at one point I remember thinking that I wasn't sure which was worse, the meetings with the companies or the meetings with the coalition.

A year and a half into my being refused entry, Chris and I were both exhausted from being separated, and I still had no idea when I was getting back there. Chris was still flying back and forth from BC to San Francisco every three or four days. Our lives were simply not sustainable trying to live in two different countries, and it looked as if there was no end in sight. So one weekend after a lot of hard conversations, Chris decided he would go back to San Francisco and resign.

But that weekend, while Chris and I discussed our future, there was a kerfuffle with the existing executive director at RAN, and he walked out. Chris arrived on Monday for a special emergency meeting of the board, and before he could announce his resignation they offered him the job of executive director—from our perspective one of the best jobs in the world. So he left Bowen intending to resign and flew home to tell me he'd become the executive director. Not exactly what we had planned.

Luckily, that same week I got the call saying cabinet had approved the Great Bear Rainforest Agreement. It was the largest single conservation decision North America had ever seen. It doubled the amount of protected forests in the region, protected Spirit Bear Island (a.k.a. Princess Royal Island), and deferred logging in one hundred large intact valleys.[3] It also mandated the provincial government to negotiate with workers, community representatives and others in government-sponsored multi-stakeholder Land and Resource Management Planning processes. In return, environmental groups agreed to suspend marketplace campaigns.

Two hours later I received a completely unrelated call from my lawyers telling me I had been approved to return to the United States.

Strangely, the bureaucracy dividing my family and the gruelling work of the negotiations ended within hours of each other.

We decided to celebrate the 2001 agreement by arranging a special tour of the Great Bear with some of our biggest funders and some potential big funders. We rented a twelve-person sailboat, *The Maple Leaf*, for a multi-day tour. The trip was supposed to leave September 12, 2001.

On September 11 I got up early, complaining about how corporate executives always want to do breakfast meetings at ungodly hours, and headed down to the MacBlo headquarters on Granville Street. There were strange excited conversations on the bus about planes and New York, but I couldn't catch what was going on. Everyone else at the meeting looked similarly bewildered. We tentatively started the meeting, but by that time more news was filtering in, so we gave up and had a TV brought into the room. And so it was that I watched history unfold and tried vainly to come to grips with the horror of people jumping from exploding buildings, while sitting with the corporate executives of some of Canada's largest logging companies. After a brief break in which everyone tried to call friends and family, we came back into the meeting room. I was at a loss as to how to proceed with a meeting that now seemed beside the point (because of course everything seemed beside the point), when the only other woman in the room did something I will always be thankful for. With a tremor in her voice, Linda Coady from MacBlo asked everyone to observe a minute of silence, and after that we simply cancelled the meeting.

Later that day I received a call from the captain of *The Maple Leaf* saying he was very sorry but the trip was booked, and he had to charge us whether we took it or not. Every flight from the United States was grounded, so no one would be joining us from outside BC. So here we were with a paid-for sailboat and a rare chance to see the remote rainforests we'd spent the past eight years trying to protect. We gathered some of our campaign team, my mother-in-law, Forrest and James MacKinnon, a reporter for Victoria's weekly, *Monday Magazine*, who went on to co-write the great book *The 100-Mile Diet*. We flew up to Prince Rupert, and for four days, cloaked in mist and fog, we sailed down the 200 miles of the Great Bear Rainforest. It was one of the most magical experiences of my life. Not only were we going to the forests that we now knew would be protected because of our work, but we were, unforgettably, processing the horror of 9/11 together in this wild, lush, pristine place. At one point the captain anchored the boat in a beautiful estuary, and we hiked up the side of a hundred-foot waterfall to massive thousand-year-old trees. One old cedar tree was the width of an average house and over three hundred feet tall.

As we were all hiking up the glorious waterfall, our guide told us to stop and crouch because we were near a spot where a rare white spirit bear regularly came to feed on the salmon. The streams were rich with salmon, and the place was littered with fish bones. Suddenly, we heard a crashing in the forest across from us. I looked over and there it was. The white bear seemed ten feet tall. For me, it was a moment of pure, raw, wildness as the bear crashed out of the forest, reached down to a pond in the river, grabbed a massive salmon and broke it in half. Blood spurted everywhere, all over its white fur. Then it started eating.

I kind of shifted my position, and the bear looked up and stared me right in the eye, and it looked so intelligent and so . . . weary. It finished its meal, turned around and lumbered back off into the forest.

SINCE WE launched the Great Bear Rainforest campaign, hundreds of companies—some of their own free will because individuals in those companies believed in these values, some with a little help—have said that they don't want to buy products from the last endangered forests on earth.

In February 2006, Greenpeace, Sierra Club and ForestEthics stood on stage with representatives from all the coastal First Nations, the government, the logging industry and the labour unions and announced the protection of five million acres of rainforest on the west coast of Canada. In 2009 the details were finalized: together we had saved 2.1 million hectares, or 5 million acres—an area half the size of

Switzerland. A fund of $120 million for local communities to help kick-start a new conservation economy as an alternative to logging, and a new system of lighter touch logging, based on ecosystem-based management, was created.[4] The negotiations had been a resounding success.

PART III

BOARD

Chapter 8

DANCING WITH THE ENEMY
LEARNING TO SEE PEOPLE, NOT POSITIONS

*We have two ears and one mouth so that we can listen
twice as much as we speak.*

EPICTETUS, THE GREEK PHILOSOPHER
ASSOCIATED WITH THE STOICS (AD 55–c.135)

KAREN MAHON WALKED into the Vancouver Greenpeace office
and said, "You're never going to believe what just happened!"

It was 1995 and Karen had just given birth to Aedan. She was
walking down the street one afternoon in Kitsilano and bumped into
someone with the same blue polka-dot stroller and a baby the same
age: Linda Coady from MacBlo. Linda was with her husband, and she
turned and said, "Dear, this is my arch-nemesis, Karen Mahon, from
Greenpeace. Karen, this is my husband."

They decided to meet for coffee—and mom to mom, person to
person, they saw each other as people for the first time.

It was a breakthrough for forest politics in Canada.

Karen came back to the office and said, "We need to meet with
this woman and work out a way to break through the logjam." At this
point we had stopped MacBlo from logging most of Clayoquot Sound,
but we had expanded our campaign to the Great Bear Rainforest.
MacBlo was logging throughout the region, so our disputes were continuing to escalate.

Karen and I met Linda, and we came up with an idea. If we could get some of our core constituency together, and she could get some of her company people to meet outside of British Columbia . . . secretly . . . and we tried to stand in each other's shoes and understand each other, maybe, just maybe, we could create a new path forward.

I WANT TO STEP BACK a bit from the journey and reflect on one of the most critical things I've learned in all my time at the Friends of Clayoquot Sound, Greenpeace, ForestEthics and PowerUp Canada. Somehow, through all the posturing in any contentious issue every day, I began to see, connect with and eventually really listen to actual people in government and industry. It may sound simplistic, but my experience is that we are way too quick to slap a label on someone (corporate flack, government stooge, hippie environmentalist). We allow such labels to get in the way of real learning and sometimes even of solutions. If you are not ensconced in the environmental movement, that revelation may seem crazy to you; but in my twenties, in the circles I was working in, it was crazy for a different reason. It was heresy.

I FIRST MET Linda Coady in 1994 when she was working in the PR department of MacBlo. Back then all the people we talked to at the company worked for the PR department. We couldn't get a meeting with anyone in senior management to save our lives. They thought we were all wing nuts and wouldn't deign to acknowledge us, never mind meet us.

Linda might have been the first person at any logging company in Canada who was given the specific task of working on environmental issues. The company would trot her out as the softer side of MacBlo. She quickly became their environmental affairs person, and I think she was the first person I met from a logging company who really talked to us about the issues instead of trying to spin them.

Once Karen made the connection with Linda, we started having these "close the door, let's really talk about it" conversations, which we had never had before with anyone from the industry. She would say, "Okay, what do you want me to do? Our business model is designed on quantity, and you're saying, not only do we have to stop logging Clayoquot Sound, which is very profitable for us, but we also have to stop clear-cutting. That means we probably have anywhere from 30 to 70 percent less wood coming through our business, and somehow we have to make our business model work. So are you saying we should shut down our company? Because I know where to go with that. I can't do anything, other than fight you."

It was a fascinating conversation, because for a lot of us our default response was "Yeah, shut down your company." We had to go back to the Greenpeace office and ask ourselves, What are we trying to achieve? Do we really think we can create enough pressure to shut down a company? Do we think the government is going to step in and regulate the industry so we don't need to do a deal with the devil? As you can imagine, these were difficult and contentious conversations. Many from within Greenpeace felt strongly that we should never talk to the company at all; talking to them face to face was a completely alien concept: for years the only "meetings" we'd had with company representatives were at the side of the road, or on a blockade, or when they were standing with the police on the other side of the block-ade lines. We heard from Linda that many at MacMillan Bloedel felt the same way about talking with Greenpeace. Both sides were en-trenched. Once we started talking with people from the company, so many people on both sides were opposed to the idea of our breathing the same air that we couldn't announce our meetings. And we had to meet on neutral ground and rent hotel boardrooms to talk. MacBlo hired a professional mediator so we could bring together a couple of leaders from each of our teams to talk about developing a long-term critical pathway.

Was there a way for MacBlo and Greenpeace to agree? Or would this be a fight for the rest of our lives? Because that's what it felt like at the time. In a moment pure of heart (or high on hormones), Chris and I had named our first son Forrest. That same year someone from Interfor named their son Timber. At times Chris and I would have nightmares that in thirty years Forrest and Timber would be having the same disputes we were having with MacBlo.

At this point we had reached the Clayoquot agreement and had not yet launched the Great Bear Rainforest campaign. Linda and several others from MacBlo agreed to meet with a group from "our side," including Adriane Carr from the Western Canada Wilderness Committee, Liz Barratt-Brown from the NRDC, Merran Smith, who was then with the Sierra Club, Karen, Chris and me, for a two-day totally off-the-record brainstorming session. We brought in some well-known academics and mediators and went to a retreat space outside San Francisco, in the middle of the redwoods. In the dining room the two "sides" sat at separate tables, not really talking to one another. We had a professional facilitator (Gifford Pinchot from the Bainbridge Institute, a sustainable-business school in Seattle) and advice from Paul Hawken (environmentalist, author and entrepreneur) who ran a workshop on natural capitalism and the green economy.

We all went into the first session on Friday night unsure what to expect. Gifford looked at me and Bill Cafferata, the chief forester from MacBlo, and said, "I want you two to go in this room alone, and I've left a couple of cold beers in there in case you need them. Tzeporah, your job is to be Bill. You got into this business because you care about forests, and you want to do the right thing, but your job is to protect the business model. And Bill, your job is to protect biodiversity, en-dangered species and old-growth forest. Both of you know that you need to reach an agreement that your constituencies will be happy with. Now go away and don't come back for two hours."

I was supposed to be Bill Cafferata?

Bill Cafferata was, to put it politely, the anti-Christ. He is a big man, about six foot five, and very scary. Tall, huge, very gruff, he repre-sented everything I was fighting against, and he was pretty much the only person on the other side who could shut me down with a glare. He'd started working with the company the year before I was born. We called him Frankenstein.

Bill and I had never said a civil word to each other. Ever. It was very, very uncomfortable in the beginning, but by eleven o'clock at night we'd broken open the beer and were screaming with laugh-ter over our crazy ideas. It turned out Frankenstein wasn't nearly as scary as I thought he was.

I had learned from him before, though.

Early in the Clayoquot campaign, I was in Nanaimo meeting a number of First Nations chiefs, and Bill was there to convince them that the logging MacBlo was planning was responsible. He had facts and figures and details at his fingertips. I had done my research, I knew what I was talking about, but the particular area that he was focusing on in that meeting was one that I hadn't been to.

At one point in the meeting I was contradicting him and he turned toward me, quite frustrated. He always had a very calm, low voice, but it was now a kind of growl. He said, "Listen, young lady, until you have mud on your boots, I don't think you should be talking about things you don't know anything about."

Not many people could silence me the way he did. As much as I disagreed with the logging plans that he was advocating, it was a moment of learning for me. I thought, *Ya know, he's right.* From then on it became a point of honour to really know what I was talking about, to have "mud on my boots."

That weekend at the retreat outside San Francisco set the stage for conversations with MacBlo about the practice of clear-cutting. I'm still not sure those conversations would have gone anywhere if MacBlo hadn't hired a new CEO from outside Canada, who had never been part of the fights. Tom Stephens was known as a fixer. He was a large part of the reason we went on the retreat at all because when he got the job earlier that year and took a look at MacBlo's reputational capital he said, "What the hell have you people been doing?"

When we got back from California, we met with Tom and presented him with the strategies we'd devised: a model in which MacBlo publicly committed to the need for old-growth and endangered species protection and new ways to log that would protect biodiversity and mimic natural systems and structures.

Clear-cutting in a temperate rainforest is not in tune with natural phenomena. In a lot of other forest ecosystems, like in the boreal forest, larger openings do occur naturally from fires, but in a temperate rainforest you would never see more than a few tree lengths of open area. They're too wet. Tree farms will never replicate that. We asked MacBlo to use the best available science and work in conjunction with

Greenpeace to find out whether this was a viable business model. The concept of the FSC hadn't taken hold yet, but Tom basically said, "I like it, Bill. Do it."

Still, many in their company and in the environmental movement would have been horrified and outraged if they had heard we were working together. Over the following months we worked behind the scenes with the MacBlo foresters and biologists. What would it look like if MacBlo set old-growth zones that were "no harvesting" areas? How much would that take away from their annual revenue? What would it look like if MacBlo changed clear-cutting? We weren't aware of this at the time, but they were so sure these talks were a waste of time that they internally named this new process "the Snark Project," after the Lewis Carroll poem about a ship of fools hunting a prize that probably doesn't exist.[1]

They spent more than $600,000 on the Snark Project, and much to everyone's shock they came up with a model based on how much tenure they had. The tenure system in BC once offered free land rights, and MacBlo had a huge area to work with, so sustainable logging was financially viable for them. If they could spread out their logging over a wider area, protect key areas of old-growth and selectively log in other areas while attempting to minimize roads that were costly and caused significant environmental damage, they would create a new model of both protection and responsible logging.

We ran their model past independent experts, asking if it would sufficiently protect biodiversity. They separately confirmed that the model would not only protect biodiversity but also shake the logging industry worldwide. An international company's announcement that it should protect more old-growth and end clear-cutting would have global ramifications.

No one could believe this was happening.

We went back to MacBlo and agreed to support and congratulate them but warned that we were still planning to launch a campaign for full protection of some of the intact areas on the coast (which later became known as the Great Bear Rainforest). Then they agreed to make history. The headlines from the announcement felt as if they'd been pulled from our dreams: "MacBlo to end clearcutting in old-growth coast forests."[2] This was front-page news across the country and picked up all over the world. The *Wall Street Journal*, the *New York Times*, the *International Herald Tribune*—everyone covered it. At the press conference, on national news, Karen handed Tom Stephens a bottle of champagne.

It was a defining moment for logging in North America. And it was a defining moment when we began to see people, not just positions. Through this process I learned that there are good people everywhere who want to do the right thing. The trick is capturing the attention of senior decision makers and convincing them to give their staff a mandate to think creatively.

Tom Stephens, who still works in the forest industry, called his time with MacBlo "one of the high points of my life." In an interview with *Forest News Watch* more than a decade later, he said, "We put together a team of professionals to look at the alternatives for logging in the unique forests of British Columbia. It was amazing that the right economic solution and the right environmental solution happened to overlap. . . . Once we had the facts down on the table and the team made their recommendation, it was one of the easiest decisions I've ever had to make."[3]

Thanks to MacBlo listening—and Karen and Linda's mutual taste in strollers—we suddenly had a seat at the table with the logging companies. Linda and I went on with several others to help create the Joint Solutions Project: Sierra Club, Greenpeace, and ForestEthics sitting down with Western Forest Products, Interfor and MacBlo to discuss what became the Great Bear Agreement. Linda became a driving force and one of the primary negotiators for the industry side. After we completed the agreement, she left the logging industry and began working for World Wildlife Fund before working on environmental issues for the 2010 Olympics in Vancouver.

The night of the MacBlo announcement, Greenpeace threw a dinner party for the company. We realized that if the company was really going to implement this new direction, it needed to empower the staff. Sure, the big announcement had to be made for the board and the CEO, but if the employees resisted, nothing would change on the ground.

We invited staff from every department to thank them for their work on the project and took them to a restaurant in downtown Vancouver. At the beginning it was decidedly awkward. We were seated at a long table, Greenpeace on one side, MacBlo on the other. Someone toasted our big announcement and the benefits of "working together," and the wine started flowing. Then one forester said something I will never forget: "You know, I've gotta thank you. I've been a forester for twenty years, and the entire time I've only been allowed to use one of the tools in my toolbox, and that's clear-cutting. Now, I'm allowed to think it through, and use my knowledge and training that I've never been able to use before. That's given a whole new meaning to my work."

It was an incredible moment. The implications of how deeply we were all shifting the ideology of Canada's approach to its forests, and how living or not living in harmony with nature impacts the people who work in the industry, were suddenly clear. My focus had always been on how we could protect forests and preserve biodiversity. The full ramifications of the cultural and ideological shift that we were effecting really hit me at that dinner. It started being less about us against them, and more about how we, as a society, craft a different way of living on the planet.

Midway through dinner all the funny stories were coming out. People from MacBlo were saying, "I thought you were going to be terrible—we were terrified of meeting with you." Then Bill Cafferata said to me, "This will be a big relief in my home life. My daughter has barely been talking to me. She's got a poster of you up on her wall."

I didn't even know he was a dad.

I laughed, and just as he took a sip of water I said, "Oh yeah, I guess you should know we nicknamed you Frankenstein."

And the anti-Christ spat his water halfway across the table.

Unfortunately, we didn't end up with the perfect eco-friendly happy ending because not long after the announcement Weyerhaeuser bought out MacBlo. Weyerhaeuser has been notoriously intransigent on these issues and did not follow through with the new plan. But that initial announcement by MacBlo shook the forest industry across the country and around the world. Until that day, industry's default position was to say that groups fighting for old-growth forests were naive at best and eco-terrorists at worst, that we were tree-hugging hippies who didn't know what we were talking about, and that they represented the side of science. But now, one of the largest logging companies in Canada was saying, "We have to do things differently."

DESPITE THE RELATIONSHIP we'd formed with MacBlo, the negotiations that came next, which involved the five logging companies (Interfor, MacMillan Bloedel, Western Forest Products, Canfor and West Fraser) operating in the Great Bear Rainforest, made it seem as if we'd gone back to the war in the woods. For a good six months we butted heads. We postured, they postured. We tortured each other and the mediator until all hours of the morning. The daily meetings were not going anywhere. We were in detailed negotiations about which valleys they would stop logging, and which they wouldn't. It was a gruelling valley-by-valley fight. The last thing any of us wanted was more time together.

Then the mediator announced he had tickets to the Elton John concert and wanted us all to join him. We stared at him as though he was crazy, but it was his party, so we went.

We walked into the small private box at the concert, and there were several First Nations leaders; Bill Dumont, the chief forester from Western Forest Products; and Patrick Armstrong, the consultant the industry had hired to dog me around Europe to find out what I was doing, whom we'd always thought of as "the creepy industry guy." There was Catherine Stewart from Greenpeace, Dr. Jody Holmes, a conservation biologist representing all the environmental groups, and Merran Smith with the Sierra Club. I was sitting there thinking this was one of the weirdest experiences of my life. There was Elton John, and here was the logging industry on one side, with the First Nations chiefs on the other.

Patrick turned to Jody and said, "Wanna dance?"

She looked at him and without missing a beat said, "Have you lost your mind?"

He said, "I'll give you a valley."

She fired right back at him, "Which one?"

Everyone had been silent for this whole exchange. We were used to screaming matches, and with Jody's deadpan response the whole room started laughing. Then we were all dancing to Elton John.

I was wearing a silk shirt with a silk jacket. As we danced I got hot, took off my jacket and forgot about it. The next morning I walked into the negotiations, and Bill Dumont pulled my jacket out of his briefcase and said, "Tzeporah, you left this last night." Not everyone had been to the concert and I froze. We all started laughing.

The mediator was right. Having those bizarre, shared experiences and seeing one another as people changed the tenor of the discussions. It didn't mean we changed our positions on the issues, but it meant we started to see the individual participants and listen in a way we hadn't before.

THE OTHER FORMATIVE EXPERIENCE for our negotiating team that year was taking formal leadership training with Robert Gass at Hollyhock. Working with the Rockwood Institute in San Francisco, Robert also brought in Bill Ury, head of the Harvard Negotiation Project, to train us in negotiation skills. Robert taught us his strategy of leading from the heart. He challenged us to remember, at all times, that no matter whom we were talking to, everyone wants to be a good person, regardless of their position; they're just stuck in a bad system. He said if you are open to people, and you can create a conversation, they're going to be more willing to work on solutions with you. If you force them to agree to something, whatever deal you make will not last.

We jokingly called this "Robert's love strategy" and did a lot of training based around it. He introduced us to meditation and his theory that healthy, centred, grounded people are more effective. And none of us qualified as healthy, centred or grounded at the time. We were spending the night in sleeping bags under our desks. We were living on takeout pizza and cheap Scotch. We were in battle mode. Robert pushed us to try breathing instead of smoking and getting up early to do yoga instead of staying up all night stressing and drinking. He kept saying, "You're all going to burn out. You've got to be whole people, and you've got to see the company and government representatives as whole people."

Not long after training with Robert, I was at a meeting in the MacBlo Tower across from the Hotel Vancouver. The environmental side was entirely composed of women. Karen turned to Jody, Merran and me in the elevator and said, "Remember the love strategy." We were all laughing as we went in, thinking, *Yeah, right. Love them.* Then we started an intense meeting, and several times Merran or Karen or I would catch each other's eye and we'd start listening instead of shouting. It totally unnerved the logging representatives. The tenor of the conversation started to shift and change, and we got much more done that day.

After the meeting I said to Bill Dumont of Western Forest Products, "I really want to understand why you think you can't do this. What are your barriers? I'm listening."

He said, "If you're really listening, then meet me tomorrow. I'm going to bring in some of my guys, and they're going to give you the numbers. They'll tell you how many people are going to lose their jobs, and then you can tell me how I should tell them the news."

I went over to Western Forest Products the next day and sat in with Bill and some of his staff. He walked me through the numbers and the people. "This guy has a family of four. He's already been off work three times this year because we've stopped and started this road three times. If we do this, he's out of work completely. And if we shut that project down, this contracting company is going to sue us, and it will cost us this much." It was the chain reaction of the real-life consequences of doing what we were asking him to do.

We started to weigh those issues and considered the other places to log that would have less ecological impact and provide some transition to a longer-term strategy for the company and those workers. We switched to real problem solving that required compromises for all parties. We agreed to a phased-in approach: a selective logging and ecosystem-based management system that would happen over a period of four to eight years.

I recognized a challenging truth when I started going down that path with Bill Dumont. As I started to see their barriers, I realized that

I could easily start compromising my ecological values. Once I started having empathy for the "bad guys," one of the hardest aspects was being heartfelt, open and clear and still sticking to my own "bottom line." I repeatedly found that while change is never easy—and you might not be popular for advocating for change—as long as you're communicating your bottom line with integrity, clarity and compassion, you will be respected. Yes, we needed to compromise to find some workable solutions, but we also needed to hold on to our ecological values and make sure that we not lose sight of our ultimate goal to permanently protect the majority of the rare rainforest valleys from industrial logging.

To make sure we were still on the right path, we had constant conversations with other environmental groups and decided the line in the sand was the intact valleys. We would not accept anything less than all those valleys being off limits. All logging outside those valleys had to use ecosystem-based management. We would negotiate on how long that would take and over what period of time. Once that decision was made, we moved forward and reached an agreement.

A couple of weeks later, we were in an intense meeting with the provincial government, First Nations and logging companies. The logging company put a proposal on the table, which was not the proposal we'd discussed at the previous meeting. They were clearly side-swiping us in front of the government and First Nations. Tension was soaring, and it was clear we were going to lose a bunch of valleys. Then Merran passed me a note that had one word on it: "Breathe." I took a deep breath and instead of lashing out I said, "I think we need to take a break and then come back in and think about this in a different way."

Everyone took a break. Merran and I breathed deeply, and we returned to try to approach the conversation in a whole new way. Instead of sending our energy all over the place, we were calm and in control. We went back in trying to find a solution. The First Nations recognized and respected this culture of conversation and took over the meeting.

The conversation went on long into the night, and that meeting was seminal in reaching the legislative agreement that we eventually achieved in 2001 to protect the five million acres of the Great Bear

Rainforest. The leadership training we did and our willingness to see beyond positions, engage in solutions and listen to the challenges that industry needed to overcome were critical elements in achieving this success. Both sides of the table began working together, found common ground and put our resources into problem solving.

Even though there were moments when it felt like the answer to corporate negotiations could be found on our yoga mats or meditation pillows, without the direct action and the intense markets campaigns we would never have gotten to the table at all.

But empathizing with one another was still only one piece of the puzzle.

Chapter 9

HARD ON THE ISSUES,
SOFT ON THE PEOPLE
CREATING FORESTETHICS

Environmentalists are whipping our ass in the battle for
the forests. You have to respect them for that.

DAVID EMERSON, THEN CEO OF CANFOR, SPEAKING TO THE
TRUCK LOGGERS ASSOCIATION'S ANNUAL GENERAL MEETING

IN 2000 WE REALIZED that the US coalition that we had founded
to work on BC forest issues (the Coastal Rainforest Coalition, or CRC)
had outgrown its coalition structure. The staff of the coalition was
inspired to create an environmental group that focused on using
market tools to protect Canada's forests. We decided to make the
CRC a stand-alone organization with a mandate to use financial
and political leverage from the marketplace to protect endangered
forests. Having recently given birth to Forrest, I was finding it hard
to do the amount of travelling my job with Greenpeace required.
I simply had fewer hours for work, and I was frustrated by how
much time I needed to spend focused internally in order to make
decisions about messaging, campaign plans and policies.

One of the first moves was for everyone from the CRC to meet in
British Columbia for a strategy retreat to talk about what we were
going to do, how we were going to run our campaigns and what
we would call ourselves. We had been debating the name for a long
time. Some people felt we couldn't lose the name Coastal Rainforest

Coalition because we'd already had it for several years. Other people wanted a different name, like the "Something Action Network" or the "Forest Markets Group." We did months of focus groups and hired a major media company to confer with us. We couldn't find anything we all agreed on. We wanted an "edge," but we also wanted a name that would be taken seriously by all the companies we would approach. One day on a hike in the Elaho Valley somebody said, "We need the word 'forest' in it." Somebody else said, "What if we combine it with 'ethics.' Because that's what we want, we want people to have ethics about how we interact with nature." And it was like those old commercials where the chocolate ended up in the peanut butter. After months of debating, at that moment we all realized our new name was ForestEthics.

ForestEthics was founded to harness the power of the marketplace to protect our incredible forests. Our mottos have been "Hard on the issues, soft on the people" and "We work with companies but we don't take no for an answer." The mandate was to shift marketplace demand to ecologically responsible products and catalyze economic diversification of forest-dependent communities. The plan was to put pressure on corporations—and use corporate buying power—to demand more responsible products to protect endangered forests. Since forming in 2000, we've had more than a hundred companies sign statements committing to FSC-certified products and not sourcing material from old-growth forests. Those agreements have catalyzed the demand for certified products from both consumers and industry and shown major logging companies that certification is worth pursuing. The companies committed to stop buying from the most egregious sources, giving us the power we needed in negotiations in the Great Bear and many other regions.

About two weeks after we became ForestEthics, a bunch of Chilean organizations approached us and wanted to learn about what we were doing in the Great Bear Rainforest because their own temperate rainforests were being logged to make way for quick-growing plantations. So began ForestEthics Chile. We tracked Chilean products and visited companies that were buying Radiata pine from Chile. We found an alternative, which is FSC-certified second-growth Radiata from New

Zealand. We showed the companies they could buy the alternative and make a political statement by not contributing to native forest destruction in Chile. We went to Home Depot, with whom we now had a relationship, and asked them to broker a discussion between several conservation groups and two companies—Arauco and Mininco—that are responsible for 80 percent of the logging in Chile. In the end we protected a million acres of native forests in Chile, and there's still a joint solutions agreement between the environmental groups and the logging companies that protects native forests in Chile today. We took the model of what we did in the Great Bear and planted it in Chile.

The initial team for ForestEthics included Liz Butler, who was a well-known American environmental organizer and was on the original board of directors for the CRC. Liz is a Harley-riding vegan with long black hair and an encyclopedia-sized Rolodex. She knows absolutely everyone, talks a mile a minute and can turn around and organize a protest of dozens of people in some remote location in half an hour anywhere in the United States. We've always had a really strong relationship because we understand each other, and our work complements each other's. Liz is brilliant at harnessing the power of grassroots activism and creating an engine for a corporate campaign. I had experience developing strategies in which to fit that engine, and I knew how to use the pressure in negotiations and lobbying once it was generated. Liz and her team were the reason we could affect companies as big as Staples. We'd look at a corporate campaign target and she'd say, "No way. Where are people going to protest? Not enough storefronts. How are people going to engage? No one knows that brand. That company's inaccessible, off the table." She is always so clear about what will work and what won't. We worked together hand-in-hand for well over a decade, primarily on US campaigns. She's now the campaign director for 350.org, one of the biggest climate networks in the world.

The team also included Kristi Chester Vance, a vivacious, brilliant communications director and an incredibly bold and creative thinker. She always managed to make the work fun, because she frequently had that slightly off-the-wall wacky idea destined to catch on. She's a very driven, very clear communicator and the person who really taught me that PR is not about that one report you're trying to get a media story on, or that one blockade you want the press to cover; it's about creating a narrative that the press can follow with good guys and bad guys—princes and dragons, David and Goliath. Building a story, charting a narrative and being prepared with reports, events, statements and actions to "feed the media beast" is an art form that few do well. At ForestEthics we won many campaigns (Staples, Office Depot, Victoria's Secret) because of the impressive combination of media savvy and grassroots organizing.

Todd Paglia is the executive director. Todd is a lawyer and breaks most of the clichés of the environmental movement. He's more comfortable in leather loafers and perfectly ironed button-down shirts than Birkenstocks and hemp-wear. Even when he came to visit me in our new home on Cortes he got off the water taxi wearing shiny leather loafers, and I laughed and told him to take off his shoes because we were going to the beach. He used to work for Ralph Nader in Washington, DC, and we persuaded him to join our group as a campaigner just before it became ForestEthics. He was the engine behind the creation of the Staples campaign, and within a couple of years he became our executive director.

The Great Bear Rainforest campaign had started before ForestEthics was founded, but many of us had worked on it as individuals or in other organizations—as I had begun work on it with Greenpeace—so it became ForestEthics' first major campaign. It was a campaign that required all our tools, amazing people and many other organizations. For years it felt as if we were in a pressure cooker, trying to build enough steam to stop the logging before it spread too far. Once we reached an agreement in 2001 for them to stop logging those sixty-nine intact valleys, the environmental partners had to agree to stop our high-profile and successful boycott campaigns. The difficulty was that those campaigns were our power base. Now we had an "agreement" with many details not worked out and no permanent legislation or safety net. If the companies decided to go ahead and log, we would have to restart the campaign, which would have been very difficult to do. Campaigns require time to build awareness and interest. They can't be stopped and started easily. This, of course, is a familiar dilemma for many in social and environmental campaigns, because no solution is perfect at the outset, and any set of negotiations requires both a leap of faith and some hard compromises. It's impossible not to question whether an agreement is strong enough, if we're getting as much as we can, or if we should continue the campaigns.

We had all spent many sleepless nights trying to decide if we had gained enough to give up our boycott campaign. The difficulty was that if we didn't make a deal, the logging companies would punch roads into the intact valleys. In 2000 the companies agreed they would not log in any of the intact valleys if we stopped targeting them in the marketplace. It took another year for the government to accept a process of planning and decision making that included the First Nations governments as equal partners and addressed long-term economic development and employment issues.

But the agreement had held. After we reached an agreement in 2001, there was still a five-year period before the Great Bear Rainforest could officially be announced, and a further three years to figure out how to make the deal work, build a new economy, finance economic diversification, and negotiate laws with government and industry to create legislation for eco-forestry, which had never been done. We created working groups with government, industry, environmental groups, First Nations and unions, and hired third-party economists and scientists. We needed to keep the companies informed to maintain the pressure on the process, but simultaneously shift most of our efforts toward identifying economic alternatives for the region and listing scientific criteria for which activities could be allowed in the region without threatening the ecological stability. It was gruelling, detailed work and not the kind of stuff I'm cut out for. So after the initial agreement was reached in 2001, I largely stepped away and took the position of campaign director at ForestEthics, overseeing the creation of a new interior rainforest campaign focused on protecting the habitat of mountain caribou in BC and a new boreal campaign.

Chapter 10

EVERY SIXTY SECONDS
SAVING CANADA'S BOREAL FOREST

There is ample evidence to show that "current" forest use and management practices are destroying our legacy, that we are cutting too many trees over too large an area and that our forest policies have been ill-advised.

Yet, on paper at least, Canada has an enlightened, sustainable forest policy.

COMPETING REALITIES: THE BOREAL FOREST AT RISK,
CANADIAN SENATE SUBCOMMITTEE ON THE BOREAL FOREST, 1999

IN THE SUMMER OF 2002, I decided to visit my grandmother who lives in the boreal forest in Northern Ontario. Forrest, who was two, and I flew into International Falls in Minnesota, right on the US–Canada border, because that was the cheapest ticket I could get from San Francisco. Then we rented a car.

As it was getting dark, I found myself driving toward one of the largest mills I'd ever seen—and it was lit up like a Christmas tree. Smoke and wood go in, and chips pour out of this massive industrial beast. I drove toward it trying to figure out where the border was and then I realized . . . the border was through the mill. You have to drive through the Boise Cascade Mill in International Falls, US, and follow the bridge to the mill in Fort Frances, Canada.

There was slurry slopping down one side and chips snowing down the other. The bridge that is the crossing between Canada and the

United States is, essentially, a pulp mill. I raced through this monstrous, belching beast as if my life depended on it. The scale and smell of it overwhelmed me. Once I was through, I sped down the highway until I saw a huge black thing up ahead. I stopped the car. A large black bear was sitting in the middle of the highway. It stood up, crossed its forepaws and looked at me.

That encounter finally made me realize where I was—in an extraordinarily beautiful part of the boreal forest. For the longest time I watched the bear, trying to figure out how to get past it, until it started lumbering slowly down the road and we followed it in our car. I felt like it was telling me to slow down, to think about what I had just seen and where I was. The bear finally ambled off and I was still driving slowly, thinking about the forest and the mill and wondering if I was up to committing to another three to five years to such a big new campaign—the protection of Canada's boreal forest.

The boreal forest stretches from coast to coast in Canada and beyond in a ring (or some say halo or crown) around the top of the earth, spreading across Siberia. In Canada alone it spans a dozen political jurisdictions, hundreds of First Nations and includes the workings of twenty different logging companies. It's an ecological gem, a refuge of wilderness, two-thirds of which are undisturbed by roads or industry. Astoundingly, the Canadian boreal contains 25 percent of the earth's remaining intact forest and is, along with the Amazon and Russian taiga, one of three places remaining on earth with large intact forest landscapes. At 1.3 billion acres, the boreal is thirteen times the size of California. It's the second largest forest in the world, and is, without a doubt, North America's largest conservation responsibility. Canada's boreal holds more freshwater in wetlands, lakes and rivers than any other place on earth. It also constitutes the world's largest storehouse of carbon, making it one of our most important defences against global warming.

The boreal also has incalculable value as habitat for wide-ranging species such as grizzly bears, wolves and caribou. It has global significance for migratory birds, an abundance of other megafauna species such as pine marten, wolverine and moose, and a diverse array of minifauna and miniflora such as insects, lichen and fungi.[1] The boreal landscape is the product of ten thousand years of post glacial evolution that has produced a vast mosaic of wetlands, forests, rivers and lakes.

Back in the car, despite recognizing the boreal's beauty and importance, I was busy rattling off all the good reasons I should not get involved in yet another prolonged forest battle. I noticed the light up ahead was really odd, and there was a weird cracking sound. I stopped the car, got out and realized it was the aurora borealis, the Northern Lights, dancing across the sky in streams of green and blue.

I woke Forrest and put a blanket on the roof of our car. We lay there watching the magic lights ripple and crackle above us. Finally, we got back in the car and drove through the dark to Lake of the Woods. The next day I called Chris and told him about our drive into the boreal and said, "Honey, I think it's starting again."

He laughed and said, "Not again. Can't we just have a normal life for a little while?"

IT WASN'T LONG after the first Great Bear Rainforest Agreement that we had started thinking about the rest of Canada's forests and doing research on the logging happening across the country. Due to the media coverage of the Great Bear Agreement, I had been fielding calls from people at places like Home Depot asking if it was okay to buy Canadian forest products again. Canada's temperate rainforests are an important part of the country's biodiversity, but they're less than 2 percent of the landmass. The majority of forests across the country were being logged at a rate of over one hectare (2.5 acres) every 60 seconds.[2] So we started thinking about the boreal and researching what was being logged, how much was protected and who was buying it. There was a lot of resistance to starting a new campaign, especially because the other fights weren't truly over. Yes, we had announced a truce, and we'd agreed to work together, but even a decade later we were still working on the Great Bear deal, trying to finalize all the protected areas and the economic diversification strategies. The truce was only the beginning of a very long process. The more research we did, the more we realized it was time to up the ante.

Unlike most other countries, Canada still has enough intact forest and wild landscapes that we have a tremendous opportunity to ensure adequate protection of environmental values, ecologically sustainable forest management and the provision of ecologically sound forest products. While polling has consistently shown that the majority of Canadians are concerned about forest loss and would like to see more wilderness protected in Canada, most logging companies in Canada haven't been listening to the majority of Canadians.

We have the capacity, the resources, the knowledge and the creativity to protect what's left of the earth's primary forests, but we need to be bold, sophisticated and critical. We need to challenge ourselves and hold corporations accountable. That means we need to look at what you're holding right now as you're reading this—if you are reading it as a hardcover or paperback and not an e-book.

Manufacturing paper is the single largest industrial consumer of forests worldwide. The Canadian boreal provides about 20 percent of the world's supply of pulp and paper products. Forty-six percent of the newsprint used in the United States is printed on paper made from boreal trees. ForestEthics started working on the boreal by identifying who was buying the paper. We discovered that companies like Victoria's Secret were producing a million catalogues a day, primarily printed on old-growth forest material from the Canadian boreal.

Paper is also the biggest component of solid waste, accounting for over 30 percent of waste that gets sent to landfills and incinerators after recycling. If the whole catalogue industry, which uses 3.6 million tons of paper a year, switched to paper with just 10 percent postconsumer recycled content, it would save enough wood to build a six-foot fence stretching seven times across Canada, and we would reduce greenhouse gas (GHG) emissions by over half a million tons. That's like taking 91,000 cars off the road for a year. US junk mail alone—the creation of it, the shipping of it—is responsible for the equivalent emissions of ten million cars every year. Because junk mail in the United States consumes 100 million trees per year, if we're able to reduce the stream by just 25 percent, it will be equal to taking a million cars off the road for a year. The US annually produces 100 billion pieces of junk mail, 90 percent of which people don't want and never read.

You've heard of "carbon accounting," carbon credits and carbon offsets? It seemed to all of us at ForestEthics that the whole life cycle of old-growth boreal forests being made into catalogues and junk mail was just "carbon ridiculous." On top of the environmental consequences, ForestEthics found studies showing that in their lifetime North American city dwellers each spend *eight months* separating and recycling their junk mail. We launched a campaign for "do not mail" legislation in the United States on the basis that it's an environmental nightmare, and because we have a right not to find this crap in our mailboxes every day.

Several campaigns worked together to put the heat on companies logging the boreal and, more than that, to shift how paper is made in North America. Within a couple of years, an industry study revealed that recycling levels in North America were at an all-time high. The study specifically stated that it was because of the increased demand for recycled materials from Office Depot and Staples, which were ForestEthics' first two campaigns.

Those two campaigns were key: the National Resources Defense Council's and Greenpeace's campaign against Kimberly-Clark, which attacked the practice of logging old-growth forests to make toilet paper and facial tissue, and ForestEthics' fight against Victoria's Secret, which is explained in more detail in the next chapter. Greenpeace hung banners off and blockaded Kimberly-Clark's factories and buildings, and spoofed their world-famous brands. It was a very conscious, combined effort to squeeze the companies on the boreal. We also scored a magical assist from Harry Potter. Nicole Rycroft and her organization, Canopy (formerly Markets Initiative), took on the newspaper, magazine and book publishing industry and turned it on its head: with the support of J.K. Rowling, Canopy made sure that the last few Harry Potter books were printed on recycled and/or FSC-certified paper.

So thanks to the boy wizard, the toilet paper campaign and underwear ads, the industry agreed to come to the table with us in 2008. We planned to start by convincing every logging company in the country to stop logging in all caribou habitat—30 million hectares (74 million acres) across the country—at a time when their mills were shutting down due to the economic downturn. Everyone said that was impossible.

Everyone hadn't met Avrim Lazar.

One of the best illustrations I've ever had of the importance of seeing people, not positions, is Avrim. He became president and CEO of the Forest Products Association of Canada (FPAC) in 2002. His primary responsibility is to represent loggers. When I met Avrim, I was used to dealing with men like Jack Munro from the International Woodworkers of America, a six-foot-four, beer-drinking, leather-jacket-wearing logger who salted every other sentence with a four-letter word.

Avrim is a sixty-something, wiry, energetic man with a PhD. I first started to know him through the radio waves because he was the guy they kept having debate me on the issues. I thought he was danger-ous. I'd say, "Logging has to be stopped in this area," or "We have to make certain changes to the industry." Normally when I'd say that, the industry rep would immediately attack and explain why they needed to log exactly the way they always had. Avrim would always agree with whatever I said, which made the industry appear more ecologically responsible. The problem was that they weren't actually doing those things he was agreeing to, and he knew it.

But partway through the boreal campaign, the mediator, Dan Johnston, said, "You need to meet with Avrim. Both of you are talking about creating an industry that's based on quality and not quantity and an industry that has a reputation for being environmentally responsible."

When we met I was totally surprised to realize Avrim is a spirit-ual, socially conscious man who told me about the progressive syna-gogue he goes to in Ottawa, where social justice issues are part of the mandate. As we ordered dinner, I discovered that he has been a strict vegetarian since his teens—is, in fact, quite militant about it and will happily go on about the carbon footprint of cattle. This was not the opponent I was expecting.

Over the next few months we met several times and brain-stormed about what a truly "green" future for the boreal logging in-dustry would look like. I was able to talk frankly with Avrim about the environmental community's skepticism concerning the industry's intentions. We knew they wanted to end the protests and the markets campaigns, but did they really want to change? Were they truly willing to log differently? Would they really leave vast amounts of forest untouched and protect threatened species? Avrim thought it was possible—if we were willing to address economic issues and work with the industry to make sure they saw benefits from the sacrifices they made. We agreed to bring together our caucuses, put everything on the table and create a joint project where the environmental community and industry would reimagine the future of logging in one of the largest forests in the world.

There were outstanding questions on both sides. If the companies agreed not to log in caribou habitat, would that mean mill closures? What does green prosperity really look like? Should the primary export of the forest industry still be wood? If the future of oil companies is to stop thinking of themselves as oil companies and start thinking of themselves as diversified energy producers that work with energy from the sun and wind, what is the future of a logging company? Does it start thinking of itself as a forest- product company?

What will the forest industry look like in twenty or thirty years? Will it have run out of accessible old-growth and be forced to diversify, or can we speed up the process of diversification, create a sustainable industry now and protect more forests?

For years logging companies have used pulp to make fabric and adhesives. The most exciting research I've seen on forest products today comes from companies that separate the components of the tree and use its chemical structure to make foam and plastics that are natural, non-toxic and biodegrade in the same way. You put the pulp in a bath and separate out its sugars and starches and chemical components. Then you use those parts to create plastics in the way that you would if you used petrochemicals to make plastics.

If resource-based companies are going to survive in an era of scarcity and climate uncertainty, they need to redefine themselves. Forestry companies need to create more jobs and value from each tree and shift their focus from cutting trees to processing wood with ingenuity, new technology and services.

Avrim was true to his word after those initial conversations. He said, "I'm going to go back to every company in Canada and ask if they will commit to a statement recognizing that we need far greater conservation in order to protect endangered species and have viable forests." And he did.

Over the next two years about a dozen senior people from both sides met monthly. All of us had to admit that collectively we had more knowledge than anyone in the country but completely differing experiences, values and foci. And collectively, none of us were outside the issues—we all lived, worked and breathed them. Because none of us was willing to compromise our values, we realized that if we worked together we might find a truly new solution.

And I think we did.

In 2010 the BBC hailed the resulting Canadian Boreal Forest Agreement as the largest forest protection deal in history with the potential to save an area the size of New Zealand.[3] But only history can judge that.

The Canadian Boreal Forest Agreement took twenty-four months of often gruelling meetings, and while we certainly didn't redefine what a forestry company will be in the twenty-first century, the industry agreed to enact new forest practices across the country and defer logging in over 30 million hectares (74 million acres) of caribou habitat while joint scientific studies were conducted and new permanent protected areas were delineated. Some environmentalists and First Nations were furious because it's a deal with the logging industry, but it's one that could protect millions of hectares of caribou habitat that was slated to be logged.

Our last meeting before brokering the deal was at a retreat in Toronto. We had spent two years drafting more than one hundred pages of details, designs and terms of reference. By this point we were on draft fifty-six. We've gone from another war in the woods to collectively believing that Canada can lead the world in redefining the logging industry's relationship with nature. The funny thing is that what really saved the boreal wasn't the fight over lumber; it was a fight over lingerie.

Chapter 11

VICTORIA'S DIRTY SECRET
MOVING FROM LUMBER TO LINGERIE

*Unless you protect more forests—and you're not logging
an endangered species' habitat—I can't buy paper from
you. I definitely can't buy paper from you if there are
protesters attached.*

VICTORIA'S SECRET SENIOR EXECUTIVE TOM KATZENMEYER

IN A MEETING WITH THE ONTARIO GOVERNMENT

A CRITICAL PIECE of the puzzle that led to the Canadian Boreal
Forest Agreement was the Victoria's Dirty Secret campaign. Avrim was
critical to the success of the negotiations, but I suspect the primary
motivator for most of the logging companies at the table was avoiding
another high-profile campaign targeting one of their customers.

Once ForestEthics launched the boreal campaign, we started to do
chain-of-custody research to see who was buying the most lumber
from the boreal forest and what products they were making. We over-
laid that research with maps of the most important areas to protect.
Some of the most ecologically vital areas are in the Rocky Mountain
foothills, the bridge between the mountain ecosystems and the boreal
ecosystems. Canada had already protected some big areas (Jasper and
Banff), but these areas are not connected by corridors, so caribou and
other species in the area cannot roam through their habitats.

We initially decided to focus on the boreal forest in the Rocky
Mountain foothills. Our research showed that the mill in Hinton,

Alberta, was producing a huge amount of paper for catalogues. With a little bit of digging we discovered that the top six catalogue companies in North America were all buying from the boreal, and all their catalogues contained less than 10 percent recycled content.

We contacted all the companies and met with several to ask them to use recycled paper, reduce the number of catalogues they produced and make a commitment not to buy from the boreal. We also prepared background information and analysis on each company. In order to hold the catalogue industry accountable for its impact on the forests and to protect the boreal, we knew we needed a high-profile public campaign. We set aside two days for a strategy meeting to decide which of the six companies to pursue. We knew we needed to pick one company in order to create a high-profile campaign and focus our efforts.

We soon covered the walls in matrices showing which company had the most storefronts that would be accessible for protest, which had the worst record of environmental responsibility and paper procurement policy, and which bought the most paper.

Everyone in the office had his or her own pet catalogue company. One person fought vehemently to target L.L. Bean because they publicly marketed how green they were while buying old-growth forest for their catalogues. Another person argued that we should go after the Sears Christmas wish book, because it's the mother of all catalogues.

And on it went.

After that first night of arguing in circles, I suggested we take a break, go to dinner and not talk about forests or catalogues. We came back the next morning, and I went around the room and said, "In your gut, what do you want to work on most, and what do you think is going to be really successful?"

Every single person in the room said, "Victoria's Secret," because the idea of going up against a lingerie company was just too much fun.

Sometimes in doing this kind of campaigning we let our intellect get in the way and forget that our head and heart have to be aligned for us to be successful. It's hard work, and you need to align with purpose, passion and values because that's what we get out of it. God knows it's not the salary. If you constantly force yourself into a place you shouldn't be, you'll burn out. If you're doing a job that provides a great paycheque, security or benefits you need for your family, that's a whole different thing. But that's not why you do this work—even when there is a paycheque attached. You do this because you want to make a change in the world, and you want to feel part of something bigger. Regardless of how you think about an issue, if it's not what you're excited about, if it's not what keeps you up at night, it's not going to be your best work. Before choosing a campaign it's always important to "find the juice": what piece of it excites you? What it really comes down to is giving an honest answer to the question, What do you want to work on for the next couple of years?

VICTORIA'S SECRET was producing a million catalogues a day— yes, you read it right, *a million catalogues a day.* They mailed almost 400 million catalogues a year, and the majority of their paper came from Canada's old-growth forests.[1] We approached them and told them what our research had found and offered to help them "green" their catalogue. Their initial response was . . . to mostly ignore us.

Because our campaign was against using wood from the boreal, the logging industry and British Columbia government organized a tour of the area for all the catalogue companies. Some of our friends inside the companies made a point of refusing to go unless ForestEthics was also present. So, on a crisp autumn weekend, I found myself in the surreal position of touring the forests and logging operations of Alberta with some of the largest catalogue companies in the world. At the time I was once again a new mom and trying to balance my commitment to breastfeeding Quinn with the travel my job demanded. The result was that on this particular weekend I was not only crashing the industry boys' club (it was quite common for me to be the only woman in the room on these industry tours) but also doing it with a six-month-old baby and my mother-in-law in tow.

I knew the day was going to be a disaster when we got on the plush tour bus and the PR flack for International Paper calmly handed out a new agenda blithely explaining that a couple of stops had to be cut to save time and get us to our resort in the Rockies for cocktail hour.

While everyone else nodded in good spirits as they oohed and aahed at the stunning Rocky Mountain landscape, my heart sank. I had been negotiating the tour and schedule with the company for weeks, and now they had cut our stops at some of the most devastated areas. In the end it was just as I had feared: International Paper took the buyers for the catalogue companies to protected areas, then took them to selective logging areas and said, "This is the way of the future. Doesn't this look like a beautiful logging operation?" Everyone nodded agreeably. Having visited the region many times to do research and discuss the issues with the local community, I knew we were standing in a rare ecologically responsible experimental logging operation and that less than a mile away behind the trees that lined the highway was a scarred clear-cut landscape that went on as far as the eye could see.

I asked, "How much of the logging you're doing today is selective logging, and how much is clear-cutting?" The fact was that over 90 percent of the logging in the region was conventional clear-cutting, but it took repeated questioning to get International Paper to admit it in front of their customers. Later that day, after quietly threatening to "go ballistic in the middle of your goddamn tour," I had the tour organizers agree to stop the bus in a small clear-cut we were passing. Regardless, the sight seemed to have little effect on the customers who were annoyed at being delayed from reaching their resort and cocktails.

It was incredibly frustrating: we had millions of dollars of consumer power in the forest with us, but the individuals who were on the tour were very happy to lap up the drivel being shovelled at them by the logging company and then amble off to have steaks at a posh retreat in Banff National Park. The logging and paper companies had managed to create such a relaxed environment and jocular culture on the tour that hard questions or critiques seemed gauche. It's impolite to bite the hand that feeds you, and this hand was feeding us an enormous line of bullshit coated in foie gras. Looking back, I see that tour as an opportunity to be "inside the beast" but also one of the failures in our campaign's early days. Being one of the only women there (not to mention operating on very little sleep due to Quinn's habit that year of waking up every two or three hours) and one of the only dissenting voices, I found myself awkward and fairly ineffective in what felt like a privileged moment within the old boys' network.

At the end of that tour, Victoria's Secret renewed a two-year contract with International Paper and the Hinton mill for paper made from clear-cutting the habitat of threatened caribou, primarily because the paper was cheap and it was easy for them to continue their cozy relationship with International Paper. They also thought ForestEthics was too small to have an impact on them.

They were wrong.

Back at the office we had been digesting our failure on the tour and brainstorming how we could regain the upper hand. It turned out the upper hand came in the form of a model wearing cheap lingerie and carrying a chainsaw.

The idea of a brand attack on Victoria's Secret in the form of a mock ad came to us during a strategy meeting in which we were analyzing the company and what would influence them. We realized Victoria's Secret invested heavily in the image, based on sex and possibility, that they created in the minds of millions of women. The most powerful action we could undertake was to threaten that image. A corporation's brand is usually one of its most valuable assets. How customers or investors perceive the company has a direct impact on its bottom line. We knew that if we could threaten the Victoria's Secret brand, the company would take notice.

We found a model via Craigslist. In the beginning, the feminists among us were horrified. We even tried shooting the image with transvestites in order to ensure that we were not also objectifying women and trading in the glorification of a mostly unattainable body image. While memorable, the ad that resulted just didn't cut it because there was no way anyone would confuse it with a Victoria's Secret ad. In the end we decided to get as close to the brand as we could without getting sued, and made sure our model, though beautiful, was "not quite hot enough" to be a Victoria's Secret model (we later heard this was one of the things that upset the company most).

The caption was "Victoria's Dirty Secret."

I had a last-minute panic attack that as a feminist I couldn't support an ad showing a woman in lingerie holding a chainsaw. I e-mailed the picture to two of my feminist heroes: Gloria Steinem and Judy Rebick. They both thought the brand attack was so clear that the image was not objectification; rather, it was a parody of Victoria's Secret ads in every way. So we took out a full-page ad in the *New York Times*. The newspaper initially refused to run the ad because it was too suggestive and maybe even violent (our guess was that their opposition came more from the fact that Victoria's Secret is a huge advertising client). We pointed out that they ran Victoria's Secret ads daily and that several of their movie ads had scantily clad women holding M-16s. Finally, they agreed to run the ad, but not before first questioning all our data, for which we had exhaustive references.

That single ad, running once, was half our campaign budget: $30,000.

It was a classic low-budget non-governmental organization (NGO) strategy: make your paid media so controversial that it earns you coverage you could never afford to buy. A media storm erupted. Papers like *USA Today* reported on the controversy and ran the ad again. Estimates vary, but we likely achieved the equivalent of a $1.5 million media buy with one ad.

We followed the ad with serious grassroots organizing around the United States. People who were concerned about these issues signed up on the ForestEthics website and sent over ten thousand letters to the Victoria's Secret CEO. We staged 852 unique protests outside Victoria's Secret stores in the next twenty-four months. In November 2005 we held a rally outside their annual fashion show in New York City. That Christmas we issued a postcard with a photo of Victoria's Secret CEO Leslie Wexner, with a devil on one shoulder and an angel on the other, and the cutline "You can make all the difference. Protect our forests." We mailed a postcard directly to him. We hired local organizers in the CEO's hometown to go door to door with our materials and to leaflet outside the headquarters.

Within six months of the campaign starting, Victoria's Secret came to us and said, "We want to talk."

We began meeting with senior executives who realized that their company had made a mistake in renewing their contract for paper from the boreal, but they now had a legally binding two-year deal. Also, they consumed so much paper that it was going to be difficult if not impossible to source a greener catalogue. Discussions started within the industry over who could make catalogue paper with a higher recycled or FSC fibre content. Tom Katzenmeyer of Victoria's Secret's parent company, Limited Brands, asked us if, behind the scenes, we would help to devise procurement guidelines to aid in their discussions with suppliers who seemed to be obfuscating the issues in order to avoid changing their supply. The next year and a half was a truly difficult dance in which we worked hand in hand with the company while still maintaining high-profile protests at their stores. This kind of inside-outside strategy is essential in any set of protracted negotiations. If the heat goes away, the impetus for change peters out at the same time as the company or government is coming to terms with the real work that will be required to make the changes necessary to reach a deal. If the recognition of just how difficult the road ahead is hits at the same time the pressure is reduced, it can kill the negotiations before an agreement is reached.

I remember one day late in the campaign that was particularly problematic (though Tom, Todd Paglia and I managed to laugh about it years later). Tom had flown to San Francisco with several other senior executives to meet with Todd and me. We were an hour into the meeting and making some good progress when Todd's BlackBerry started buzzing. Before he could reach over to shut it off, mine rang. Two seconds later Tom's rang. We all looked at one another and agreed to take a break. As we were sitting in the meeting devising a solutions package, grassroots volunteers had set up a protest at the Victoria's Secret store across from Macy's in New York. It's their biggest store and does over $40 million in business every year. To Tom's credit, he understood why we insisted on continuing our campaign until a final agreement was reached, and must have worked some magic inside the company to get them to engage in the negotiations while the campaign raged outside the boardroom.

On December 6, 2006, in a joint press conference, Tom and I announced to reporters from across North America (and many government officials as well as paper and logging companies that we knew from the online report had quietly joined the telepress conference) that Victoria's Secret/Limited Brands and ForestEthics had reached a landmark agreement to work together to transform the way catalogue paper was made in North America. Victoria's Secret would no longer buy from the Hinton mill. In fact, they agreed to no longer source from any company that was logging endangered forests or endangered caribou habitat in the boreal. They also committed to dramatically increasing recycled fibre content and giving a preference to FSC fibre. In addition, they pledged $1 million in research to protect the boreal forest and to jointly advocate with us for greater forest protection in general. The logging industry reps were livid.

It seemed too good to be true, but for once it wasn't. Victoria's Secret/Limited Brands were true to their word. Over the next two years Tom Katzenmeyer flew to Ontario, Alberta and British Columbia with me to lobby the governments to protect more forests and warn that they had to improve their logging practices if they were going to hold on to their customers.

On one memorable spring day in Toronto, Tom and I met with officials from the ministry of natural resources and the premier's office. As usual, the meeting opened with one of the top bureaucrats giving an overview of why the logging in the province was "sustainable" and even "world class." At one point he told us, "Many of our studies show caribou actually like clear-cuts." For once I didn't have to respond by countering with study after study. Before I could say a word, Tom leaned forward in his chair and said, "I don't think you understand. I'm here because your lack of environmental regulation has become a problem for me, and I'm the customer. I buy $100,000,000 worth of paper every two years, and I want to buy from Canada, but I can't unless you provide recycled fibre, and more Forest Stewardship Council fibre. Unless you protect more forests—and you're not logging an endangered species' habitat—I can't buy paper from you. I definitely can't buy paper from you if there are protesters attached. So until she's happy, I'm not happy." And Tom flashed a smile at me.

You could have heard a pine needle drop.

I realized we had harnessed a whole new power through this collaboration with industry. It's definitely a very different experience to be sitting in a meeting with politicians when you have the financial power of the market behind you.

In late 2007 and into 2008, which was a weak time for the US economy, Victoria's Secret did $5.6 billion total US sales; $3.7 billion of that came from the stores, $1.4 billion from the catalogue and their website. They have 60 million customers. As Tom said, they buy a lot of paper.[2]

The government might have been willing to play chicken with environmental groups, but they weren't ignoring a customer with Tom's buying power. The following year, the Ontario government announced the permanent protection of 50 million acres of forest, an area half the size of California.

Of course a decision this big does not come about as a result of one campaign initiative or even one campaign or one organization. It was the result of many years and many hands. That said, the legacy has been huge. People inside the government and inside the industry have told me that the Victoria's Secret campaign and the related lobby meetings had a significant impact on protecting the boreal forest.

In 2008 Tom and I shared a stage at a Hollyhock event titled "Strange Bedfellows: Corporate and Environmental Alliances for Powerful Change." That night we told stories that the other had never heard.

Tom was startled to discover how and why we'd chosen to target Victoria's Secret, but he understood. As he said, "The other thing they could have done was go after the logging companies or the Canadian government or International Paper, who was selling the pulp to us, but that's not very sexy at all, and who's going to join in demonstrations against International Paper? I don't even know who they are, where they are, what they are; it's just this nameless, faceless corporation. So to go after an iconic brand, I think was very, very shrewd on your part."

Tom explained that they initially ignored our requests because they "weren't in a listening mode." He noted that before our campaign Victoria's Secret prided itself on its green policies. "We care about the environment, and we do all kinds of other things in terms of recycling and waste reduction, the lighting in the stores and all this other stuff, but we chose, for whatever reason, to just simply renew the contract." He said that one of the lessons they learned as a corporation was to listen. "We're a values-driven company. . . . It matters how we play the game." And he noted that it mattered not just to their company but to their customers and their shareholders.

Another tactic that affected the shareholders was our attending the shareholder meetings. Todd, ForestEthics' executive director, started going to meetings with local activists and giving impassioned pleas to save the boreal. "It was a very, very, very moving thing," recalled Tom. "One of the women who came actually cried because it was so moving, and everybody was very touched by this. That actually happened two years in a row.

"ForestEthics also did a lot of activities on college campuses," Tom continued, "which is kind of going right at our customer base. . . . They had one of our shareholders called Domini Social Investments, which is a socially responsible investment firm, propose a shareholder resolution on this issue. Talk about putting the fear of God into a company.

"This is what was going on behind the scenes. This campaign starts and we start talking. And we basically knew going into this that they were going to want to keep the pressure on us even though we were in negotiations. So it wasn't a situation where we could say, hey, lay off and we'll talk to you. These folks were well down [in] a campaign. They were getting a lot of visibility. It was good for everything else they were working on. It was a very viable thing for them, so they're not going to back off the campaign. And why would they trust us? We didn't listen to them the first time around. We had to get our credibility back."

He talked about how we worked together to develop their procurement process and craft the Request for Information (RFI) that was used to choose the paper companies. "Once the proposals came in we didn't actually let them see the financials of the proposals," said Tom, "but we let them see the answers to the environmental questions that came back. . . . We learned so much, even though we have paper experts and people who know how to procure paper from around the world. It was just a giant 'aha moment' for us that an outside entity, an outside NGO, could have as much knowledge. So we learned a lot, and I think we're a lot smarter because of it today."

Since Victoria's Secret let us in on their procurement process, ForestEthics has also been invited to advise other groups, including Dell, Seventh Generation and Estée Lauder.

As we talked about the agreement, someone in the audience asked if we took money from the company.

The answer was no.

Victoria's Secret offered us money. Most companies do. I have often felt torn about it because there are points where you honestly think, *We should just take their money and use it for good. Then we could hire more campaigners, or we could have some money to help First Nations communities.* And, in fact, that's the decision that many organizations make.

Greenpeace and ForestEthics have never taken funds from any corporations that could potentially be a target, because if you were to become financially indebted to the company it would be hard to maintain your objectivity and integrity. But during the Victoria's Secret campaign we did come up with what I think was a very clever way to use their money, without taking it. We encouraged them, as part of the agreement that they made with us, to commit to putting $1 million toward advocacy, science and mapping to ensure greater forest protection. To decide where that money went, we created a board of directors, which I was on. I called a bunch of the organizations that I knew needed funding to get the good work done—like Global Forest Watch—but no money ever went to ForestEthics, and it didn't affect our capacity to act independently.

THE RELATIONSHIP with Tom may sound too good to be true, but this kind of relationship building is one of two keys toward making headway in the corporate world.

I. ENGAGE SENIOR MANAGEMENT

If you don't reach them, they won't invest the resources that are necessary to become ecologically responsible. They may create a better public relations strategy, but that's not the same as taking on your concerns as a project that they need to manage with deliverables and a real budget. Significant change will not happen unless you involve senior management.

We used a number of different strategies to reach senior management. We couldn't get our e-mails and faxes and letters to the senior management team at Victoria's Secret/ Limited Brands, because we couldn't get past the gatekeepers. On Valentine's Day, we sent dozens of organic roses (with the note, "Victoria's Secret, Don't Break Our Hearts. Help Us Protect Forests!" included) to everyone on the team—who's not going to accept a delivery of flowers? That got the attention of senior management.

2. FIND CHAMPIONS

I don't think we would have made a lot of progress with Victoria's Secret without connecting with Tom. You need to find someone with whom you can build a relationship, someone who, on a personal level, wants to see the company behave responsibly, the same way Linda Coady and Bill Cafferata did at MacBlo.

Once you find your champion, it's crucial to build a relationship. We didn't just have meetings with Tom, we went out, ate together and talked at length, and we were gut-honest in our conversations. From the very beginning, I let Tom know our campaign would continue until significant commitments to change had been made, because that was where our power lay. You may be doing things the other person doesn't like, but you need to maintain that power base while you're in negotiations. I've seen negotiations fail for NGOs when they let go of that power too soon and didn't maintain it during negotiations.

Tom told me a few things I didn't know, like the fact that his company had hired a PR company that specialized in crisis management to deal with us, and hired another company to offer advice in order to avoid their stock values taking a major hit because of the protests.

He also described how this experience affected their policies in other ways. Limited Brands is in the beauty and personal care business, and a lot of their products are in plastic and glass bottles made overseas. They've started dealing with the state government in their home base in Ohio to develop local bottlers and shorten the length of their supply chain. He admitted that even our most outrageous demands were getting some traction. "We are beginning to understand that cataloging may be an outmoded business model. Maybe. People are actually saying this now. Because our business is shifting to the internet. Sixty percent of our revenue, $1.4 billion, is now done on the Internet. So there's a whole dynamic changing here, and people can do catalogue quick-orders from their cellphone now. So there's all kinds of stuff that we're testing. . . . It has definitely caused a mindset change."

One of my favourite stories about Tom's outreach and advocacy is when he came to meet with BC minister of forests Pat Bell and our inland temperate rainforest campaigner, Candace Batycki. I called Candace before the meeting and she was nervous. I was talking her through what happened in Toronto when she said, "There's a really big black car pulling up. Oh my God, I think it's him. I gotta go." Then she hung up.

She'd never met Tom before and didn't know what to expect. We were at a key point of negotiations on caribou issues in BC, and it was very tense. After the meeting Candace called me again, but she sounded shaky, as if she was about to cry. I panicked. Tom was so great in Toronto. "What happened?"

Candace said, "He said things better than I could have imagined in my wildest dreams. I had to pick the assistant deputy minister's jaw up off the floor, and then we came out of the meeting and there was the big black car and he just got in and was whisked away, and now I'm standing here on the legislature lawn thinking, Who was that masked man?"

Because of the success ForestEthics had with Staples, Office Depot and Limited Brands, whenever I go into a boardroom now everyone looks at me as if I'm Michael Moore or a reporter from *60 Minutes*. The companies are worried because they know the public wants to see that they are environmentally responsible, and they're willing to change faster now. People are voting with their dollars at checkouts. Ultimately when doing the green thing affects their profit margin, the companies have to care. But of course corporate leadership is not enough. We still need better laws, not just better lingerie catalogues.

Chapter 12

GREEN IS THE NEW BLACK
CAMPAIGNING IN TINSELTOWN

In the 'hood we say ride that shit till the wheels fall off.

VAN JONES

"OH, HONEY, green is the new black." The neon-bright voice on the other end of the phone belonged to Nicole Landers, a PR wizard from Los Angeles.

Landers and some people from Warner Brothers were on a conference call, talking about flying me to Hollywood for the opening of the eco-documentary *The 11th Hour*, produced and narrated by Leonardo DiCaprio. "We've got a number of designers in LA who want to dress you for the red carpet," chirped Landers.

I was on my BlackBerry, driving a rented Prius north of San Francisco to a senior management retreat for ForestEthics. It was 2007, the boreal campaign was ongoing, we had just won the Victoria's Secret campaign and a couple of minutes before this call, I'd been wondering how we could increase our efforts to save the habitat for BC's mountain caribou in the inland temperate rainforest. Now I was Cinderella, being dressed for the ball, and the girly part of me was thinking, *I'm going to LA, getting dressed by an LA designer, walking the red carpet and meeting Leonardo DiCaprio!*

Then Landers said, "We just need to know your measurements. What size are you?"

"I'm a twelve," I said.

Dead silence on the other end of the phone.

These are people who usually talk so fast that I can never get a word in edgewise. But now they were silent . . . until several voices started talking at once.

"Oh, we didn't realize," said one mortified woman.

"We . . . we saw your picture and it looked good," stuttered another, trying not to sound as if I was deformed. And failing.

"We had no idea," whispered a third, as if I'd just revealed I had days to live.

Finally, Landers explained the dilemma as delicately as possible. "Honey"—she paused before delivering the death sentence—"LA designers don't design above a size six."

For a moment, all the body image issues I'd ever had came crashing in on me: my insecurity, memories of my brief flirtation with bulimia. Suddenly I was thinking, I shouldn't do this. I couldn't do this. I had no business going to LA and walking the red carpet, I was a cow. Suddenly I was Cinderella after midnight, my chariot replaced by a pumpkin, my gala gown by Birkenstocks and a really big Gore-Tex jacket.

Then I remembered that just before receiving the verdict that I was too fat to be seen in public, I'd been worrying about raising the profile of the threat to critical wildlife habitat, and realized this whole Hollywood ride could be a fantastic new way to get our message out. I might not end up being known for my striking figure on the red carpet, but I would be known for my work. Nothing above a size six?

"Well, honey," I said, "they make 'em big up north. Just have them get me two, 'cause I'm coming and I'm a twelve."

They all started laughing.

"I'm sure we'll find something," said Landers. "We love you. We'll find you a dress."

Size twelve or not, I was going to Hollywood.

THE ROAD TO HOLLYWOOD started in 2006 at the Bioneers conference in Marin County. An annual eco-themed melting pot of scientists, journalists, activists, philanthropists and some of the greatest visionaries of the environmental movement, Bioneers is where I met Van Jones, a Civil Rights activist and environmentalist; Janine Benyus, the author of *Biomimicry*; Lois Gibbs of Love Canal fame; and two of the world's most important green thinkers, Paul Hawken, entrepreneur and author of *The Ecology of Commerce, Natural Capitalism* and *Blessed Unrest*, and Bill McKibben, author of *The End of Nature* and *Eaarth*.

It's a place where new ideas are seeded, strategies take root, deals are made and projects are launched. In 2006 I was giving a speech to five thousand people, the largest group I'd ever spoken to—and it was being webcast live to another twenty thousand. I agonized over the speech, what to say, how to say it and, when I was done, came up with something entirely new. Instead of simply analyzing the issues out loud and drowning my audience in statistics and righteous indignation, I followed some of my communications training and set the issues within real-world stories. This was the first time I told the story of my journey from the Clayoquot campaign to the fight for the boreal. The whole blockades to boardrooms journey. While I was working on this speech, I started to realize the lessons I'd learned from each fight and how they all fit into the big picture. I started to visualize this book you're reading now.

The conference had just started, and I was at one of the cocktail parties for the speakers. I went outside and overheard about a half-dozen people talking at super-caffeinated speed.

"We've got David Suzuki saying this, Mikhail Gorbachev's saying this, and Paul Hawken's saying this—but we don't have anyone talking about the state of the world's forests."

Not being shy I turned to them and said, "If you really want to show the state of the world's forests, use the World Resources Institute data, which show that 80 percent of the world's intact forests are already gone. We only have about 20 percent left, and the majority of that is in Canada, Russia and Brazil. And in all three countries we're losing the forests at incredible rates. Seventy-two countries have lost all their frontier forests—areas large enough to maintain ecosystem services and biodiversity. And the US has already lost 95 percent of its old-growth forests, so US markets have turned to Canada, and the majority of Canada's old-growth forest is being logged to make newspapers and magazines in the United States."

In slow motion they turned to me, "Who *are* you?"

Within a couple of minutes Leila and Nadia Conners—the directors and producers of *The 11th Hour*—had talked me into flying to Hollywood to be interviewed for the film.

TWO WEEKS LATER, I arrived and hit a wall of heat as soon as I got off the plane.

A chauffeur held a sign with my name on it, and he took me off to a big black car. It was all as I'd imagined, except we didn't drive to a studio—they were filming in a hotel. When I arrived at the hotel, the scene was surreal. I walked by a room where Archbishop Desmond Tutu was having his makeup done. Then a small, powerful woman came over and invited me for lunch. I sat down and ate salad with Irmelin DiCaprio. She's a smart cookie, really knows the issues and she's a great adviser for her son, who wasn't on the set. After lunch with Irmelin, I went up to the suite where they were filming, sat on a chair and was interviewed for two hours about the world's forests— their condition, and how industrial logging threatens them. I also talked about Canada, and how logging and deforestation contribute to global warming. Then the limo drove me back to the airport and I flew home. A year later I got a call from Nadia saying they'd interviewed more than three hundred people, chosen seventy-two, and my interview had made the cut. I was one of the only women in the film, one of only three Canadians, alongside David Suzuki and Wade Davis, and one of the youngest participants.

I went to LA, saw the screening and was really impressed with the film. A month later I received a call telling me that Warner Brothers had bought the film, and they were doing a red-carpet opening in LA. They wanted to fly me back for the premiere. I remember thinking, *How much carbon have I spent already, going back and forth for this? It's a good film, but I'm only in it for fourteen seconds. Is it really worth taking more time away from my kids, going all the way to LA . . .*

I was debating it when I had two conversations that made me decide to leap in with both feet. I called my sister Corinne, who's always one of my touchstones, and she practically shouted, "Are you crazy? They're offering to send you to LA, and you get to walk the red carpet, and meet Leonardo DiCaprio, and they're going to dress you? When are you ever going to get a chance to do something like that again? We are so going to Hollywood!" I'd also put the news about the invitation as a status update on my Facebook page: "Hey, I'm in DiCaprio's *11th Hour* film. I'm debating whether or not to go down to the red carpet to LA."

Van Jones wrote, "In the 'hood we say ride that shit till the wheels fall off." I read Van's message, thinking, *That's right. I'm a campaigner and this is a new tool falling into my lap. I can either be cynical or I can get organized.*

So after talking it through with Kristi Chester Vance, our communications director at ForestEthics, we decided to hire an LA PR agent to try and use the moment to get more attention and traction on our campaigns to protect endangered caribou. Our PR agent told us the smartest thing we could do was hold our own premiere because all of LA wanted to see DiCaprio's new film, but there were only three hundred seats at the red carpet premiere. Suddenly we were renting our own theatre, doing our own screening, and the PR agents went to work.

I arrived with Corinne the next day, and from the moment we stepped off the plane I was put in the hands of an army of women who rushed me from makeup, hair and nail appointments to dress fittings and interviews. And yes, they did get me a size twelve. They found eco-designer Linda Loudermilk, who designs for real women with real bodies. The tunic was made from FSC-certified wood fibre with a cutout tree design in the back filled with lace. The pants were made from organic bamboo. My hair looked shellacked.

The day of the premiere, I was on CTV National news, CNN and even *Entertainment Tonight.* I was chauffeured in a Zenn electric car to the premiere at the Arclight Cinemas in Hollywood, where I walked the red carpet.

I'd been surrounded by media before, but this was like nothing I'd ever done or seen. There were rows of reporters practically climbing over one another, firing words and aiming their flashbulbs at me. "Look here! Look here! Tzeporah! Look here!" And I was wondering, where do I look? I felt totally goofy. Once they'd finished with their "look heres" and flashing bulbs, they wanted to ask questions.

I reached the first reporter, who asked, "Who're you wearing?" I told them about my outfit. Then it was, "Who did your hair?" and "What shoes are you wearing?" Finally, I got to a guy from the *Chicago Tribune* who asked a serious and thoughtful question about the economic impact of the United States using less wood from Canada. For a moment it was as if he was talking Greek. Then I realized he was the only person actually speaking my language. I stepped forward, and we had a real conversation until the carpet sweeper pulled me away. I handed the reporter my card and told him to call me for a proper interview. And he did. I realized that in a situation like this you have only fifteen seconds, and you can spend it answering questions about shoes or hair, or you can turn whatever question you get into a moment to talk about the issues.

Then I went in and watched the film. When I came on screen, my fourteen seconds had turned into nine seconds, and I was talking only about the state of the world's forests. They'd cut the part about Canada, which was in my press release. I texted Kristi during the screening, then raced out of the theatre afterwards and called her in a panic.

She told me not to worry. "You're talking about Canada now. You just talked about Canada with *ET*. No one's going to remember exactly what you said in the film."

So I just kept on talking about Canada, and she was right. No one actually checked the movie to see what I'd really said or, if they did, they didn't remember. I talked about forests in the film, and now I was talking about forests. Doing this type of work, you worry so much about exactly what you're saying and being precise in the messaging, but most people remember only general subjects: Canada, forest, controversy. I'd been so worried about my one sound bite, but it didn't really matter—I still got the message across.

When the premiere finished, we went to the after-party, and there were all these stunningly beautiful people wandering around. Corinne and I were watching, laughing and sipping martinis. Someone came and shuttled us to a VIP area, which is just a part of the bar that's cordoned off, and I found myself in a lineup waiting to meet Leonardo DiCaprio. He was sitting in a little booth with his friends, and there was a line of people waiting to shake his hand. Security guards were everywhere. I felt kind of silly, but . . . My turn came. I shook his hand, and he said, "Thanks so much for being in the film." A lot of the Hollywood people I'd met really didn't understand environmental issues. They had an honest curiosity, but their knowledge was very superficial, and I didn't know what to expect when I met him. He looked me right in the eyes, unlike most of the other people I'd met that night who had looked past me for the person to whom they should really be talking. DiCaprio was very present, and he asked, "Do you think we have a chance?"

I laughed. "Oh! We're going to have a real conversation."

He laughed.

I said, "I think we do. But I think the question is how do we use the new mainstream interest in the issues and even this movie to galvanize political change?"

And he said, "I don't know, that's your job."

Then to my astonishment we had a real and informed conversation about cap-and-trade, and whether the United States would ever set a true price on carbon before his handlers dragged me away so the rest of the lineup could have their few minutes with him.

I took out my BlackBerry and called my kids, because I realized that Tobey Maguire was sitting with DiCaprio, and Val Kilmer was standing on the other side of me. Forrest answered the phone. I said, "Mommy's standing between Spider-Man and Batman. Should I go meet one of them? Which one first?"

Eventually the evening ended, and Corinne and I went back to our hotel room, which was the cheapest place we could find in Hollywood that didn't make us cringe. I was so tired that I didn't wash my face, even though I was wearing a mask of makeup. I just threw my pyjamas on and fell into bed. The next morning I had an interview with *Canada AM*, which has a huge audience, but because I was in LA and the show is live from Toronto I had to be up at five in the morning to do it. They were sending a car, the driver didn't know the number of our room, and the front desk wasn't open. In my dreams I heard beeping. Then my BlackBerry started going off. I finally stumbled up and grabbed the BlackBerry. It was Nicole Landers. The car had been driving up and down the block, honking, for forty-five minutes. I was supposed to be on the air in eighteen minutes.

I was across the city from the studio, I was in my pyjamas and I hadn't even washed my face. But that's the great thing about having yourself shellacked. I ran into the bathroom, looked in the mirror, and I looked pretty much the way I had the night before. I wiped off the smears and ran outside in my pyjamas, holding my high heels and my suit. I jumped into the back of the limo and shouted, "Drive!" I changed into my suit, and when we got to the building I flew out the door, high heels still in my hands. There was a security guard waiting. "Are you the Canadian woman who's supposed to be on that Canadian show? You're live in ninety seconds!" We ran to the elevator, they threw me into the studio, stuck the ear bud in, and I heard, "You're live in ten, nine, eight . . ."

I hadn't put on my shoes, so I dropped them under the table. I was totally dazed. I'd had three hours sleep and no coffee. I had no idea what I was going to say when the camera turned on. Then there was a woman talking in my ear.

People all over Canada watched this interview and later told me it was fabulous. The interviewer asked, "So what's Leo like?" and I just went on autopilot. I clearly remembered the lesson from the red carpet, though, because I said something like "He's really great. And the thing is, he's really concerned." Then I started talking about the threats to the forests, global warming and junk mail. I only know that's what I said because a transcript was sent to me by a university professor who uses it in her class as an example of "media management."

When the lights went down, the woman who was filming came into the room with the guard, looked at me and directed me to the coffee.

THAT NIGHT at our screening, I gave a little talk after the film, and it went really well—standing ovation kind of well. Landers said people don't usually get excited like that in LA if you're not a superstar, so she was thrilled. Cisco Furniture had offered to do the after-party for our premiere for free, because then they'd have people walking around their showroom. Then acrobats who had trained with Cirque du Soleil offered to do a performance.

Suddenly our little screening had turned into an A-list event full of people I didn't know. They'd come to see *The 11th Hour,* but the price of admission was hearing about ForestEthics.

We had planned our own little "green carpet" for any celebs who happened to attend. Sharon Lawrence, a great actor who's really knowledgeable and engaged in the issues, had agreed to help me host the evening. There were a couple of other actors coming, so we had a bit of press interest. We started working the carpet, and there were four or five press people there. Then Adrian Grenier from *Entourage* came in. He told me that he was building an eco-friendly house in New York. The funny thing is that I was trying very hard not to laugh, because he was standing beside me with his hand on my back as we were smiling at the camera, and all my friends who were behind the cameras were swooning and giving me "oh my God!" faces.

Just as the film was about to start, two women walked in. I kept looking at one of them thinking, *Who is that? Why does that person look so much like . . .* It took me a minute to process it, and I realized it was because I'd seen her face a million times, but in real life, Paris Hilton is tiny and almost ethereal, as if she might blow away. She was standing by the door, looking kind of shy and uncomfortable. A woman from her side walked over and said, "We have about forty-five seconds before those doors burst open with media and security, and Paris wants to know if you want your picture taken with her, and if you can come and brief her." It all flashed through my head. Paris Hilton. She was just in jail. Do I really want my issue associated with her? What the hell does she know about Canadian forests? Any time something huge happens, there's a part of you that thinks, *This could fail miserably.*

Then I remembered Van Jones and thought, *This is one of the most famous people in the world . . . time to ride this shit.*

I walked over and chatted with her. She said, "I'd really like to support some environmental causes, and I heard you're a really great group. Tell me what you do."

I told her about the rainforest victory, and how ForestEthics was trying to kick-start a campaign in the boreal. We talked for about thirty seconds before what looked like a hundred people with cameras barged in. Then a wave of security guards pushed us away and cordoned us off onto the carpet. A thousand flashbulbs started popping. People were screaming, "What are you wearing?" and "Why are you here?"

Hilton kept talking to me as though nothing was happening as the paparazzi kept yelling for her attention. About two minutes later, her assistant tugged her sleeve and said, "I think we're ready." Hilton said, "Okay, Tzeporah, it was great to meet you. Should we have our picture taken?" She turned and half looked down, and she moved her shoulder, and she kind of bent her knees, and I was thinking, *Oh, she's gotta pee!* because in real life the pose she did looked slightly contorted. When you see the photos, I'm facing the cameras like a deer in the headlights, which is exactly what you're not supposed to do, because it makes you look the size of a house. She's turned sideways, and twisted slightly with one shoulder down, which I was later told is exactly what you're supposed to do. So she looks tiny and elegant, and I look like a stunned moose.

As the photographers and reporters called to her, she kept talking to me as if we were the only people in the room and said, "It was great to meet you. I'd love to get a copy of the film. If you can just walk me nonchalantly to the green room, I'm going to try to slip out the back door." So we went to the green room, the security guards followed, and she said goodbye and disappeared out the back door. As soon as the press realized she'd left, they all rushed out the door and, tires screeching, cars doing U-turns, they followed her home.

After the party, at about one in the morning, I regrouped with the ForestEthics volunteers. The five of us sat around our dingy hotel room eating veggie burgers, drinking beer and emptying our pockets and evening bags of all the business cards we'd collected.

Later that morning I got up and checked my voice mail. The mailbox was full. Then I called to check my other voice mail. That mailbox was full too. Then the phone started ringing, and it was someone from the ForestEthics office in San Francisco saying, "Our phones are going crazy. You need to look online."

I went online and saw newspaper after newspaper had picked up the picture of Paris Hilton and me. It was everywhere. People from Greenpeace in the UK, whom I hadn't talked to in years, were calling and e-mailing to say they'd seen the picture. I also got a wave of enthusiasm and interest in the issues on my Facebook page and from all over the place from fourteen-year-old girls.

My niece was going crazy. Now she wanted to know about the issues Auntie Tzeporah was working on because she and her friends saw a picture of me with Paris Hilton. News of that two-minute meeting made the front page of almost every newspaper in Canada, in full colour, above the fold. The picture appeared in twelve countries, in hundreds of articles. For the next three days my phone rang nonstop. I did interview after interview after interview, and they all started the same way: "What's Paris like?" and "Did you really get to meet Leo?" And I would gently steer the conversation to the real issues.

About two weeks later, Hilton was photographed in Toronto walking down Queen Street wearing a T-shirt that read, "What if this was the last tree?" And our meeting was back in the news again. Paris Hilton had turned green.

I have received considerable flack about the "Paris moment" from some of my critics. That it was an attention-getting stunt, that many Hollywood celebrities use the issues to add depth to their reputations, that I was using their fame to create a platform to talk about the issues. Well, sure. All that is partly true. Does that mean it's bad? Engaging celebrities means we reach audiences that would not normally be exposed to environmental issues at all. Huge audiences. Given the urgency of the issues, in my opinion the more attention-getting stunts the better.

I ARRIVED IN VANCOUVER completely exhausted. I spent some time debriefing with the Canadian staff, and they wanted to know whether we could do a premiere for the film on our own turf. We were at a critical moment in the campaign to protect mountain caribou that are dependent on the inland temperate rainforest. The BC government was being intransigent, even though the research and science were on our side. Caribou habitat was being logged and their numbers were dwindling rapidly. Like any species that requires a large range for its habitat, the mountain caribou was the canary in this particular coal mine. Mountain caribou were historically found across southeastern British Columbia and as far south as central Idaho. Herds were interconnected, permitting genetic exchange. Currently mountain caribou live in thirteen isolated herds. The southernmost herd, known as the South Selkirk, crosses the US–Canada border in the Selkirk Mountains south of Nelson, BC, and north of Spokane, Washington. Mountain caribou numbers have plummeted from about 2,450 animals in 1997 to 1,900 today. Many herds have been reduced by half, and some herds now have fewer than fifty individuals. During that same time period the logging industry made short work of cutting down more than half of the region's oldest trees.

For a couple of years we'd been trying to raise awareness about those forests, but we were victims of our own success. Because the Great Bear campaign had been such an enormous victory, everyone—the public, reporters, companies that bought the wood—had this notion that Canada was now green, and Canadian logging was sustainable. Trying to build the new campaigns to protect the boreal forest was like slogging uphill. But I realized maybe this was our chance. Maybe we could redo what we'd done in LA. Millions of Canadians had read about the DiCaprio film, and it hadn't had a Canadian premiere.

ONE OF THE BASIC tenets for good campaigning: repeat, repeat, repeat. People have to hear something several times before it becomes real. The job of a campaigner is to find every moment to bring those issues into the spotlight. I called Warner Brothers and asked if we could premiere the film in Vancouver. We picked a date, booked a theatre, sent a notice to all the TV shows and films shooting in the city and invited people to walk our green carpet.

We had been doing a postcard campaign, asking Canadians to sign a giant card to the premier, and we had several thousand signatures. But it had not made any impact on the government. This is the grunt work of social change. You talk to thousands of people, and you get maybe one line in a newspaper. I think it was Candace Batycki, who was running the inland rainforest campaign for ForestEthics, who said, "Can we get the stars to sign the postcards?"

The night of the premiere the publicist told me to drag over any stars to sign the postcard so we could get photos of them. I spend pretty much all my time either working or with my kids. Ask me who stars in something my kids watch and I'll know. But shows for adults, I have no idea. So she said, "Oh for heaven's sake! If they look stunningly beautiful, sandblasted and shellacked, bring them to me."

It worked. Three hundred people flooded into the theatre. Once in a while someone would look as if she'd just stepped out of a catalogue, and I'd say, "Get her!" I would stand with her on the green carpet and ask her to sign the postcard.

When we showed the film, I spoke, along with Gregor Robertson, then the co-chair of the New Democratic Party's Caucus Climate Change Task Force, who became the mayor of Vancouver and was elected on a promise to make it "the greenest city in the world." We were just starting the after-party when a reporter from the *Vancouver Sun* walked in and handed me a copy of the next day's paper that was hot off the press. On the front page, above the fold, in colour, there was a photo of me and Marlee Matlin signing a postcard to the premier, calling on him to protect mountain caribou. Front page, above the fold, in colour. As a campaigner, you can't ask for anything more. I climbed on top of a table, announced it to the room and we had a great party.

Two days later a government official called me and said, "Oh, God! First it's women in lingerie, then it's that guy from *Titanic,* and now you're on the front page of the paper with a star from *The L Word.* Enough already! We've gotta talk."

I'd always known decision makers care about power and money. That's what the markets campaigns were about. But in that moment I realized that by engaging celebrities, we had the capacity to get past the converted and reach a wider audience—a wide-enough audience to make politicians nervous.

There's never any one thing that you can credit to winning a campaign, because there's no question that the scientific reports—the years and months of painstaking research—the endless meetings with industry, bureaucrats and government, and all the public organizing build up and have a huge effect. With the mountain caribou, for example, ForestEthics worked with several organizations on the campaign. And a number of amazing individuals, from both government and NGOs, contributed to the agreement that was eventually struck.

But there is no question that the profile that the Marlee Matlin article generated was the straw that broke the camel's back. Less than two months after that front-page photo, the government announced it was protecting 2.2 million hectares (5.5 million acres) of caribou habitat in old-growth inland temperate rainforests, which was all the winter calving grounds of caribou, so it gave the caribou—and our forests—a fighting chance.[1]

After that experience, I realized that celebrity power is not only accessible and effective but a lot of the celebrities really want to engage. They don't necessarily have access to the issues, or ways to get involved; they're just people who care. Since then I've been doing "celebrity-organizing" workshops for other activists. I tell people that it's not just about the celebrities showing up and having a photo taken; you need to ask them to say a few words, brief them on the issue, get them to sign a postcard or an open letter. That not only involves the celebrities but it's also more newsworthy than having them smile at the cameras.

I also suggest making a wish list based on the audience you're trying to reach. Far too often in the environmental movement I hear people say, "We have to do a public campaign. We have to engage the public." The public is a big thing, and we don't have the financial capacity to do major communications campaigns that reach everyone. We're not Coke. We're not Walmart. And even those companies target specific markets.

So my questions are, Who do you want to reach? And who do *they* care about?

If your swing vote is women over fifty, you might not want Lady Gaga as your celeb sponsor, but you might want Celine Dion. Just because you like Lady Gaga doesn't mean that she will be effective in reaching your audience.

For me, the fact that *Vanity Fair* and *Rolling Stone* did green issues and Paris Hilton wore a tree T-shirt is reason to be hopeful. Our job as environmentalists used to be to kick open the door to issues to get people to notice. We don't have to do that as often anymore since there is more widespread awareness of environmental issues. Now we can focus on pushing or developing solutions and working with decision makers to identify the appropriate legislation.

Ironically, I knew the value of star power from my experience with Midnight Oil in Clayoquot Sound, but Greenpeace lined up that concert and it didn't occur to me that any other organization I worked with after that time would have that kind of reach. Why weren't celebrities involved with ForestEthics? We hadn't tried to approach them. Celebrities seem a bit exotic, and real people don't get to touch them. Maybe Greenpeace or the World Wildlife Federation could get celebrity endorsements for their work, but not me. I just never saw that as an option for us.

So make your wish list and don't be afraid to try to find these people, because you're probably fewer than six degrees away from everyone—even Paris Hilton. And if you're not, don't be afraid to cold-call; you never know who's willing to show up to help a good cause.

At the time of the Clayoquot blockades in 1993, over 98 percent of all the logging in Canada's ancient rainforest was large-scale, industrial clear-cutting. This image of a clear-cut in Clayoquot Sound shows the destruction left behind, and only hints at the devastation to local wildlife, their habitats, and water systems.

Valerie Langer blockading clear-cut logging by cantilevering herself off the Kennedy Lake Bridge in Clayoquot Sound in one of the very early protests in the late eighties.

By mid-July 1993, hundreds of people were flooding into our Peace Camp in Clayoquot Sound every day. Teachers, students, business people and hippies rolled up their sleeves and created a strange and wonderful community in the middle of a clear-cut. Every afternoon we ran peacekeeping and civil disobedience workshops. Every night we facilitated a meeting explaining what would happen the next day and the legal risks involved. Every morning at 4:00 we headed to the blockades.

In the summer of 1993 the Friends of Clayoquot Sound invited Australian rock band Midnight Oil to visit the blockades and perform to raise awareness of the fight to save the old-growth forests. The lead singer, Peter Garrett, who went on to become Australia's minister for the environment, heritage and the arts, was on Greenpeace International's board at the time. Their performance attracted three to five thousand spectators and helped the protests gain international media attention.

An image of me with my fist in the air after the opening day of the blockades appeared on the front page of the national newspaper. When it landed on their doorstep, my family flew across the country to make sure I was safe and hadn't in fact lost my mind. Moved by the extensive clear-cut logging, my sister and her husband (both business executives, pictured above) decided to join the blockades. The idea of them being arrested stressed me out so much I begged them to get off the bridge so I could do my job!

My soon-to-be husband, Chris Hatch, was arrested in Clayoquot Sound for blocking the road with leaders from Greenpeace UK, Germany, the Netherlands and the US. The arrests resulted in dramatically increased international media coverage and awareness. It was also a good move for us within Greenpeace Canada because once executive directors were arrested they were more determined to get involved and win the campaign. After he was released from jail, I remember Thilo Bode, the executive director of Greenpeace Germany and later Greenpeace International, declaring, "Zee Canadian government and za logging companies vill pay for this!"

The protests in Clayoquot Sound were one of the largest acts of civil disobedience in Canada's history. Ten thousand people from all walks of life joined the protests in 1993 and close to one thousand were arrested.

Our lawyers had counselled us that we could expect community service hours for blockading the road. No one predicted that the courts would send hundreds of people to jail for months on end, some of whom had blockaded the logging for less than ten minutes.

Protesting the continued logging of Clayoquot Sound outside the Ministry of Forests in 1993 with Garth Lenz, Val Langer and Karen Mahon.

When the logging continued in Clayoquot in 1994 after the massive blockades were ended, it was hard to maintain momentum in the campaign. Hundreds were in trials and going to jail. That year was one of the hardest of my life. On this day in particular, it hit me that I was no longer taking a break from "real life" to help save the rainforests—this work had become my "real life."

AN OPEN LETTER

The Honourable Colin Gabelmann
Attorney General of British Columbia

Dear Minister,

On Monday, June 20th environmentalist Tzeporah Berman stands trial in Victoria, facing charges related to clear-cut logging protests in Clayoquot Sound. It is our understanding that Ms. Berman acted solely as a peacekeeper and that she broke no law or court order. Nevertheless she faces criminal charges and a potentially serious jail sentence for allegedly "aiding and abetting" protesters who blockaded logging roads to voice their opposition to the clearcutting of Clayoquot Sound. We are writing to express our concern over these charges.

The current charges clearly violate Ms. Berman's right to protest and her freedom to organize other people who freely participate in an act of non-violent civil disobedience. Singling out and arresting a protest organizer in this way is an act of intimidation and harassment. Finally, we are concerned that these charges represent a violation of Ms. Berman's right to free speech.

The issue of clearcutting the old growth of Clayoquot Sound is a serious one and people must have the right to express their opinion and peacefully organize for what they believe without fear of arrest and potentially long jail sentences. We therefore appeal to you to instruct the Crown Attorneys in your department to review again the evidence before them and halt the charges immediately.

Sincerely,

Saul Arbess, anthropologist
Margaret Atwood, author
Maude Barlow, Chair
  Council of Canadians
Diana Barrington, actress
Peter Blyer, Council of
  Canadians
Meg Buckley-Potter
June Callwood, writer
Joan Candioo
Bruce Cockburn, musician
Paul Copeland, lawyer
Nita Daniels-Levine
William Deverell, author
Jan Eastman
Dr. Bristol Foster, biologist
Ursula Franklin, professor

Peter Garret,
  singer – Midnight Oil
Anton Gross
Donna Gross
Josh Gross
Richard Gross
Mavis Gilly
Angela Hryniuk, artist
Mel Hurtig
Jane Jacobs, author
Norman Jewison
Robert Kennedy Jr.
Dr. Crystal Kleiman
Valerie Langer
Jack Layton, politician
Hart Levine
Greg McDade, lawyer

Jim McFarlane
Kathy McGregor
Maureen McPherson
Alice McQuade
Mel Morlliet
Farley Mowat, author
Elsie Murphy
Susan Musgrave
Michael Ondaatje, author
Robert Osleeb, wood worker
Stuart Parker
Eric Peterson, actor
Ken Pogue
Stephen Reid
Svend Robinson, M.P.
Peter Ronald
Rick Salutin, journalist

Robin Skelton
Roger Smeeth, architect
Dr. David Suzuki
Karen Title
Ray Travers, forester
Rick Turner
Judy Tyabji
Myra Waller
Tom Westwater
Carrol Whitwell
Michael C. Williams,
  businessman
Florence Wilson
Jane Woodland
Ross Woodland
Ray Worley

Responses: c/o 1726 Commercial Drive, Vancouver, BC V5N 4A3 • Phone 253-7701

I was charged with 857 counts of criminal aiding and abetting for my work coordinating the blockades in Clayoquot Sound. Luckily I not only had one of the best lawyers in BC, I also had my sisters and Chris at my side. The trial lasted five days, at the end of which the judge expressed dismay that he couldn't lock me up, but he said there was no legal basis for the charges. Here Chris and I are leaving the courthouse ecstatic that I no longer face six years in jail!

I have had a few opportunities to see the rare white spirit bear in the Great Bear Rainforest in British Columbia. With their majesty and almost incorporeal presence, they have become an inspiration for my work. The term "spirit bear" comes from First Nations tradition, which holds that the white Kermode bear (normally brown but with a recessive gene) are to be revered and protected.

ForestEthics' full-page ad in the *New York Times* was so controversial it was reported in the media across the US and Canada, resulting in a multi-million-dollar impact for our $30,000 expenditure. At the time, Victoria's Secret was printing *a million catalogues a day*, primarily made from Canada's boreal forests.

Greenpeace's first blockade in the newly named Great Bear Rainforest on the northwest coast of Canada, May 1997. We lived in this clear-cut for fourteen days and also organized simultaneous protests at Canadian embassies across Europe and the United States.

In 1995 we began working with the Nuxalk in Canada's Great Bear Rainforest. In this picture, the late Chief Ed Moody (K'watsinas) participates in an action against the ship the *Grebe Arrow* in Belgium, exporting paper made from Canadian rainforests. He would go on to travel around the world speaking about the issues and protesting in front of Interfor's corporate customers. On several occasions he worked with the Rainforest Action Network and Greenpeace on "stolen goods actions," where he and others from the Nuxalk walked into a Home Depot and, with cameras rolling, walked back out with lumber, declaring it stolen from their traditional territories.

My first cell phone was the size of a brick and required its own briefcase. Here, in 1996, we have occupied one of the largest log barges in the world, the *Haida Brave* near Squamish, BC, to protest the export of Canada's raw timber.

A Greenpeace protester being hosed in an attempt to remove him from an anchor chain.

In the nineties, we organized protests around the world to block wood and paper exports from British Columbia rainforests. Protests like these compelled industry reps and governments to come to the table with environmental organizations and discuss the issues. British Columbia's environmentalists were successful in creating a debate over the lack of protection for Canada's ancient rainforests.

By far one of the funniest campaigns I have ever seen. This was how Greenpeace UK campaigned in 1999 to stop the import of genetically engineered soybeans into Europe a few weeks after US president Bill Clinton's Monica Lewinsky scandal.

The five minutes I spent with Paris Hilton at the launch of *The 11th Hour* in Los Angeles were arguably the most surreal but productive campaigning minutes of my life so far. This image led to over a hundred newspaper stories in thirteen countries and gave ForestEthics a global platform for its campaigns to protect Canada's old-growth forests. *Thank you, Paris!*

When Oscar-winning actor Marlee Matlin, at the Canadian premiere of *The 11th Hour,* signed this postcard calling on the British Columbia government to protect the inland temperate rainforest caribou habitat, it made the front page above the fold of the *Vancouver Sun.* The BC government agreed to protect 2.2 million hectares (5.4 million acres) of caribou habitat less than a year later.

In 2009 I accepted an invitation to be one of many Canadian torchbearers in the Vancouver Winter Olympics. I carried the (gas-powered!) Olympic torch on an electric scooter to raise awareness about the potential of zero-emission transportation alternatives.

The *Deepwater Horizon* oil spill in the Gulf of Mexico was, of course, one of the worst environmental disasters in our history. We sent a scientific team and one of our ships to research the damage in the Gulf. Previously unknown impacts are still being discovered today, and I expect the legacy will impact the planet for decades. Despite the disaster, in 2011 Obama re-approved deepwater drilling in the Gulf and other regions.

One of my favourite cartoons . . .

In November 2009, *Reader's Digest* brought the story of the Clayoquot Sound blockades and other key moments in the last twenty years of the environmental movement to its 5.9 million monthly readers.

When the oil spill in Dalian, China, happened in 2010, one of the courageous firefighters, Zhang Liang, was killed. The Greenpeace rapid response team was at the site within hours. Photographer Lu Guang captured this horrific image, which won a World Press Photo award.

After the *Deepwater Horizon* spill in the Gulf of Mexico in April 2010, our team at Greenpeace International decided to harness the moment by shining a light on dangerous drilling in one of the most fragile and ecologically important places on earth: the Arctic. We sent our ship the *Esperanza* to the Arctic and occupied the drill rig right under the nose of the Danish Navy. We were successful in slowing down—but not yet stopping—the drilling and increasing international awareness.

When most people think tar sands, they think desert, but the reality is that Canada's tar sands are under the boreal forest—one of the most intact, original forests left. Canada's tar sands are now widely considered to be the largest, most destructive industrial project on earth. In 2008 Greenpeace occupied this Syncrude operation and blockaded the pipe that sends toxic sludge into unlined open-pit lakes. Every day, the tar sands development pumps 1.8 billion litres (475,509,694 gallons) of toxic water into open unlined pits.

Greenpeace's campaign to get Facebook to use renewable energy instead of coal and nuclear has over 700,000 members around the world and has included protests in several countries. As the IT sector rapidly expands, so too will its carbon footprint unless there is a significant increase in the use of renewable electricity. Cloud computing, which relies on centralized data storage infrastructure to deliver real-time information from the internet, is one of the fastest-growing sources of electricity consumption worldwide. In fact, if the internet were a country it would be the fifth-largest consumer of electricity in the world. Here I am in Dublin, Ireland, in 2011 protesting in front of one of Facebook's headquarters.

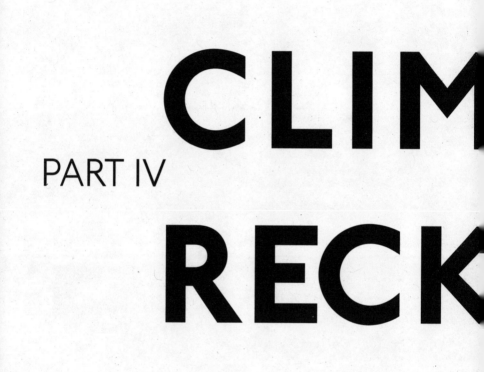

PART IV

CLIM

RECK

ATE
ONING

Chapter 13

THE ATMOSPHERE DOESN'T NEGOTIATE

CHANGING MY FOCUS TO THE KEY CHALLENGE OF OUR AGE

Abrupt and potentially catastrophic climate changes are not only possible but likely in the future. The world is teetering on the brink of abrupt climate change: a change that will be so rapid and unexpected that human and natural systems will have difficulty adapting to it.

THE US NATIONAL RESEARCH COUNCIL

THE NIGHT BEFORE I left for the United Nations Framework Convention on Climate Change (UNFCCC) negotiations in Bali in 2007, I heard my two boys talking in their bunk beds. "I hate it when Mommy goes away," said Quinn, then five.

"I know, but Mommy's going to save the climate," said Forrest, who was nine. Forrest's confidence in me was crushing and motivating at the same time.

I was due for a sabbatical. When we created ForestEthics we'd built in the principle that after you were there for seven years, you could take a three-month paid break. I was planning to enjoy my time off and recharge, and I knew I needed it because I was dissatisfied with my work. We were having huge successes like the Victoria's Secret campaign, but I was finding myself short-tempered, frustrated and annoyed. It felt as if no one was doing enough. None of our ideas were good enough. The progress was not fast enough.

I'd started seeing reports about the impacts of climate change, the increased fires in the boreal, the pine beetle infestations in British Columbia and the desertification of the Amazon. There was this little voice in the back of my head saying, *You got into this because you wanted to protect forests, and now it's pretty clear that industrial logging may not be the greatest impact on forests today.*

But there was a much bigger voice saying, *Thank God someone else is working on that.* I was happy to listen to this voice because I didn't know how to deal with climate change. I worked on logging issues. But the voice persisted, and that year I started researching climate matters from a forest-issues perspective. How does industrial logging impact global warming? How is global warming impacting the health of our forests?

This research led to an invitation from a number of environmental groups to speak in Bali on the impacts of logging on global warming, the impacts of global warming on the boreal and the importance of the boreal forest as a carbon storehouse. In a mad scramble right before Bali I thought, "How can I have an impact in Bali? And what is the conversation that needs to happen there?"

My focus was the forests, but I was worried about Canada's tar sands because I'd just read *Stupid to the Last Drop: How Alberta Is Bringing Environmental Armageddon to Canada (and Doesn't Seem to Care)* by William Marsden, and loved it. So I called his publisher, Louise Dennys, the executive vice-president of Random House of Canada, and told her how much I loved the book, how important it was and that I was going to the United Nations Climate Change Conference, and wondered if she could spare a few copies. She was happy to oblige. I went to Bali dragging two hockey bags full of copies of *Stupid to the Last Drop.*

Intense conversations started for me the second I landed, as conference delegates found one another in the baggage claim and the visa lines. Before I had even collected my baggage I had given out several copies of *Stupid to the Last Drop* that I had in my briefcase. I eventually handed a copy to the minister of energy for Alberta, and I distributed them at all the briefings and Canadian government press conferences. It made them crazy, in large part because Canada, like so many other countries in Bali, was trying to portray itself as a climate leader while hiding its growing oil developments.

In the shuttle to the hotel I was at a loss to explain to academics from France and Germany why so few people realized that Canada was creating the largest and most destructive fossil fuel projects in the world and had become the biggest exporter of oil to the United States.

As a Canadian I came to Bali with the knowledge that under Stephen Harper's Conservative government we had scuttled the potential of a significant agreement at the Commonwealth talks that year in New York, which would have committed many countries to strong mandatory reductions in fossil fuel emissions. I was also painfully aware that we were one of the few countries that had reneged on our commitments under the Kyoto Protocol and were balking at making any new commitments.

According to independent international rankings, Canada is second to last among industrialized and emerging countries for the effectiveness of its national government climate policies and fifty-seventh out of sixty major countries on climate change performance. In fact, Canada ranks just behind China and ahead of only Australia, Kazakhstan and Saudi Arabia.[1]

What I have discovered from my research is that Canadians themselves do care. Across the country people are taking steps to make their own lifestyles more carbon conscious—eating locally, taking the bus, changing to more efficient light bulbs—and yet our emissions are going up, not down, primarily because of heavy industry. We have yet to see a politician with the courage to address that issue, and to advocate for, never mind implement, the tough laws needed to regulate industry, because political terms are short and it's very difficult for a politician to see past the next election. Oil money is becoming a major part of our economy,[2] and so far, only the bravest politicians are willing to say, "Hold on. We have to change direction." The year before Bali, the Liberal leader, Stéphane Dion, had proposed a price on pollution that would have been a great start. Unfortunately, he campaigned earnestly on the importance of a carbon tax instead of framing the end goal or vision of what the change could create.

His opponents jumped all over it, and their fear-mongering about price increases played a big role in ruining his run for prime minister in 2008.

In the lineups at the airport, many were agreeing that despite similar depressing stories in many of our countries (the one big outlier that year was Australia, where the prime minister was elected on a climate platform after a particularly smart campaign that focused on building a safe future for our children), Bali offered a new opportunity to reinvigorate a global agreement on climate change.

It was stimulating to be surrounded by thousands of people talking about solutions, and it felt great to be doing something tangible and immersing myself in the climate conversation. My bubble burst when the Canadian government came out opposing hard emissions reductions targets internationally and taking positions that seemed designed to stall or slow negotiations. It was the oddest thing to watch as one after another, the scientists and UN officials and all my environmental colleagues from around the world made statements condemning Canada.

After hearing that, every morning I'd get up at five and go to the main coordinating office to check the agenda, which was larger than an encyclopedia. I'd flip through it, underlining and highlighting sessions I thought I should attend. I went from international panel to international panel and learned more than I ever wanted to know about the coming impacts of climate change. What blew me away most was not just the statistics but that so many scientists were unable to stop themselves from crying.

The second day in Bali, Canada had the dubious honour of receiving the Fossil Award of the Day for a leaked memo that showed Canadian delegates had been instructed to agree to nothing short of binding targets for all countries. The memo went on to propose that Canada push for a "special circumstances" addendum. The positions were designed to derail the negotiations in Bali. The Harper government knew full well that China would never agree to be treated the same as the "developed countries" that had created the mess to begin with, let alone agree to special circumstances for Canada and other oil-producing nations. The result was that Canada could hide behind

China, and the Harper government was left with a very convenient excuse to do nothing.[3]

I delivered my speech, and it was a tough one to make because I'd never felt less proud of being Canadian. So that's what I talked about.

"Today I stand here as a Canadian, ashamed. Ashamed that while the international community struggles to fight global warming, Canada is developing the largest fossil fuel project in the world, the Alberta tar sands. Ashamed that my government has reneged on our Kyoto commitments and is refusing to commit to strong absolute emissions reduction targets and, more than that, holding up important international agreements that would chart a path forward."

Then I laid out for them just how much climate change had already changed Canadian forests. Ten million hectares (25 million acres) of forest are completely dead due to pine beetle infestations. The pine beetle is an innocuous little bug that used to die every winter when the temperature dropped below minus forty degrees. The problem is that the beetles don't die seasonally anymore because it doesn't get cold enough. The result is that pine beetles are eating their way through British Columbia's old-growth forest.

There were over a thousand environmentalists in Bali for the climate talks. At the end of every day hundreds would meet and vote on which countries did the most to hurt the potential for progress in fighting climate change. Canada won first, second and third place. On the third day, Canada's minister of environment, John Baird, finally arrived, just in time to win all three days' Fossil Awards.

There was one thing to admire about Baird: his chutzpah. With full recognition of how he disgusted some of the most committed and informed people from around the world, he waltzed into the non-governmental organizations' reception and grabbed a beer.

I couldn't pass up the moment. After debating the issues with him for half an hour, I can safely say that chutzpah was all I found to admire. Talking to Minister Baird was a little like debating Bill O'Reilly. He was clever, but he didn't listen for a second. The minister spent a lot of time trying to tell me that the Liberals had done a worse job than he was doing. When I finally got him off his partisan rant and tried to steer him to a conversation about the art of the possible, he moved on to blaming ineffective environmentalists for Canada's rise in emissions.

I reminded him that he was the environment minister and that his government might perhaps have a teeny bit of responsibility for whether Canada actually stepped up to the plate and set strong absolute emissions reductions targets, thereby protecting Canada's international reputation.

He argued that 20 percent reductions by 2050 was a strong target. Maybe, just maybe, he would have been right if he meant a 20 percent reduction from 1990 levels, but he confirmed that he was talking about 20 percent from 2006 levels. That would be like treating a sucking chest wound with a bandage. He stated that those reductions were the most Canada could manage. I told him he was underestimating the knowledge, the commitment and the courage of Canadians.

Perhaps just as shocking as Baird's posturing and weak environmental agenda was the response he received from the hordes of environmentalists who were cursing him and the Canadian government from a distance but were unwilling to talk to him or the rest of his contingent.

While I was running around grabbing knowledgeable people like Steve Kretzmann from Oil Change and Dale Marshall from the David Suzuki Foundation to engage with him, I was chastised by some who thought we should save the debating and lobbying for the daytime and not bother him with the issues in the evening. Amazing. In my mind there is no question that we have to take every opportunity to engage decision makers, to encourage debate, to hold accountable those who have the power to make change. The environment minister was at a climate change conference, and hell, I was respectful—I completely refrained from throwing him in the pool.

I had been reading scary statistics and apocalyptic predictions for years. But now, surrounded by twenty thousand people from over two hundred countries and witnessing the complete failure of governments to reach a strong plan to address the problems, I hit rock bottom.

I flew home to British Columbia fighting such acute despair and fear that I found it hard to breathe. I couldn't stop picturing my little boys in their bunk bed and Forrest confidently assuring his brother that "Mommy was saving the climate."

To be clear, I am an optimist. I have been faced with some pretty big challenges in my work and have always been able to see a path forward, to rally the troops, to see no challenge as too big.

But this felt too big. Too frightening. Too fast. We were supposed to fix this by 2020? We had less than two decades to transform to a low-carbon economy. To transform our energy grid, our transportation systems and our food systems, protect what was left of our primary forests, stop the development of the tar sands in Canada, stop all new coal plants, decommission the old ones . . .

That night when I got home, Quinn, who had just been introduced to computer games, asked me if I had won in Bali.

I tearfully told him that I didn't think so.

His response made me stop in my tracks: "Did you at least level up, Mommy?"

When the United Nations Millennium Ecosystem Assessment Report tells us that "Human activity is putting such strain on the natural functions of earth that the ability of the planet's ecosystems to sustain future generations can no longer be taken for granted,"[4] what is "levelling up"?

In the weeks following Bali I was in despair. I spent my days on the floor in my pyjamas playing Lego with my boys. I spent my nights on the couch with potato chips and *Battlestar Galactica*, simply trying to escape. That was my strategy for dealing with this new crisis, because I realized it was forcing me to question everything I do. What was the point of my work in the world? What was the point of anything?

It was hearing the author Barbara Kingsolver on CBC Radio one afternoon that finally snapped me out of my funk. She said that in the face of pressing environmental challenges, "Optimism is the only moral choice."

After that I asked myself the tough questions. If we really don't have much time, what should we be doing? Should we learn how to grow our own food? Should we just focus on making sure that our family is well set up to deal with the 50 percent increase in the severity and frequency of violent storms? Was I ready to give up hope on mitigating, slowing down or stopping global warming, and focus on adapting our lifestyles to a very different planet?

To be frank, the idea of focusing on our own personal lifestyle and preparedness made me even more depressed. It just seemed defeatist. So selfish. So small. And what about my own work? How could I as an environmentalist be talking about a crisis yet be unwilling to dramatically change my own work and focus?

From my place of despair I began to wonder how others were dealing with this dilemma. What strategies were they employing to fight climate change? My curiosity and search for answers got me off the couch and functioning, but it wasn't until months later that I began to feel a deep sense of purpose, that my despair began to lift.

I spent a good two months of my life down the policy rabbit hole, and when I finally emerged I was angry. I have two university degrees, I had worked in the environmental movement for fifteen years, campaigned against and later advised some of the largest corporations in the world, and I could not figure out how to usefully engage in the climate debate or even what immediate objectives I was supposed to be fighting for. If I couldn't figure out the environmental agenda, how could we expect a soccer mom who cares about global warming and has maybe fifteen minutes in her day between work and dinner and packing lunches to think about it and take action?

All the environmental groups' websites I surveyed had complex policy platforms calling for various percentage reductions in emissions by certain dates, with other dates identified as benchmark years. The policy prescriptions to get us to those emissions reductions were even more complex. I spent weeks tied in knots over carbon tax versus cap-and-trade, or cap-and-auction, until I felt that I had a handle on it and began to look at what these groups thought I should do to engage. For the most part, after telling me that life as we know it was doomed, I was told to eat locally and change my light bulbs. The actions proposed were so oversimplified that they were laughable, given the scale of the problem.

—

AS GLOBAL WARMING increasingly threatens the lifestyles—and lives—of people around the world, carbon—namely, whether emissions diminish or increase—will increasingly define "right" and "wrong."

In 2005 the United Nations released the Millennium Ecosystem Report, the first comprehensive analysis of the condition of the world in relation to climate change. The report was the collaborative project of thirteen hundred experts from ninety-five countries, and proved the existence of rapid climate change. It warned that "human activity is causing such a strain on the natural functions of the earth that the ability of the planet to support human well-being is now in question." The report cautioned that two-thirds of the services that nature provides to humans are in decline worldwide, and that climate change is humanity's biggest threat. More people are now forced to leave their homes because of environmental disaster than because of war.

What makes the document so chilling is that it's a conservative assessment and most scientists I've met believe it soft-pedals the dangers we're facing.[5]

In *The Future of Life*, Edward O. Wilson wrote, "The last frontiers of the world are effectively gone. Species of plants and animals are disappearing a hundred or more times faster than before the coming of humanity, and as many as half may be gone by the end of this century."[6] Scientists estimate that there are between ten and one hundred million species on the planet. While we have names for approximately two million of these species, we have little idea how the vast majority function and interact, or the roles they individually and collectively play in maintaining the biosphere.

We are, in effect, burning the library before we have read the books. We now know that taxol from the bark of the yew tree can fight uterine cancer. Before that discovery, yews in British Columbia were burned as collateral waste in clear-cuts because they weren't considered a commercially viable species. Every day new species become extinct due to habitat loss, not just as the result of clear-cut logging and other industrial development but due to habitat changes that are the result of climate change.

The year 2010 tied with 2005 as the hottest in recorded history. The ten hottest years on record have all occurred since 1998.[7] Glaciers are retreating and ice caps are melting. Projections from the Intergovernmental Panel on Climate Change (IPCC) indicate that by 2020, between 75 million and 250 million people in Africa will be exposed to increased water stress due to climate change. In some countries, yields from rain-fed agriculture could be reduced by up to 50 percent.[8] The human toll is beyond comprehension: Christian Aid estimates one billion people will be displaced globally by 2050.[9] These are some of the reasons why the US Defense Department reports that climate change is now among the greatest threats to international security,[10] and the US Environmental Protection Agency has begun to regulate carbon dioxide emissions as a threat to human health.[11]

The sad truth is that even if we make climate change our number-one priority, we cannot stop global warming at today's levels—we have emitted enough heat-trapping gases (carbon, methane) that they will continue to heat the planet for years to come. The writer and environmentalist Bill McKibben argues that we have already created a "new" planet, new in that its composition is so clearly different from the planet we have known in the past that he calls it "Eaarth." McKibben recognizes that drastic impacts on life are all but inevitable.[12]

Still, we have a chance—and a responsibility—to modulate the negative outcome. But what does it mean to "get climate change under control"—and how do we do that?

Sometimes people say to me, "One or two degrees doesn't seem like much." The difference between average global temperatures today and during the last major ice age is only five degrees.

Scientists have defined a tipping point in the buildup of greenhouse gases in the atmosphere, after which the impacts on the earth will create a domino effect that we can no longer control. The atmosphere doesn't negotiate. Increase the amount of carbon dioxide and other heat-trapping gases in the atmosphere, and the earth's temperature rises. The sea ice melts and reduces the reflective quality needed to bounce the sunlight away. The oceans absorb more carbon, increasing their acidity. These effects roll into themselves and magnify one another.

When I went to Bali, I was still working for ForestEthics and increasing my involvement in addressing climate change through forest issues. Bali opened my eyes to the problem and gave me the resources I needed to help make climate change comprehensible to others. There had to be a way to explain the problem. More important, there needed to be a way to communicate solutions and engage enough people that politicians would care. I was sure of it.

ON A RAINY DAY in January 2008, I made the tough decision to leave my safe job and the work that I knew so well to focus my efforts directly on climate change. I was on fire about creating a group that focused on Canada's energy policy and could communicate the issues simply and with mass appeal. I knew that the Harper government was just not going to pass the laws that we needed to rein in oil development and hold big industry accountable unless we could engage more Canadians. I love ForestEthics and they continue to do great work, but educating people on clean energy and climate change is not their primary focus. I couldn't find an organization that concentrated on making the issues accessible—translating complex policy issues into everyday language—and offered people from all walks of life the information they need to engage in a meaningful way. I also wanted to be part of an organization that recognizes the political ramifications of inaction and will call for massive change beyond lifestyle choices—new laws, not just new light bulbs.

In February in Vancouver, Chris and I sat with a group of friends and colleagues. We discussed the fact that we were all having these conversations with our family and friends, that it seemed there was an increased awareness of the issues, yet people felt alone and ineffective in dealing with the problems. We agreed to develop a campaign and strategy to harness the concerns of Canadians and mobilize a political force that called for stronger laws to address global warming.

The awakening to the disastrous effects of climate change that I experienced in Bali had knocked me down for months. Now, with this coalition that searched for practical solutions and addressed Canadians' concerns, I had journeyed from despair to empowerment.

We founded PowerUp Canada the following September and raised money from a couple of philanthropic foundations who share our goals. Our first action was to spend almost our entire budget on polling Canadians to find out what they knew about global warming, and their primary concerns. The results were astonishing. The majority of people believed that Canadians were global leaders on environmental issues, and that Canada was one of the most environmentally responsible countries. When we told Canadians that we had weaker laws than almost any other industrialized country, and that Canada is one of the top ten polluters in the world, they were horrified.[13]

The polls showed that Canadians, almost more than any other group, consider global warming to be one of the most important issues, yet we have some of the most regressive polices, which actually allow our emissions to rise.

Working with a small coalition, Chris and I started building a strategic plan based on power mapping and a realization that with this issue, like all the ones that we had worked on so far, what the government cares about is money and votes. The Harper government especially cared about votes in BC, Ontario and Quebec because they needed those votes to win a majority. We needed to harness power, to create a politically savvy and informed constituency, and that required reaching out to unlikely allies. Our capacity to make change lies in connecting with the Canadian public because they do care. The politicians are going to do the right thing only if the voters tell them to.

The other thing the polling revealed, which confirmed my own experience, was that while the majority of Canadians were worried about global warming, they really didn't understand it—in part because the conversation has been too technical. As a result, they were not really engaged in the issues. When we asked Canadians to identify the cause of global warming, they were less likely to blame the tar sands than they were to say, "I use too many plastic bags." That was an eye-opener. When we asked what Canadians needed to do to stop climate change, people would respond, "I should use fewer plastic bags" or "I should walk to work more." Environmentalism seemed to be all about guilt.

It was clear that when it comes to climate and carbon, all too often environmentalists have been communicating complex details of our policy priorities, when we need to focus on the big picture and build broad public understanding. We need to develop a public narrative that the majority can follow. We absolutely need to ensure that the public has access to our data and research, but for the most part we need to talk about detailed policy recommendations with decision makers while sharing our vision of what we are trying to achieve. If we focus on clearly making the connection between lack of regulation and rising emissions, we can build an understanding of the need for stronger legislation and help the majority of the public move past guilt and into action.

Under Stephen Harper, our federal government is doing almost nothing to develop a new clean-energy economy. In another global study we ranked thirty-first in developing clean energy and clean technology.[14] To put that in perspective, we ranked just below those global superpowers Kazakhstan and Slovakia. Canada is not only losing the race, we're not even in the game.

I met with an acquaintance in the Prime Minister's Office and asked her to help me understand. I explained that I had seen the polls. Canadians care about global warming. We have some of the worst environmental laws and policies in the world, even behind China. The UK is committed to carbon-neutral homes. President Obama is spending six times as much per capita as we are to create green jobs, move toward renewable energy and turn the United States toward a low-carbon economy. Why weren't we doing these things in Canada?

She said, "These are difficult changes, and Canadians do really care. They simply don't understand it, and they aren't organized."

In general, the Canadian public is confused. Concerned but confused.

There is no doubt energy issues are complicated, but it isn't rocket science. Complex books that analyze and present our required clean energy systems, the kind of policy frameworks we need, and whether a global agreement on climate change is feasible or even desirable are a dime a dozen these days. As I mentioned in the introduction, the purpose of this book is not to rehash the data—that's not my cup of tea, and might bore you to death.

I frequently talk to family members and friends who care, who have former US vice president Al Gore's *An Inconvenient Truth* on

DVD, but aside from changing their light bulbs, walking to work and perhaps writing a cheque to an environmental group, they simply don't know what to do or how to reconcile their busy lives with the crazy doomsday scenarios we read in the newspaper. "Honey, the UN reports that two-thirds of the ecosystem services necessary for human well-being are now in decline. Did you pick up milk?"

In Europe these days the public seems to be at least a decade ahead of North Americans in environmental awareness—whether the issue is recycling, conservation or forestry. Selective logging started in Scandinavia decades ago, long before there were huge debates on the practice of clear-cutting. It didn't happen in Canada until the '90s. I suspect that's because Europe simply has less wild space. Canadians are lulled into thinking that we are environmentally responsible because our country is physically so green. We have more intact forests than almost any country in the world. We have more green space as a result, because we have a very small population in a big country. We've grown up believing that the bush and nature are a part of our national psyche, part of our culture. We've got a caribou on our quarter, a beaver on our nickel and a polar bear on our toonie. Not to mention the loonie.

But having a lot of green space doesn't mean you're green. And in fact we're not. We are one of the top ten polluters in the world. We're less energy efficient and produce more garbage per capita than almost any other country in the world.[15]

A lot of people believe we're not going to get serious about addressing climate change in North America until we can see and feel and experience the impacts. People have felt those impacts in Europe. Major cities have flooded, and heat waves have caused people to drop in the street in England and France. There is no question that Europe needs to do much more, but many countries are far ahead of the United States and Canada in creating a low-carbon economy and addressing global warming.

It seems to me, in watching these issues play out over the past few years, that we are beginning to understand that we can harness the power of the wind, sun, water, and other renewable resources to turn on our lights and travel from point A to point B. But what will it really take to ensure that a widespread shift to using clean energy happens while we still have forests and can maintain a reasonably stable climate? To ensure that we can help develop an economy so future generations have meaningful and gainful employment?

From my perspective, here's the bottom line: We need to limit pollution. We need to make polluters pay for their emissions and waste, and then use that money to fund retrofits and clean energy. We need to stop treating the atmosphere like an ashtray, and that means stiff limits (or "hard caps," as the policy wonks keep telling me) on pollution across the board, including the tar sands. As much as we can, we have to reduce our dependency on oil and fossil fuels. We need to increase conservation and efficiency to the utmost of our abilities and support government leaders who share these goals. We must dramatically increase our sources of renewable power and move to a low-carbon economy. Such a step requires the involvement of all levels of government and industry, and, I hope, will eventually lead to a global agreement to take fair, decisive and legally binding action to fight climate change.

But how do we, as individuals and citizens' groups, make sure all this gets done? We need to commit to talking about these issues, teaching our children and questioning our daily actions. Changing our lifestyles is not just about buying the right product; it's about engaging in civil society, writing to your elected officials or joining one or more of the incredible organizations that are working to funnel and organize public concern into action, such as the Sierra Club, Environmental Defence, the David Suzuki Foundation, the Pembina Institute and Greenpeace.

We live in a strange society with an overdeveloped consumption muscle and an underdeveloped engagement muscle. This is our moment to get involved, to volunteer, to take risks. Our situation demands that we take action immediately, but changing quickly will be messy. We're not always going to agree on the best way forward, yet these are important debates to have, provided that they come from a place of purpose and intention that recognizes the need to find solutions together.

—

POST-BALI, the biggest disconnect for me was between what the environmental groups were saying about the issues and what people heard and needed to know. I wanted to work in a different way that would help a majority of people act on the issue of our lifetime. I wanted to create a vision and campaign on solutions, but first I needed to understand the source of Canada's contempt for climate-change policies. And that meant I had to get mud on my boots again—really sticky mud. It was time to visit the tar sands.

Chapter 14

CANADA'S MORDOR
VISITING THE ALBERTA TAR SANDS

It is truly nuts. But you know, junkies find veins in their toes. It seems reasonable, to them, because they've lost sight of the rest of their lives.

AL GORE IN AN INTERVIEW ON THE
CANADIAN TAR SANDS, *ROLLING STONE*

ONE COLD FALL DAY in 2008, I drove the highway between Fort McMurray and Calgary at sunset. I was with the photographer Colin Finlay, and we both took pictures. I remember marvelling at the beauty of the region, how the setting sun glinted off the surrounding lakes. Then I checked the map to get my bearings, and it hit me that I wasn't looking at lakes but at toxic "ponds." I knew these tailings ponds existed, but for some reason I thought they would be behind barbed wire or at least warning signs. But these open pits full of toxic effluent lap right up to the side of the highway. I had never witnessed a more surreal sight.

As of 2011, there were 130 square kilometres (50 square miles) of toxic ponds in Alberta.[1] One of the dams that holds those toxic ponds back from the beautiful Athabasca River is the second-largest dam in the world, second only to the Three Gorges Dam in China.[2]

The ponds are so toxic that the oil companies fire cannons every few seconds to scare off the birds. The birds that do make it past the cannons encounter little scarecrows floating in the ponds. The helicopter

219

pilot I met in the bar of our hotel in Fort McMurray told me that there are people employed by the oil companies just to rake the dead birds off the top of the tailing ponds. In 2008 the cannons at Syncrude's Aurora pond were out of operation—the company blamed a spring snowstorm—and sixteen hundred ducks landed on the water.[3] They began to die immediately. This travesty became national news and swiftly spread around the world. In 2010 an Alberta provincial court judge found the company guilty of the birds' deaths and fined them $3 million.[4] The irony is that these same toxic ponds threaten downstream communities, but it took the ducks to make it a mainstream issue.

In another sad irony, the Alberta government responded to the dead-duck situation by spending $25 million on a public relations campaign to brand tar sands oil as "friendly oil" and the United States' answer to energy security problems. The tar sands is the second-largest oil reserve in the world after Saudi Arabia's,[5] and holds 179 billion barrels. Burning this oil would result in twenty-five times the world's annual carbon emissions. There is nothing secure about dramatically increasing our global warming impact or poisoning Canadians and Americans. Canada's federal government has now joined Alberta's effort under the new banner of "ethical oil." I imagine George Orwell would be impressed by the sheer chutzpah of trying to rebrand this controversial, dirty oil as "ethical."

This "ethical oil" is poisoning people. The morning after our drive past the toxic ponds, Colin Finlay, Todd Paglia and the actress Neve Campbell (whom I had brought to the tar sands to help us raise awareness on the issues) met with George Poitras, former chief of the Mikisew Cree First Nation in Alberta. He told us about his community members dying from rare cancers and other chronic diseases and that the government and industry had refused to address the issues.

The chiefs were interested to meet with us and discuss working with environmental organizations, but I have a sneaking suspicion that they were actually most thrilled to meet Neve. As soon as our meeting was over, they asked to have their pictures taken with her, and later that night those media-savvy chiefs sent out a press release referencing the famous horror film in which Neve had starred: "Scream Star Horrified by Tar Sands." They made national news.

My friend Steve Kallick had worked in Alaska during the *Exxon Valdez* oil spill. When I called him from Fort McMurray, he told me that he had just met with some of the scientists he had worked with in Alaska. They told him that their tests showed the water held three-thousand times the toxicity of the *Valdez* spill, and the breach of one dam would poison the entire basin of the Mackenzie, one of the world's largest and most pristine rivers.[6]

I wanted to take Neve Campbell to the tar sands and get ForestEthics campaigning on the issue, because this Alberta megaproject is important on many different levels. The tar sands reveal the desperate lengths we are willing to go to to keep the fossil fuel economy going. The toxic landscape and carbon emissions are disastrous enough, but those are only the direct impacts. Allowing the growth of the tar sands is also a driving reason behind the Canadian government's unwillingness to legislate a cap on Canada's carbon emissions. Unlike most developed countries, Canada's global warming emissions are still skyrocketing, and fully half of the growth is coming from Alberta.[7] As Rick Smith, executive director of Environmental Defence and co-author of *Slow Death by Rubber Duck*, explains, "Canadian climate policy is being held hostage by the tar sands."[8]

This domestic reality has awful global implications. Canada has consistently refused to abide by the commitments it agreed to under the Kyoto Protocol. Not only have we flagrantly overshot our targets for emissions reductions, but we are also no longer even pretending to try. Canada has seriously undermined the international community's efforts toward climate policy to date. And at one international meeting after another, insiders have described Canada working behind the scenes to scuttle progress on future commitments.[9]

The tar sands are the biggest fossil-fuel development on the planet, many say the biggest industrial development of any kind. The Carbon Dioxide Information Analysis Center lists 207 nations by order of carbon emissions. The tar sands has higher emissions than 145 of them.[10]

But even those numbers understate the problem, because the tar sands are also the bleeding edge of a whole new energy frontier known in the industry as "unconventionals." Sounds benign, but what it means is that as we run out of easy oil reserves that gush out of the ground, the industry has shifted its sights to exploiting more compli-cated resources. Deepwater drilling in dangerous seas is already under way, and companies are eager to move into the thawing Arctic. It gets even more "unconventional" than that: extracting methane from coal seams, natural gas from shale, shale oil, gasoline from coal, under-ground gasification of coal. There are even projects afoot to extract the mind-boggling amounts of methane frozen under polar seas, known as methane hydrates. No one really knows the size of these unconven-tional sources, but to give just one example, the US Geological Survey recently did some recalculations and determined that tapping uncon-ventionals would give Venezuela more reserves of heavy oil than there is bitumen in the Alberta tar sands or crude in Saudi Arabia.[11]

We already know that there is too much carbon in the atmosphere. We cannot afford to double down on ever dirtier supplies of fossil fuels. Instead, we must choose a different path: clean, renewable energy. The tar sands have started Canada and the world down a path of unconventional fossil fuels. It is a course that we must abandon.

MANY PEOPLE PICTURE the tar sands as desert and imagine that the oil is located under a gigantic stretch of sand, but it actually lies underneath the boreal, the second-largest intact forest left in the world and one of the planet's major sources of fresh water. At a time when we should be figuring out not only how to stem global warming but how we're going to adapt to a changing climate, we're destroying the healthy, functioning ecosystems that are our natural air and water filtration systems. These forests hold the key to our ability to function in a world with a changing climate. We are strip-mining for oil in the centre of Canada.

The tar sands are different from most oil developments that require drilling to get oil. At the tar sands they're scraping away what the com-panies refer to as the "overburden," which the rest of us would call "forest." The tar sands development is literally clawing away at the planet, moving earth into the biggest trucks in the world, each carry-ing four hundred tons of soil. Those trucks travel to large facilities where steam is pumped through the earth to separate the oil from the clay and sand. That process uses an enormous amount of resources.

Each year 4,241 million cubic feet (394 million cubic metres) of water is used from the Athabasca River. Ninety percent of the water used is polluted in the process. Every barrel of bitumen ("the heaviest, thickest form of petroleum," according to *The Canadian Encyclopedia*) pollutes between 2 and 4.5 barrels of fresh water. The used water is then pumped into unlined tailings ponds with rimmed earth dams and left there to settle. Every day, the tar sands development pumps 1.8 billion litres (2.2 billion gallons) of toxic water into leaking open-pit lakes.[12]

Producing each barrel of oil from the tar sands creates more greenhouse gas (GHG) emissions than producing a conventional barrel of oil due to the energy needed to access and process that oil. Each day more than 300 million cubic feet (91 million cubic metres) of natural gas is used to extract the oil in the oil sands. That's enough to heat more than 3 million Canadian homes.[13]

Using all this natural gas to produce oil never did make economic sense, but since the price of oil has increased, the development of the tar sands is escalating dramatically. Canada is now the single largest source of foreign oil for the United States, exporting about 1 million barrels a day. In the United States, billions of dollars are being funnelled into the expansion of Midwestern refineries so they can handle the dirty crude and bitumen. The toxic impact of those new refineries across the Midwest will be devastating because this is dirty, dirty oil.

You don't have to stretch your imagination to determine what being the largest source of foreign oil for the United States may mean for Canadian security. You can play it out yourself in the video game based on Tom Clancy's book *EndWar,* in which both Russia and the United States invade Canada in a battle over the tar sands.

FOURTEEN ENVIRONMENTAL organizations and five First Nations groups on both sides of the border are collaborating in the most incredibly effective coalition I've ever seen in my life, to bring the story of the tar sands to the world and to rebrand it as "dirty oil." The result is that we're now seeing companies in the tar sands scrambling to figure out how they can continue their operations in a "clean" way. The French mining company Total, for example, announced last year that it would do two projects in 2012 without tailings ponds. Suncor has recently announced that it can "reclaim" the tailings ponds. On reading these press releases, I didn't know whether to be happy or cry. On the one hand, it's clear that all the scrutiny has forced them to try to clean up their act; but on the other hand, is it really possible to have "clean tar sands"? Even if the toxic impacts are reduced, we are still keeping society hooked on oil and not addressing the issue of fossil-fuel emissions.

The other shocking implication of this new rush to "clean up" is that some of the announcements and my conversations with executives from the oil industry have made me realize that *we could have done this all along.* Even though technologies exist to develop the oil with less toxic impact, until there are regulations that require industry to change it will not. Individual companies may believe that being greener is the right thing, but without regulation it's not a level playing field, and the companies feel they can't afford to spend money that their competitors aren't spending.

The other reason we haven't seen more responsible practices is the entirely predictable logic: why be careful with how much clean water you are poisoning when the water is free? All the water that the oil companies are using, those lakes they're poisoning—do you know how much they pay for it? Nothing.

One of the things changing today, and changing so quickly that we can barely keep track of it, is the way we define "the environment." Right now our economic systems treat the environment as what economists call an "externality," something that is not valued and often not even considered in decision-making processes—as if we don't need to breathe clean air and drink clean water. That's why you have a system where oil companies can take fresh water and turn it into toxic sludge because poisoning our drinking water is free. There is no cost for destroying species' habitat, threatening a species or contributing to a species' extinction. Every elementary textbook on economics discusses the problems of externalities that need to be dealt with in a public policy framework.

The only way to "internalize" externalities is through government action. The government has the power to ban certain activities, limit others and make the true cost to the environment part of the cost of doing business. There's no reason why tar sands developers can't be properly regulated for their use of water when there are limits and fines in place for pollution. Frequently, however, fines are set so low that they are simply worked into the budget. That's exactly what happens with logging: "Oops, we weren't supposed to take that cedar? Sorry, here's our $150 fine." And the cedar is worth $20,000. Imagine how safe our roads would be if drivers were fined only a quarter each time they were caught speeding.

TAR SANDS DEVELOPMENT locks North America into a high-carbon future, feeds our addiction to oil, delays the transition to clean energy sources and threatens to derail efforts to stave off a catastrophic global warming cycle. If North America is to play any meaningful role in halting global warming, phasing out development in the tar sands is critical.

Tar sands emissions will account for 44 percent of the total increase in Canada's emissions from 2006 to 2020. At the current rate of development, the GHG emissions from tar sands will erase everything we are doing as individuals and all the good work by other provinces.

Under the Harper government's "intensity targets" (the commitment to decrease emissions per barrel of oil but not requiring a reduction overall), the tar sands can continue pumping out dirty oil and increasing carbon emissions at an incredible rate.

Prime Minister Harper also touts work on carbon capture and storage (CCS) as the solution to our increasing emissions, but no one has proven that CCS can safely be accomplished at the scale the government suggests. CCS basically means the industry tries to capture the carbon and store it permanently underground. CCS is the Loch Ness Monster of the fossil-fuel industry—industry claims to believe in it but never seems able to prove that it exists. Right now it's more of a PR tool for Alberta and the Harper government to say that they're developing clean technologies and working on CCS, even though they have no proof that it's viable. I think it's a mistake for governments to be throwing public money after CCS in the way they're doing and not putting that money into cleaner technologies and renewables that have been proven effective.

The oil and coal industries have been saying CCS is possible for many years now. If we really want to accelerate innovation and give them the opportunity to develop those new technologies for the future, it will happen if companies are simply not able to operate without innovating as a result of regulations. "Necessity is the mother of invention," as they say. In the United Kingdom, Greenpeace and other groups have called the government's and industries' bluff on CCS by simply saying, "Fine, if you believe it's possible, commit to not building any more coal plants unless CCS can be proven. Require all new operations to have CCS." Since CCS is unproven, new coal plant development in the United Kingdom has ground to a halt. Considering a new Harvard study has just shown that CCS is so ridiculously expensive it is likely cost-prohibitive, and a new Duke University study has proven that carbon dioxide (CO_2) leakage results in toxic contamination of drinking water, so far CCS is simply a very expensive pipe dream.[14]

THE GOOD NEWS is that if you look at the polls, Albertans support a moratorium on tar sands development. They're scared because the rapid pace of development is affecting every facet of their lives, from cities expanding without social infrastructure, to reduced water quality and quantity, to the concerns about the toxic ponds leaching into the soil and water. The other good news is that the markets are changing, and new low-carbon fuel standards may force Alberta to clean up its act. Meanwhile, solar and wind power have moved from being cottage industries to being the fastest-growing sources of electricity globally.

Perhaps the best news of all is that this issue is in the news. Environmental groups and First Nations are working to oppose new refineries and refinery upgrades. ForestEthics is doing markets work to encourage major fleet companies to adopt low-carbon fuel standards and refuse to buy oil from the tar sands. They've identified which refineries are selling it and which refineries are not. They're working with groups in the United States on municipal resolutions against tar sands oil, supporting legal challenges with First Nations, researching the toxic impacts and water scarcity and engaging investors. But will it be enough in the face of the incessant demand for oil and the United States' determination to reduce its dependence on oil reserves in the Middle East? Because, let's face it, it's hard for people in Nebraska or Idaho or any other state to worry about boreal forests or toxic impacts on First Nations communities that they have never heard of if the alternative involves American kids being shipped home in body bags.

Recently, when faced with these issues because of an impending decision over a controversial new pipeline to import Canada's oil to the United States, Secretary of State Hillary Rodham Clinton referred to growing concerns over energy security (many reporters noted that this is now code for "easier to get it from Canada than Saudi Arabia and co."), and she acknowledged that while oil from Canada was "dirty," the United States was likely to sign off on the pipeline because it hadn't yet gotten its "act together as a country and figure[d] out that clean, renewable energy is in both [its] economic interests and the interests of the planet."[15]

A COUPLE OF YEARS after visiting the tar sands, I found myself reflecting on my trip as I waited for the ferry to take me back to Cortes Island for the last time before I moved to Amsterdam. It was ten o'clock in the morning. I was in Campbell River, and I started talking to a stranger outside a café near the ferry terminal. As we sat there he pulled a flask out of his back pocket and dumped some Scotch into his coffee. I said, "It's a little early to be drinking."

And he said, "That depends on where you're coming from or where you're going."

"So where are you coming from and where are you going?"

He said, "I just came down from the Yukon, where I was busy destroying the earth, and now I'm on my way to Fort McMurray to live in hell. I'm an engineer. I work in the oil fields, and like most of my buddies I drink to forget what I'm doing."

I said, "Now you've got a good story for your buddies, because I work for Greenpeace International to help coordinate their global climate and energy campaign."

He stood up and shook my hand and said, "I'm really glad to meet ya. And I admire you for doing that work, and I hope you don't hate us, 'cause if I could figure out something else to do, I would certainly do it."

Chapter 15

THE SUICIDE PACT
ATTENDING THE COPENHAGEN
CLIMATE CONFERENCE

*We can remain the world's leading importer of foreign oil
or . . . become the world's leading exporter of renewable
energy. We can allow climate change to wreak unnatural
havoc or we can create jobs preventing its worst effects.*

US President Barack Obama, March 23, 2009[1]

A FOUR-STAR GENERAL sat next to me, our knees practically
touching, as he warned the world that climate change is "a survival
issue for human civilization as we know it." Instead of a military
uniform, US General Wesley Clark was decked out in a grey designer
suit and baby blue tie as he spoke about sustainability, pragmatism
and politics. He wasn't wearing his medals, but he had the posture, intensity and gravitas of a career soldier. This is not your parents' image
of a tree hugger. Or mine.

Ten years ago General Clark was Supreme Allied Commander for
NATO, leading approximately seventy-five thousand troops from
nearly forty countries in the war in Kosovo. I'd been a fan of his since
he broke from the pack of military figures and not only recognized
that global warming is human caused and urgent but began to speak
out about how the impacts of warming were a serious security threat.

The general and I were sitting in Copenhagen's historic City Hall
Square, temporarily renamed Copenhagen "Hopenhagen Square" by

the host city. A sixty-five-foot plastic model of our planet, covered with corporate logos including Coke and McDonald's, dominated the roadside displays of green—or at least greener—technologies. We were in one of the half-dozen or so sci-fi-style glass trailer cubes punctuating the street displays.

Both of us were invited speakers at the Global Observatory Project, which the billionaire businessman/philanthropist Richard Branson and his luminary friends like Archbishop Desmond Tutu had set up to comment and report on, engage with and analyze the climate negotiations. The title of the event was "Reasons to Act," and we talked about whether it's possible to persuade people to change their behaviour out of hope instead of fear. As I listened to the general describe how long climate change has been on the US military's radar, it was clear that fear hasn't done the job.

"I was looking at the energy security issue for the United States military back in the early 1970s when we first realized that we were no longer an oil-exporting country, we were an oil-importing country," said Clark. "I remember cheering when we tried to look at solar and wind back in the '70s. I remember the early ethanol efforts—and one by one they got slowed and delayed and sidetracked. And so now we've had to pick up all this and get going again."

It was heartbreaking to hear the general talk about solutions that were raised—and dismissed—forty years ago. It's the curse of cheap energy. When oil still costs less than coal, it's tough for people to believe we're running out of it. I sat beside him, and when asked to speak on the environmental implications of climate change, I rattled off some of today's nightmare statistics—statistics that wouldn't have existed if that last generation had paid attention, if Jimmy Carter hadn't practically been laughed out of office for covering the White House roof with solar panels that were ripped down the moment Ronald Reagan took office.[2]

The general grunted in agreement, then offered a reminder of the human cost of not acting. "When we said in the early '70s that someday we might have to put US troops into the Persian Gulf to maintain access to energy resources, people didn't believe it. Now it's banal. We've spent trillions of dollars, we've lost thousands of lives, we've disrupted the entire ecosystem in the region, and there's no end in sight to this."

He warned that because the economies of China and India have improved, it's vital for everyone to switch to renewable energy sources before those countries catch up to North American levels of consumption. "Even if you didn't believe in global warming, you simply can't have 7 billion people trying to live like 300 million Americans live. There aren't enough resources on the planet." We talked about growing resource conflicts in many countries and civil wars as a result of water scarcity and displacement due to the increase in violent storms.

After the session, the general and I shook hands, and he presented me with his card and asked me to stay in touch. The idea that he and I are on the same side gave me hope.

GEORGE MONBIOT, the rock star of climate-change journalists and author of the bestselling *Heat: How to Stop the Planet from Burning* (among other books), visited Toronto a few weeks before Copenhagen to figure out how Canada became a "corrupt petro-state."

On November 30, 2009, he wrote in the *Guardian:* "When you think of Canada, which qualities come to mind? The world's peacekeeper, the friendly nation, a liberal counterweight to the harsher pieties of its southern neighbour, decent, civilised, fair, well-governed? Think again. This country's government is now behaving with all the sophistication of a chimpanzee's tea party." He went on to refer to his trip to Canada as one in which he watched "the astonishing spectacle of a beautiful, cultured nation turning itself into a corrupt petro-state." In his conclusion, he set the stage for the climate negotiations to come: "Until now I believed that the nation that has done most to sabotage a new climate change agreement was the United States. I was wrong. The real villain is Canada. Unless we can stop it, the harm done by Canada in December 2009 will outweigh a century of good works."

Just before leaving for Copenhagen I met with Steve Kelly, the chief of staff for Canada's environment minister. I was optimistic because he had agreed to meet me and several other environmentalists. But he didn't want to talk, he wanted to lecture us. Kelly said, "If you think that you can limit the oil sands and limit industry and limit fossil fuels and put a tough cap on carbon and not destroy the economy, then you don't live in the real world."

I said, "I think California is in my real world. And they're already reducing emissions and working hard to build renewable energy sources."

He replied, "So now you think California is the same as Canada?"

I said, "Their economy and their population are a similar size."

He rolled his eyes, leaned back in his chair and snorted. "That's a good one. California is the same as Canada."

"I didn't say that it's the exact same as Canada. I said that it has an equivalent size of economy that is having success in reducing emissions and putting limits on pollution."

Meeting Kelly was an eye-opener. With PowerUp Canada, I had been working with politicians from across the country and many from around the world. I was used to discussing the social, economic and political barriers to change, but this was the first time I was actually forced to debate whether basic policy prescriptions already working in other jurisdictions were necessary or feasible. Besides being floored that we seemed to have a chief of staff for the minister of environment who clearly didn't care about the environment, I had not in almost twenty years of lobbying government ever met one who was this rude and belligerent and who clearly had such little knowledge of the environment and climate change. In the face of what the United Nations says is the greatest crisis we've ever faced, when virtually every scientist in the world is warning us we have to reduce emissions as quickly as possible and move to a low-carbon economy, Kelly was essentially saying, We're not doing that in a hurry. Don't see the need to and can't be bothered.

Switching tactics, I decided to at least get some clarity on their intentions around the tar sands. I attempted to create a dialogue about their current policy plans. "I understand that right now you are working inside the government, pre-Copenhagen, to design our cap-and-trade programme to limit pollution. What I'm hoping is that today we could have a discussion about what that's going to look like. The greatest portion of our rise in emissions is coming from the tar sands. That's the critical issue for Canada, so let's talk about it. What are the ways that you are looking at designing the cap-and-trade system to address that?"

He turned to me and said, "This government will put in place a cap-and-trade system that will include the tar sands."

I knew that from reading the *Globe and Mail*. I didn't have to come all the way to Ottawa to meet with the minister's chief of staff to learn that. Gritting my teeth, I replied, "Yes, I know. What I'm asking you is what kind of design are you thinking about in order to ensure that emissions continue to go down? Are you thinking about auctioning the permits? Will there be a hard cap on the oil sands or are you still looking at intensity targets? Can we have a conversation about it?"

He repeated the same line: "Our government is committed to putting in place a cap-and-trade system that will include the tar sands."

"You're saying you're not willing to have a conversation with me about it?"

"I'm saying I don't think you can hear very well."

I was floored. He would not even have a conversation about any of the critical issues.

By the time I left his office, I was seeing red and walking so briskly that I tripped and fell flat on the concrete in front of the Parliament Buildings and cracked my head on the cement. There I was, dead centre in front of Parliament with MPs all around me. My shoes had fallen off, and I was flat out on the concrete, all four limbs splayed. A fitting end to the day.

The most frustrating thing about my meeting with Kelly was that I had been trying to convince all the groups we were working with that we had to give the Conservatives the benefit of the doubt because climate politics defies left-right labels. Who would have imagined that right-wing icon Arnold Schwarzenegger was going to be a climate hero? Who would have thought German Chancellor Angela Merkel would be so concerned about climate issues?

There are so many examples of the right stepping up and doing an admirable job on climate policy. I'd been talking about this in all the strategy meetings, saying that we had to give the government a chance to make sane climate choices. You don't have to be right or left to care about climate change, because it's an energy security issue now, it's an economic issue. I've had conversations with Preston Manning—one of Canada's most iconic right wingers—about these issues and found enormous common ground. So I went to Ottawa determined to find a way to work with the right. I failed miserably.

As I write this, the votes in the 2011 federal election have just been tallied, giving Harper's Conservatives a majority. The Liberal Party, which had cap-and-trade as part of its platform, was decimated and left with fewer seats than at any other time in history. The NDP, which barely mentioned the environment in its campaign, made history when it replaced the Liberals as the Official Opposition. The one bright light on the environmental front is that Canada elected its first Green member of Parliament, Elizabeth May. Elizabeth is a force to be reckoned with and I have no doubt she will do everything in her power to challenge the government's lack of action on climate and clean energy. That said, given Harper's track record, the election results do not bode well for climate leadership in Canada in the coming years.

FLYING INTO COPENHAGEN from London, I discovered I was sitting next to the chief climate negotiator for Liberia. I asked him how it was going.

He looked at me as if I was an idiot. "Well, today people are dying, and more people will die tomorrow, and so far nothing we've done will help them."

What do you say to that? Would you like my pretzels?

I was on the flight to the world's largest climate conference because I was worried about the future for my children, my family, my country. He was on the flight because people in his country were dying every day. They're running out of water. They're running out of food. They don't have the infrastructure to deal with the increase in violent storms. He seemed so completely disheartened, past the point of being angry, less like a negotiator than a mourner.

I started to think past my own national interest and contemplate the importance that a global deal in Copenhagen would have for other countries around the world. The buildup to the conference in Copenhagen had already helped raise global awareness of the problems of climate change, so now it had to deliver something that could give us all reasons to hope.

My seatmate and I spoke again as we collected our luggage, and I told him about our debates back in Canada over tar sands (which he knew about) but also the debates and opposition to wind farms and run-of-river hydro power. He was amazed at Canada's regressive position in the negotiations and the opposition to renewable energy projects. With a weary look, he said, "It's nice you still have the time to talk about whether to build windmills or not, but we're more focused on figuring out how many people are going to die this year because of drought."

So I certainly didn't arrive in Copenhagen brimming with optimism. I was depressed by my meetings in Ottawa and reeling from the reports I was reading on the current impacts of climate change and numerous depressing analyses of the unlikelihood of a global deal. Besides the resistance from Canada, US legislation had to pass in order for President Obama to have the capacity to really commit to emissions reductions. China and India were holding their cards pretty close to their chest. Many developed countries were still posturing and claiming they wouldn't sign a deal to seriously reduce global warming until developing countries committed to some targets, despite the fact that the mess we are in was caused primarily by the carbon-wealthy nations spewing poison into our atmosphere for the past fifty years. All that being said, I have to admit I was still hoping for a miraculous breakthrough. I was holding on to the signs of hope in Obama's speeches. This was a president who'd said, "Our future on this planet depends on our willingness to address the challenge posed by carbon pollution. And our future as a nation depends upon our willingness to embrace this challenge as an opportunity to lead the world in pursuit of new discovery."[3] Besides Obama's speeches, back in November 2009 I also had hope because China and many other countries were aggressively investing in renewables, and the month before we had seen the biggest global protest and rallies in history.[4]

Copenhagen was the third major global negotiation on climate change. The first conference was in Kyoto in 1997, the second in Bali ten years later. Two basic topics were being negotiated in Copenhagen at the United Nations Framework Convention on Climate Change, also referred to as COP15: by how much countries would reduce their GHG emissions (the scientific benchmark that was used in the earlier agreements was 40 percent from 1990 levels by 2020), and how many resources would be allocated to developing countries.

Ultimately COP15 was all about negotiating the space that's left in the atmosphere and who pays for it. Those trade-offs dealt with what's referred to as "climate change justice." The big questions, which today are sadly still outstanding, were these: can we actually work together, globally, on new technologies that will help us produce energy from the sun and the wind and the ocean? Can we actually exchange technologies between countries without considering them national secrets? How do we deal with the reality that the majority of the world's population doesn't consume the majority of the earth's resources? Can developed countries actually fund developing countries to skip right over the industrial wave that makes them dependent on fossil fuels?

The talks were also set to deal with reducing tropical deforestation, since 22 percent of our GHG emissions come from the logging and destruction of mostly tropical rainforest.

I am not sure what I expected out of Copenhagen. I suppose that like most people I harboured a hope that we could pull a rabbit out of a hat, like the Montreal Protocol that banned CFCs and created a global treaty that successfully reduced the size of holes in the ozone layer.[5] The 1987 agreement is "perhaps the single most successful international agreement to date," according to former secretary-general of the United Nations Kofi Annan. And it still impacts climate because it commits developed countries to act first to phase out CFCs and other ozone-depleting chemicals, with phase-outs by developing countries following.

With that success in mind, I hoped that maybe, just maybe, the world's leaders would buckle down and get it done. Having been to Bali, knowing what a bind Obama was in (he couldn't very well leap ahead of a climate bill that was still stalled in Congress) and being acutely aware of how intransigent the Canadian government had been on the issues, I knew intellectually that little was likely to be accomplished. Still, I followed the progress and hoped, because I always believed there were two vital streams worth watching at COP15: the negotiations and agreements on how to move forward to address this as a planet; and an escalation of engagement and public concern in countries around the world, which was more of a success, in part because of the failure of the former. Copenhagen galvanized a citizens' movement over the fact that we need to move as quickly as possible to protect our kids and create new economies.

At the beginning of the first day of negotiations, the leaders of the developing nations, led by Africa, walked out of the talks, in large part because Canada, the United States and other countries wanted to throw out the Kyoto Protocol, which Canada was already ignoring, and start again. They came back the next day, once scrapping Kyoto was taken off the table, but the tone was set.

I've been told that I tend to think thirty thousand feet up. If that's true, George Monbiot thinks a hundred thousand feet up. One afternoon in Copenhagen we met for coffee in the hallway of the People's Forum and talked about what could be done. His stats and projections were even less encouraging than mine. He referenced a recent article about the science of climate change and global warming, which said that if you want to limit the earth's warming to two degrees, the maximum that can be used, forever, is 60 percent of the existing stores of fossil fuels on the earth. If this is the constraint of our energy system the question that we need to be asking, as a society, as human beings—regardless of political boundaries—is this: What are the best uses of that 60 percent over the next thousand years? Which is not to say that you don't use any of it. Just to fuel a renewable economy, you need some fossil fuels for our current technologies. Monbiot had cut through all the noise to sum up the essential conversation that our society should be having. At the end of our chat, he left me with some advice that still affects my thinking on what we need to do: "If you really want a campaign to stop climate change, you need a global campaign to leave fossil fuel in the ground.

That's all we can do if we're going to save humans and the majority of living systems on the planet. That's all we have time for. We need to leave it in the ground."

I walked away thinking about my little piece of the earth. Canada. The only nation that reneged on Kyoto. And I knew it was not going to happen. Not with our current government. Not unless Canadians demanded it.

We torture 1.9 million barrels of dirty oil out of the tar sands every day. The reality of the climate era is that of course we need to leave fossil fuel in the ground. We can no longer afford to extract and burn the world's remaining big carbon reserves without destabilizing the climate. That said, I've also sat in on meetings with government and industry and heard the stats about how many billions of dollars this dirty oil is pumping into our economy, how many hospitals are funded by turning fresh water into toxic sludge. I've listened to government and industry say, "We need a balance. We need a balance."

I have worked hard in the past couple of decades to find a balance, to find common ground, but in this case I'm truly stumped. How do you define "balance" in an era of ecological devastation? "Balance" used to mean that a company would have some impact on the environment that was acceptable given the economic benefits. But in the climate era, how do you define "economic benefit"? In ten years, we're going to have huge economic costs as a result of dislocation and droughts and famine, so what exactly is the "balance" and where's the "benefit?" Sir Nicholas Stern, former chief economist of the World Bank, has estimated that the cost of inaction on climate change could be as high as $9.6 trillion a year.[6]

THE "HOPE" at what some marketers named Hopenhagen frequently came from the most unlikely sources.

Guvernator Schwarzenegger electrified delegates with a speech demanding a "planetary transformation" and proposing a UN summit for provinces, territories, states and cities. One morning I woke up to the inspiring news that Canada had committed $13 billion to combating global warming, agreed to cut greenhouse gases to 40 percent below 1990 levels by 2020 and 80 percent by 2050, and was offering 1 percent of our country's GDP to aid Africa. For a brief second I was so thankful that clearer heads had prevailed . . . until I remembered my meeting at the federal energy minister's office and reality kicked in even before my first cup of coffee. More depressing was the fact that those targets are not only plausible but below the levels for which developing nations were lobbying Canada. I'd spent enough time talking to our federal representatives to know there were only two possible explanations for this bold new declaration by the Harper government: it was a hoax, or I was still asleep.

I was awake.

The global tricksters known as the Yes Men had used an elaborate press release and two expertly designed websites to force the Canadian government to admit that our country had no inspiring vision for dealing with global warming.[7] The prank didn't stop there; it included a fake press release from the Ugandan delegation praising Canada and a web link to a fake press conference. Thanks to the Yes Men's prank, the real news was even more embarrassing. The headline in the *Guardian* read, "Copenhagen Spoof Shames Canada on the Truth about Its Emissions." *Maclean's,* Canada's major news weekly, ran a story titled "Suddenly, the World Hates Canada."

German Watch (an NGO dedicated to observing and analyzing European political, economic and environmental policies) released its annual Climate Performance Index,[8] ranking fifty-seven countries on their climate laws, policies and performance. Canada ranked fifty-sixth out of fifty-seven, topping only Saudi Arabia. The index noted, "Canada's current government still has not recognised the basic necessity to take climate policy seriously—domestically and on an international level."

That day, on behalf of PowerUp Canada, I released a report titled "Falling Behind: Canada and US Efforts on Clean Energy and Global Warming," which pointed out that the Canadian government's official claim at Copenhagen that Canada was matching the United States' efforts was a boldfaced lie. As Canada's emissions kept rising, US emissions were dropping. The United States' CO_2 emissions appear to have peaked while Canada's long-term trajectory is still upward, largely due to oil and gas production. Meanwhile, Obama had committed to outspending Harper 14 to 1 per capita on clean energy.

We found out why the world had reason to hate Canada after journalists released a leaked government document analyzing Canadian climate policy. Here we were, at the United Nations summit, waiting for our government to give us something, some laws that would reduce emissions, some policies indicating they were going to show climate leadership—and what we got instead were the contents of a secret policy document revealing that Canada's government was proposing to reduce the requirements for dropping emissions on mining, heavy industry and the oil and gas industry three times lower than what was planned in 2008.[9] Every other country was talking about how to reduce pollution, and Canada's official agenda was to grow our emissions.

The fact that China has stronger vehicle emission laws than Canada should be embarrassing for all Canadians. The fact that Japan is escalating its production of electric vehicles faster than Canada and the United States should make us cringe. But as long as the tar sands keep pumping out dirty oil, the Canadian government would rather be a global eco-pariah, regardless of the ultimate costs to our country and our planet. The attitude toward Canada was perfectly summed up on the last day of the Copenhagen negotiations when three activists scaled the High Commission office in London, pulled down the Canadian flag and dipped it in crude oil.

The same day that oil dripped from Canada's flag, I presented an award to Gordon Campbell, then premier of British Columbia, on behalf of almost a dozen of Canada's biggest environmental groups including the David Suzuki Foundation, TckTckTck, WWF Canada, ForestEthics and PowerUp Canada. The honour was for the potentially suicidal political decision to introduce North America's first economy-wide carbon tax. We also gave awards to the governments of Nova Scotia, Ontario and Quebec, and to several Canadian mayors for their climate initiatives to make the point to both our federal government and the rest of the world that there is climate leadership in Canada.

To kick our Parliament in that direction, PowerUp Canada and Green Cross International released a letter to the prime minister asking that he stop being so defeatist and dedicate his energy to creating a green economy. Former Canadian prime minister Kim Campbell signed on to it and so did former president of the USSR Mikhail Gorbachev and former British prime minister Margaret Thatcher. Canadian environmentalists had also collected over 125,000 signatures from Canadians calling on the prime minister to support a strong agreement in Copenhagen. The polls in Canada showed that the majority of Canadians wanted strong leadership on climate change. Canadians are still waiting. And so is the rest of the world.

THE AMERICAN PRESIDENT, elected on a platform of hope, offered proposals in Copenhagen so weak that we should all have spent the night keening. Hundreds of people gathered around the city in candlelight vigils. Bill McKibben and many, many others fasted to protest the lack of progress. It felt as if the whole city was holding its breath. I stayed up for as long as I could function, sitting at the desk in my small room, in a hotel where activists were talking, computing and arguing in every hallway, and I wrote my thoughts for our future.

I realized the key thing to do was build the base. We needed to determine how to reach out to the greater civil society, citizens' groups and unlikely allies. This is the grunt work of social change. It's about list building, constituency building and continuous engagement because, until we have a truly broader movement, and until these issues are vote determinative, our elected leaders will not make the hard changes they need to make.

I realized this wasn't just about getting people to sign a petition. It's about building a knowledge base in these communities. It's about building the capacity of the communities to engage themselves. It's not about telling people what you think they need to know. It's about helping them build the capacity to fight for themselves.

To do this we need to communicate outside our own bubble and start talking in a language that speaks to those constituencies. So it's not about presenting a single message, it's about crafting different messages designed for different constituencies. What the Indo-Canadian community cares about in Burnaby is not going to be the same thing that the Jewish community cares about in North York.

I realized that we also need to hit the streets and build on the incredible work of 350.org, an advocacy coalition that is part of a global movement campaigning for recognition of the safe limits to holding carbon dioxide in the atmosphere, and the work of Bill McKibben. We need to make it clear to the superpowers that these issues matter to the people who vote for them. And to do that we need to get down and dirty and focus on the oil and coal. As George Monbiot said, the fight now is to keep fossil fuels in the ground. The coal plants, the tar sands and now the push into the fragile Arctic are the poster children of our failure to address this crisis.

We also need to stop beating up on our own. We don't have time to waste fighting those who are on the same side. That doesn't mean there isn't room for constructive and critical dialogue, but if we're going to turn this supertanker in the right direction, we need to focus on the targets we can agree on. We need to stop trying to reach consensus on every step we need to take. Progress is messy. There is no perfect, single, simple solution. We need both ends of the continuum—we need radical action, but we also need the mainstream. Those calling for a paradigm shift to immediately shut down the tar sands and coal mines are right. But so are the people working to ensure strong legislation and that the markets put a price on carbon and recognizing the need for a market mechanism, and even—yes—green capitalism, to ensure carbon reduction, to stimulate clean energy investment.

Finally, we can't push only our federal governments about targets without dealing with the smaller communities in our countries. We need to focus on cities, states, territories and provinces, which is where the change is actually happening. We're not seeing movement in Ottawa or Washington, but we are seeing it in BC and California.

SOMEHOW, THROUGH the fog of disappointment and grief in Copenhagen, a path forward seemed clear to me. When I finished writing, I went to sleep for three hours. I woke up and the Copenhagen

Accord had been tabled—an unambitious, not legally binding document with several blank pages for countries to fill in their own emissions targets—and the plenary was still going on. Different countries were speaking to the new accord, but the United States, China and India had already declared this a done deal and left.

I was sitting on my bed in my hotel room. I grabbed my laptop and pulled up a transcript to see what I'd missed over the three hours I'd been sleeping, because you could get verbatim transcripts. I read that many developing countries were trying to find the diplomatic language to ask, How is this possible? This is not the agreement we want. It's not even legally binding. It's not at all what we were talking about, and now it's done? This isn't democracy. This isn't the United Nations at all.

And that's when I read the Sudan speech—and I'll never forget the delegate's words: "This document is murderous. It condemns Africa. You're asking us to sign on to a suicide pact." Because from the perspective of what is now referred to as the "vulnerable nations"— countries that are already feeling the impacts of global warming— that's what this was: a suicide pact.

The negotiator from Sudan, Lumumba Di-Aping, who headed the G-77 group[10] representing 130 countries, compared the deal to the Holocaust. "If you allow emissions to continue going up from this moment—and you reach an agreement that is not legally binding— which means there is no crisis action at this point—then people are going to die. This agreement sentences people to death.

"This document threatens the lives, and the livelihoods, of millions of people in developing countries, and the existence of the African continent," continued Di-Aping. "It condemns and turns Africa into a furnace. Because 2 degrees Celsius becomes 3.5 degrees, according to IPCC AR-4 Regional Report, Working Group Number Two. L-9 asks Africa to sign a suicide pact. An incineration pact. In order to maintain the economic dominance of [a] few countries. L-9 is devoid of any sense of responsibility, morality, and it is a solution based on values— the same very values in our opinion that turned six million people into furnaces. Mr. Prime Minister, no one, no Obama, or yourself, can force Africa to destroy herself. And I want to say this on record. There is nobody—no African president or prime minister, has been mandated, or given a mandate to destroy, or aid and abet in destroying Africa."

The other delegates yelled and pounded their gavels. Germany demanded that this be struck from the UN record. And it was. Eventually they had it struck from the plenary records but not before it was excerpted widely in the media.[11] I've read a lot of what's out there, I've met with the leading climate experts, I've been in one of the movies warning us the end is near, and I still really didn't get it until that moment. You can say that climate change is the moral challenge of our age, but it's all just words until you are looking at someone like Di-Aping, or the ambassador on my flight, who have the grief of their nations etched in their faces.

And it's not just the developing countries that are suffering. While standing in the hallway after his panel speech, the mayor of Melbourne told me, "Last year, we had seven days in a row that were over 40 degrees centigrade, and 173 people died in bush fires. It was so hot that our public transportation simply failed. Our electricity grid collapsed and started to melt. The city, in fact, collapsed." As I write this a year later, floods in Queensland, Australia, have ravaged an area the size of France and Germany combined, over 340 people have lost their lives to flooding in Southeast Brazil and one million people have lost their homes to flooding in Sri Lanka. I wonder how much more of this will be required before our countries' leaders feel a strong enough sense of urgency to act?

BEFORE I FLEW HOME, I was lucky enough to meet with the thirty-member Canadian Youth Climate Delegation. We all went for pizza, and I was reminded again why we have to hope, why we have reason to hope, and why we have to keep fighting.

These kids were all starting from a position of "We're screwed." They don't need to be convinced that climate change is real; they need to be convinced that they can have an impact, that it's not already too late. And these are the kids who are already active, the ones who cared enough to come to Copenhagen. We got together to talk about strategies for campaigns, but the two most common questions I was asked during our one-on-one conversations were, How do I deal with depression and burnout, and is this worth it or is it already too late?

Our kids shouldn't have to be thinking like that. Nobody should.

I interviewed the head of the youth delegation, twenty-one-year-old Jasmeet Sidhu, for my video blog, and she explained, "We're here because we feel that this is our future that's being negotiated. In 2050 a lot of these negotiators won't be here, but we will. We'll have children, we'll have jobs, and we just feel that our voices are not being heard in the negotiating process. We need to be here to let our government know that we are representing many youth and many people across Canada, and we want to see a future with clean jobs, without tar sands, and a future where Canadians can be proud of the role the Canadian government is playing here."

THE FAILURE OF THE Copenhagen negotiations left a bad taste in everybody's mouth, but for me the feeling of despair was tempered by the contrast between what went on inside the buildings and the view from the shore looking at the endless rows of windmills—tangible evidence that an alternative scenario is possible. Denmark produces more than 20 percent of its energy from wind, while Canada produces less than 1 percent. In the United States it's only 2 percent.

The fact that Obama empowered the Environmental Protection Agency to make legal challenges against refinery upgrades to processed tar-sands oil and against coal plants and the fact that Obama personally went to Copenhagen means those measures will have a significant impact on both the culture and on the economics of these issues as we move forward.

Granted that today the blush has gone a bit off the rose. I was sorry in some ways to see the Obama administration take on health care before climate in their first term because I knew they couldn't handle juggling both hot potatoes at once. That said, I fully recognize I have the luxury to say that because I live in a country that believes the state should actually support and protect its citizens no matter their income bracket. While I'm disappointed that there are no comprehensive climate laws in the United States, I think Obama is not getting the credit he deserves for empowering the EPA and for his support for the expansion of renewables.

Copenhagen brought India and China to the table for the first time. It transformed geopolitics to create a powerful new coalition between Brazil, South Africa, Asia, India and China. It also galvanized a global movement that, though a little battle weary, seems more mature and smarter, less willing to hang our hats on global negotiations. Copenhagen forced the realization that ultimately change needs to start at home, and we need to get our own countries to shift domestic energy policy and galvanize public opinion so our leaders will have greater social licence when they get to the table.

Huge questions still exist for me today about the role of local communities in decision making and how we ensure that government decisions and regulations take into account local perspectives, yet at the same time address larger social and ecological perspectives. In Clayoquot we had a community that was torn apart because of a desperate need for local jobs and revenue and a need to address past and present injustices. That rift was widened and complicated by the fact that provincially and nationally we had a forest industry based on a model of exploiting natural resources as quickly as possible to feed global markets.

Those issues continue to play out around the world. Today we see China moving faster to install clean energy systems than any other country in the world. Greenpeace China reports that a new wind turbine is erected in their country every two hours. Many say this is the scale and pace of development we all need to reach if we are going to replace dirty coal and oil quickly enough to avoid runaway climate change.

I wonder as I watch the protests over wind farms in communities around the world, from Cape Wind in the United States to rural England and the lakeshores of Ontario in Canada, if China is ahead of the pack because they are not a democratic society. Local communities in China don't have a hell of a lot of say in whether wind turbines pop up in their village or in places like Shanghai. When the problems are global, what is the role of the local communities in land use and development decision making when we know that many in local communities will have trouble seeing past their property value, or views, or their need for local jobs? And how much should their opinions and parochial concerns matter? Sometimes NIMBYism (not in my backyard) can hold the democratic process hostage as much as corrupt governments or corporations.

I remember a conference a few years earlier when the prime minister of Denmark was speaking about the high price on carbon they had instituted, that they were decreasing their emissions, increasing their quality of life and increasing community engagement. People there are involved in the transition to a greener environment and excited about it. They have more jobs and a stronger economy today than when they started. During one of the breaks I asked him, "How are you doing this? How did you get the social licence to do what you did?"

And he said, "I had no choice as prime minister. Civil society demanded it."

Unfortunately the effect of the climate conference in Copenhagen on civil society elsewhere was quite the opposite. Poll after poll in the past year saw people disengaging. In some cases there was a rise in climate skepticism either because of controversy over the science of climate change (manufactured by companies like Koch Industries, ExxonMobil and others)[12] or because people simply can't believe that science with such severe implications could be true if our governments are refusing to act. Even in the shadow of the *Deepwater Horizon* oil spill in the Gulf of Mexico in 2010, there was less reporting of climate issues, less engagement by civil society and a lower sense of urgency in the polls. It would be enough to send me right back into the depression that followed the Bali negotiations if I weren't now in a position to see such exciting campaigns happening around the world and if we hadn't had a breakthrough of sorts at the next UNFCCC conference in Cancun.

I didn't go to Cancun, so luckily you don't need to live through another climate conference with me. I honestly wasn't sure I could take it since my first two were such roller-coaster rides. I was also pretty skeptical about what could realistically happen in Cancun and what impact I or other environmentalists could have by flying all the way there. Others at Greenpeace advised that we should send a delegation to track and try to influence the proceedings, and hold protests and photogenic actions to raise media interest in the issues. So in my new job I helped to marshal the funds and organize a plan, and I was glad I did. Our team flew a hot-air balloon with a climate message over the Mayan pyramids, sank models of iconic structures from around the world like the Statue of Liberty under water and, working with the global alliance TckTckTck, we created a beautiful image of hundreds of people on the sand in a formation that from the air read "Hope?" Media outlets around the world picked up these images, which did result in increased discussion and coverage.

I think the results of the Cancun conference surprised all of us. The delegates patched together and made progress on some of the key elements of a global deal, such as the rules for how adaptation will be financed and who will be responsible, and the transition to a low-carbon economy in developing nations. The emerging consensus is that because of this last round of negotiations, there is renewed opportunity for a global deal on climate change.

Chapter 16

SHADES OF GREEN
SEARCHING FOR RADICAL PRAGMATISM

*If you are not willing to negotiate with those who walk
the halls of power and work on solutions, then you are
not campaigning—you are just complaining.*

TZEPORAH BERMAN ON CBC RADIO, APRIL 2010,
INTERVIEWED ABOUT THE CAMPAIGN THAT HAD BEEN
LAUNCHED TO "SAVE GREENPEACE" FROM . . . HERSELF

IN 2009 THE Ontario government announced plans to replace its
entire fleet of vehicles with electric cars. It was a bold move and a first
in Canada, so on behalf of PowerUp Canada I put out a press release
applauding them for their decision. I logged on to an environmental
listserv group that I've been a member of since they invented listserv groups, and discovered that I was the subject of a full-out attack
campaign. How dare I applaud electric cars? Didn't I realize that by
celebrating the government for switching to electric cars, I was only
promoting consumption and encouraging more cars to be built? I
responded that while I think promoting better public transportation
systems and cycling is critical, our society is not going to give up
cars anytime soon. Since transportation is a huge part of the climate
change problem, Ontario's plan was a great example of a government
taking a leadership role in reducing our dependence on fossil fuels.

The attacks against me ramped up. How dare I call myself an environmentalist if I'm in favour of cars? The government needs to stop
using cars altogether. We all do.

Finally, in a moment of utter frustration, I typed, "How many of you have given up your cars and stopped driving?"

For the first time I can remember, the listserv went silent.

This listserv skirmish over electric cars is unfortunately only one example of some of the many ugly debates over strategy and "positions" in which I have been embroiled in the past few years. Don't get me wrong—a debate over what needs to happen and how is essential to designing a path toward a sustainable society, and it's essential that environmental campaigns create and encourage that debate. Sadly, all too often environmental groups take positions that shut down debate or seem so far from today's economic and social realities that they don't illuminate a solution; they simply create a fight no one can win. Decision makers will never accept a solution so far removed from reality that they cannot see how to afford it without other negative consequences. So how do we stretch the art of the possible, as we did in the Great Bear Rainforest, while at the same time taking a position that's politically viable and not completely out of whack?

In my work I have tried to carefully advocate for radical change that will illuminate a new direction to really help us change course and mitigate the worst environmental consequences of industrial activity, while identifying some clear steps forward that will help us move from A (status quo) to B (a new sustainable vision). I think of this walk along the dividing line as a kind of radical pragmatism. The solution must be radical enough to result in a meaningful change of direction, but pragmatic enough that a next step can be identified that is politically and economically feasible. As usual, there are no easy answers here, and I have to warn you, trying to chart this kind of pathway usually means that you can't make everyone happy. In fact, engaging in this process has often meant that pretty much every single stakeholder gets upset at one point or another.

WHEN WE LAUNCHED the Great Bear Rainforest campaign, all sides attacked us. Industry, government and even some environmental groups felt that calling for all the remaining pristine valleys to be permanently protected was too radical. Industry accused us of threatening jobs and the economy. Some environmental groups told us the campaign would cripple industry. Government maintained that it had "world-class logging" and no further protection was required. First Nations stayed mostly silent, and several told us to leave them out of it, to devise a solution with industry and government and not put them in the middle. Behind the scenes, several environmentalists criticized us for being too radical and asking for too much forest protection. They attacked our credibility with funders but at that point avoided a public split in the movement. Five years later when we had finally reached an early fragile agreement with the industry—it would suspend logging in pristine areas, and we would suspend our campaigns—First Nations groups attacked us because by then some of the leadership had changed and several leaders felt they should have been included from the beginning.

Flash-forward another five years, and we were standing on the stage with government, industry and First Nations announcing a joint agreement that everyone was happy with, one that protects all those intact valleys and defines new logging rules in the rest of the forest. But here's the kicker: after all that, some very vocal environmental groups attacked us for "selling out" because they believed that there should simply be no logging in old-growth forests. The thing is, on a purely ecological basis I agree with them. At a time in our history when few areas of old-growth forests remain on the planet, and we know that increased industrial activity in these last wild areas is threatening the very life systems that sustain us—combined with the knowledge that these fragile tattered remnants now face a double threat from the increase of fires and bug infestations due to a warming planet—yup, of course I agree with them. That said, had we advocated in 1996 for no logging at all on the entire west coast of Canada we would never have reached an agreement with industry to stop sending bulldozers into those last pristine areas.

What we tried to do in the Great Bear Rainforest campaign was develop a demand set that was radical (protect all the remaining intact valleys) but also pragmatic (allow some logging in already fragmented areas of the forests). In order to make sure that this campaign resulted in a new forward direction, we built into the agreement the commitment to conservation-based economic diversification.

In the Great Bear Rainforest, and now in the boreal, senior management of some of the largest logging companies in the world have agreed to set aside huge areas of forest that they were planning to log, and they are now collaborating with scientists, First Nations and environmental groups to design selective logging practices and science-based analyses of where conservation is needed to protect endangered species and ecosystem services. That isn't just radical—a decade earlier it was unimaginable. Large-scale clear-cut logging with little or no conservation was the norm. At the same time, it is pragmatic in that we are not simply beating our heads against a wall by arguing for all logging to end and refusing to enter into discussions with industry until they offer to close down their mills and recycle their chainsaws.

Just saying no until we are blue in the face will not save our forests or our planet.

Our critics within the environmental movement have argued that if we continue only to campaign and don't enter into negotiations with industry we could protect it all. I simply don't believe it's possible for the environmental movement to build adequate financial pressure to shut off enough markets to force every forestry company out of business. Believe me, I've tried. There will always be a market for forest products.

We can create an incredible amount of noise in Europe and the United States. We can get IKEA, Home Depot and Staples to say they won't buy old-growth wood—to cancel contracts and commit to a preference for recycled paper or products certified by the Forest Stewardship Council. But then the logging companies that harvest old-growth forests will just turn around and look for new markets in Asia. And in fact in the early days of our campaigns that's what they were doing.

We are not big enough as a movement, yet, to have that kind of global reach. So we have to use the pressure that we create to preserve as much land as we can.

Some people regard any work with corporations or governments as selling out. Forgive me for stating the obvious, but those are the guys with power. To think that we can just strong-arm them into shutting down or make enough noise until the government passes stronger environmental laws is beyond naive. Even when we've got science on our side, as we did when I was a student on Vancouver Island and could prove that marbled murrelets were dependent on the old-growth forests, it's rarely enough. When we win the occasional victory thanks to a high-profile protest campaign, the result rarely sticks. If you take the cigarettes away from a smoker, he won't smoke that day, but he damn well will as soon as he gets his ass to the store. There are numerous examples of parks being reopened for logging or mining years after they were originally protected. In Clayoquot Sound we continue to fight new logging in the pristine areas every couple of years because although we created enough profile and power to stop the majority of the logging, we didn't have the knowledge or expertise to negotiate an agreement that would create long-term collaboration to develop real economic alternatives. If we are going to see actual change and greater support for the values we hold dear in the time frame necessary to make the changes, we can't just say no and protest, we have to be willing to constructively engage and design processes that get all parties to *yes* and create lasting alternative solutions to critical problems.

We have to be a movement that creates solutions instead of just pointing out problems. Campaigns are a means to an end, not an end in themselves.

MY WORK IN climate and energy issues has been much more difficult and controversial than even the Great Bear Rainforest or boreal campaigns. I see now from the vantage point of the international work I'm doing that what I went through in 2009 and 2010 at home in British Columbia is playing out around the world (though thankfully in a less personal and aggressive way than what I experienced). Environmental and citizens' groups are coming to terms with the fact that we can't necessarily rely on the political left to be climate leaders. Moreover, the "solutions" that we have been proposing for years are a lot messier in reality than those solar panels and windmills looked on the cover of *Mother Earth News*.

The backlash against renewable energy in BC is a case study in proxy campaigns against climate solutions. I've had people all over the world ask me, "How did BC go so quickly from North American climate hero to a hotbed of backlash?" The other question they ask is some variation of "Is the fossil-fuel industry orchestrating this?"

I wish they were. It seems possible that the fossil-fuel industry is simply gobsmacked by their good fortune, as an alliance of politicians, unions, resource nationalists and wilderness advocates do their work for them by opposing new renewable energy build-out and vilifying those of us trying to support it as an alternative economic development to oil, coal and gas. A friend of mine aptly called this accidental coalition the "fossil fuels forever campaign."

The backlash in BC has ranged from efforts to keep outdated fossil-fuel plants on line, to eliminating energy conservation measures like two-tiered pricing, to an "axe the tax" campaign to abolish North America's first carbon tax, to protesting the use of smart meters and the building of a smart grid. We've also had "wilderness" campaigns—and I use the quotation marks because some of these campaigns do not distinguish between intact areas and those that are already industrialized—to stop run-of-river hydro, wind farms, biomass and other renewable energy options.

British Columbia is infamous in Canada for its bizarre politics and for treating politics as a blood sport, and the fight over the carbon tax was provincial politics at its most provincial. The politicians can't resist populist hot buttons about cheap energy, the unions put ideology ahead of job creation, and wilderness advocates seek to "protect" previously logged areas from run-of-river hydro developments while ignoring that the remaining ecological integrity of those same river valleys is surely doomed by the perpetuation of our fossil-fuel dependence. And it is all happening as if BC were an island cut off from the wider world of climate change and the global race for a green economy.

The tumult is all the more bizarre considering that it started only a couple of years after climate scientists awakened BC's former premier Gordon Campbell (who was right of centre) to the approaching catastrophe. After a first term that was decidedly anti-environmental, during which BC became the only jurisdiction in the world not to have an environment ministry, Campbell decisively ended North America's intransigence on global warming by committing to the first economy-wide carbon tax in North America that put a price on pollution across all sectors. He vaulted into partnership with California's Governor Schwarzenegger by promising to explore clean technologies together and create a regional cap-and-trade system that controlled dangerous GHG emissions (the Western Climate Initiative).

But even as the Obama team began studying and adopting the Campbell-Schwarzenegger model, the airwaves and public meetings in BC abounded with calls to reverse conservation measures, to "axe the tax" and to freeze renewable energy projects. One of the biggest fights was over whether BC should maintain a leadership role against global warming. The left-of-centre New Democratic Party staked out a position that internal strategists guessed would be popular with the blue-collar vote. They decided to campaign against a carbon tax and smart meters in homes on the basis that these measures would hike up gas and electricity prices.[1] They also called for a moratorium on renewable energy projects that were proposed by Independent Power Producers (i.e., corporations), instead of the state-run utility.

And the question had to be asked: if "Super, Natural British Columbia"—the birthplace of Greenpeace—can't add a few cents to a litre of gas or the price of electricity, if BC can't implement smart meters, or if it puts a moratorium on renewable energy, then what hope is there that we privileged (spoiled?) industrialized nations will lead a charge to save the developing world from drought, starvation and inundation? The most inexcusable factor in the backlash against the green economy in BC is that its campaign strategists read the same reports as the rest of us do. They can use a calculator. They know full well that we are in an urgent race against the clock, that we need to replace fossil fuels, which provide three-quarters of BC's energy (less than a quarter of total energy consumed—not just electricity but all energy—is at present hydroelectricity and other emission-free sources), that a failure to act is a moral crime against much of humanity and half the species on the planet. They know that implementing all the proposed conservation, carbon restrictions and renewable energy projects only just begins to meet the task at hand. The challenge is so great and our projected demand of electricity so high that even if we build every renewable power project currently being discussed in the region, even with all the distributed renewable energy sources and aggressive conservation, we would only begin to supply the electric cars, homes and clean industry of tomorrow.

That's obvious from some basic math. To vote against cap-and-trade or carbon taxes, or to campaign against renewable energy companies being allowed on the grid or against energy conservation, is to act against the reports of the Nobel laureates on climate science and policy.

TRUE TO FORM, I waded right into the middle of the local debate over green power while being interviewed on a popular talk-radio show about recommendations that PowerUp Canada had made to the federal government for developing a low-carbon green economy. I had heard that groups were organizing to oppose run-of-river hydro power projects in British Columbia. When the interviewer asked what we need to do to create a green economy here at home, I mentioned that new renewable power development was critical and that I was concerned about the opposition to run-of-river. I said that if we were serious about switching to a lower-carbon economy, the knee-jerk opposition to "new development," especially these run-of-river projects, needed to be rethought.

You think I would have learned by this time not to walk right out into the middle of a battle and yell, "Shoot me!" but apparently I hadn't. My phone started ringing off the hook with calls from irate environmentalists and left-wing idealists who opposed all private power production. For many people, the issue wasn't how green the power was, but who was funding and potentially profiting from it. Others argued that there was no "green" way to do hydro power and that these run-of-river operations were destroying rivers and salmon habitat.

Time to get mud on my boots.

Luckily Chief Ken Brown of the Klahoose First Nation in BC had heard the interview and called me a couple of days later with an invitation to fly by helicopter to the Toba Inlet, a stunningly beautiful remote inlet on the province's coast. He asked me to take a look at a run-of-river power project that they were developing with a private corporation. I knew these projects were controversial because of their potential for new roads in the wilderness or their negative effect on salmon habitat, and I was pretty nervous about seeing a project up close. Until this point, I had spent most of my adult life trying to keep development *out* of these remote forest valleys. At the same time, I knew that hydro power is one of the best sources of low-carbon energy production, and in the climate era it is a pretty good alternative to coal.

Despite my reservations, I was impressed with what I saw that day up in the Toba Inlet. The First Nations were onboard. The company had worked to minimize the impact on local wildlife. They were using existing old logging roads, not building new ones. The area was not old-growth forest. They were harnessing the power from falling water high up at the point where the glacier melts and returning the water to the falls well above any salmon habitat. Unlike hydro dams, this operation resulted in little or no flooding. The project appeared to be about as low impact as possible and able to generate renewable, clean power for a region that still gets the bulk of its energy from fossil fuels.

I started speaking out more vocally in support of these projects, much to the dismay of several of my colleagues in the environmental movement. I received a call from an environmentalist, someone who had fought in many of the same battles I had, someone who had previously been on my side. She was furious. She told me I had twenty-four hours to "recant" or she would "destroy me": she would tell all PowerUp Canada's funders that I'd sold out and was no longer a "real environmentalist."

I told Chris about the call. I was shaken. I found myself flashing back to the death threats I'd faced more than a decade earlier.

He laughed. "Does she want you to wear a hair shirt too?"

I hadn't asked, but I'm sure she wouldn't have objected.

Over the next year, I continued to campaign vocally in British Columbia in support of renewable energy projects, including run-of-river power developed in an ecologically responsible manner. I learned that the opposition to the projects locally stemmed from a couple of key and very legitimate environmental concerns but also from some entrenched ideological positions. The environmental concerns arose in part because the government was moving forward in developing renewable energy projects without first identifying essential best practices (like ensuring that new development wasn't sited in critical species habitat or wouldn't result in new roads into intact forests or harm fish-bearing streams). Meanwhile, the ideological concerns centred on a right-left debate over "public" or "private" power. Several groups maintained that government should develop and own all energy production and that "big corporations" should not be allowed to develop new power. Given the urgency of transforming to a low-carbon economy and the reality that big government-run utilities are simply not set up or designed to develop smaller scale, diverse renewable energy, I found both of these arguments inadequate reasons to oppose renewable energy projects.

Practically every Earth Day speech since the 1970s has sold the dream of a future when our energy comes from wind farms, the sun and clean hydro that will power a new economy of electric cars and zero-impact lifestyles. Now that the future is on its way, the clean-tech sector is booming, and environmentalists like me face a moment of truth.

From afar, Canadians claim to admire the successes of Germany in creating hundreds of thousands of jobs in wind and solar, or the green stimulus spending by the Obama administration. We clamour to eliminate the fossil fuels powering 80-plus percent of our energy use.[2] But when the solutions are in our own backyards and they're no longer hypothetical, some environmentalists start to grow queasy because the solutions are not perfect. In Ontario people have protested wind farms because—and this would be funny if it weren't true and tragic—they don't like how they look. In British Columbia, environmentalists have chosen left-wing rhetoric over environmental realities and protested run-of-river power.

We cannot oppose clean energy just because it is built by corporations, or because it requires "development."

Given the urgency of reducing carbon emissions, there should be no suggestion of slowing down carbon taxes and conservation measures, or putting a moratorium on renewable energy projects. We may not know the precise correlation between carbon emissions and human deaths or species extinction (Dr. James Hansen, formerly of NASA, estimated that a single new coal plant would be responsible for the destruction of four hundred species), but we know the correlation is direct. We know we have waited too long for a graceful transition. And we know that we, the privileged countries, must lead aggressively or doom our fellow humans.

Anyone who doubts that these projects can work and not destroy local economies should visit some of the projects for themselves and weigh the impacts against our default choice of catastrophic global warming. What are environmentalists saying when they start making blanket attacks on low-carbon energy because they don't like the companies funding them? Or they don't like "development" in principle?

We need to find a way to forge a new and supportive environmentalism, to get more low-carbon energy sources up and running quickly while weeding out the rogues. Our electric cars are going to need juice from somewhere. It's a messier business than righteous opposition, but the alternative is to fail at history's critical moment.

TOO OFTEN AND too easily, we make assumptions about people and their potential. "He's an industry flak." "She's just a government bureaucrat." "They're all hippies." Our own presuppositions and expectations limit our interactions with people and may force them into intractable positions. Name-calling and trying to define the "good guys" and the "bad guys" in a dispute often limit our capacity to build solutions.

I've worn a few labels myself—mother, student, environmentalist. We can rapidly become mired in the narrow world of identity politics. If corporations are bad, all their employees are sellouts.

I've tried to ignore the name-calling over the years to preserve my own sanity. When we launched the Great Bear Rainforest campaign and related markets efforts in the mid-nineties, BC Premier Glen Clark called us "enemies of the state." In 2009, when many from the left and other environmental leaders called me a sellout or worse ("Eco-Judas," "Astro-Turf Enviro," to name a few) for supporting renewable energy companies, colleagues who agreed with me told me privately that they were choosing not to participate in the debate because they were afraid of being labelled sellouts and losing their support, their financial backing or their friends. I had a funny (well, maybe not so funny) moment with a reporter who got me on the phone and said, "You can't imagine how hard it is to find an environmentalist willing to support renewable energy." I told him he wasn't looking hard enough. Leading environmentalists including Bill McKibben support renewable energy. Compare that reporter's approach to McKibben's in a recent column: "The environmental movement has reached an important point of division, between those who truly get global warming, and those who don't. . . . If we're to have any chance of heading off catastrophic temperature increase, we have to do every-thing we can imagine, all at once. Hybrid cars and planting trees, windmills, energy conservation, carbon taxes, emissions caps, closing the coal plants and pressuring our leaders."[3] Or the visionary German leader Hermann Scheer: "They fight against wind farms and small hydro as if they were coal or nuclear. The glaciers are melting. There is not one square metre on this planet that is protected, and we have to replace nuclear and coal. If people don't support wind farms, they are part of the problem, and not a part of the solution."[4]

In the climate-change era, we should not be broadly opposing re-newable energy just because it is development or it is in our backyard or because it is built by corporations. Yes, we should be arguing for laws to make sure we are creating new developments in the right place and with minimal impact but even that should be a small part of what we do.

In a utopia, somehow everything is done with zero impact—but in reality nothing can be done with zero impact. It's basic physics: everything has an impact. There's a choice and a consequence embed-ded in everything we do.

I once heard a mayor from the Pacific Northwest describing the way her town was eating itself alive. This was in the late '80s, when the debate over logging in the endangered spotted-owl habitat was dividing communities. She said, "It took me a while, but I convinced everyone that if we stand like bulls with our horns in and our rumps out, we'll just destroy each other and they win. But if we stand with our rumps in and our horns out, then we're a force to be reckoned with."

That's a lesson we're still learning within the environmental movement. Our horns are focused in toward each other way too often. The environmental movement is going through a bit of an identity crisis, and that's something we need to address. Whether the focus is wilderness politics or economics, we need to recognize that tackling carbon emissions should be the priority, and we need to be for solutions as much as we're against unsustainable or damaging development.

I'm sure that there are fossil-fuel lobbyists who watch this inner skirmish with relish. If we can stop name-calling and start seeing people, we can begin to recognize the need for diverse solutions. We need to cultivate a sense of fierce friendship and create an atmosphere in which we can challenge strategies. It is possible to have healthy debates about targets, demand sets and strategies without resorting to personal attacks and mean-spirited innuendos suggesting collusion. There is no one strategy to survive this challenge. It will take all of us and then some.

WHEN I STARTED this work, an environmentalist's job was to ring the early warning bell. From Rachel Carson waking us up to the impacts of pesticide use on songbirds in the '60s, to Lois Gibbs of Love Canal fame in the '80s standing up to toxics poisoning community waterways and soil, to Sheila Watt-Cloutier in the '90s causing the world to notice the real effects of climate change being felt first by indigenous communities in the Arctic, we sounded the alarm and then rallied to oppose destructive development. When I was first at Greenpeace we called these "stop" campaigns. And those were our specialty. Some environmental campaigns were "change" campaigns, and some visionaries spoke of solutions, but my take on the overarching role and predominant push was that we were trying to step in front of the bulldozers.

Today most of the world knows that we face an environmental crisis of previously unimaginable proportions. Worldwide, poll after poll has shown that people agree that environmental issues are a high priority.

In some ways the transition from blockades to boardrooms is an easy answer to the question of environmentalism's role today. It's true that I have chosen different tactics over time, but that's not because I think protest is dead and our new acceptance and awareness means all we need to do is book a boardroom or conference hall and sort it out over lunch. The decision whether to sit down and negotiate or protest is one that I repeatedly agonize over.

When BC originally won the bid for the 2010 Winter Olympics, I tried to figure out how to seize the moment and organize some high-profile protests. Canada would be on the world stage, and those of us trying to raise awareness of our government's weak laws on climate change could leverage that attention. But we ultimately realized that not only would there be issues of physical security for protesters, but protesting an event that many people around the world love could easily backfire. Friends of mine who tried to stop logging in California once hung a big banner on the Golden Gate Bridge, and it stopped all traffic on the bridge for half a day. The response? People called the radio and wrote letters to the editor complaining about "the stupid wing nuts who shut down the bridge." Few heard the protesters' message. I had a hunch that would have been the response to any Olympic action. A few years after British Columbia won the bid in 2003, I received an invitation to carry the torch. I would join the relay in Squamish, near the end of the cross-Canada run, on my forty-first birthday. Was there any reason to switch my stance from protesting and disrupting the Olympics to participating in them in this very public way? As my family sat around the dinner table, I shared my concerns. I was bemoaning all the money that was being spent on the Games, and what this says about our priorities as a country, when Forrest interrupted. "Aren't you proud to be a Canadian?"

"Yes," I said, and before I could get to the "but," Forrest asked, "Aren't you tired of always protesting everything?"

And I returned to that question: what do I stand for? Was there a way to be part of the celebration while still making a positive state-ment and raising awareness of our carbon crisis?

I accepted the invitation with one proviso: I would carry the torch while driving a zero-emissions scooter and use the moment to raise awareness of cleaner transportation options.

Not long afterwards, a Facebook group appeared called "Protest Tzeporah for being an environmental sellout for carrying the torch." The Olympic organizers called and told me they were putting extra security on my route. The media calls started coming in, and I used the interviews to talk about why I was carrying the torch on an elec-tric vehicle. I started receiving calls and e-mails from First Nations leaders who thanked me for taking part in the celebration of an Olympics that they were co-hosting. I received hundreds of e-mails from people who said "thank you for doing that" and "you really in-spired my kids" and "as a mother I really appreciated what you said about how your kids wanted you to do something positive" and "as someone who has always been interested in electric vehicles I was fascinated to see that it could actually work."

The night before the ride, an old friend who works with some of the more radical protests groups on tar sands issues called and said, "I'm hearing the word 'pie.'"

I said, "You should tell them that first of all I'm doing this to raise awareness on climate change, and second, I'm going to talk in the paper about my reservations around the Olympics and Olympic spending, and third, I'm on an electric bike. If they pie me it's dan-gerous. I could crash. And tell them that I love banana cream."

When the day arrived, I was surrounded by friends and family. My sisters had flown in from Toronto. I dressed in the official Olympics jumpsuit (note to Olympics organizers: Really? The whole world was watching and we looked like white-suited prison convicts?) and mounted the scooter. When the torch was handed to me, all went according to plan. I saw a couple of protesters on the route, holding a sign about the tar sands that read "No Tar sands. No Olympics." I tried to give them a thumbs-up without letting go of the handles. They didn't throw a pie.

Meanwhile, my family and friends ran with me beside the scooter, laughing until I handed off the flame to the next torch bearer.

I jumped in the back of the bus with the other people who carried the torch that morning. Everyone on the bus danced as we continued along the route, seeing walls of kids the same age as Forrest and Quinn excitedly waving their Canadian flags. Finally we reached the point where the last torch bearer was picked up. We went around the bus, and all the participants told their story about how they became a torch bearer and where they were from.

There was the woman who had come all the way from Spain, who had helped put the original bid together for Canada. There was the high-school student from Port Coquitlam who had entered a healthy-living contest. She was so nervous that she was shaking. The guy in front of me, the guy who handed me the flame, was senior management at Rio Tinto Alcan—one of the world's largest mining companies—and the guy sitting behind me was an oil engineer from Alaska.

I told my story about Forrest. The two men sitting in the seats in front and behind me immediately started to tell me how much their companies were doing to address climate change and how worried they were about greenhouse gases. "I know we mine coal but . . ." The whole bus started talking about the issues, and everyone had a personal connection, and I realized that's why I'd wanted to do this—to create the conversation. There I was between a guy who mines coal and a guy who builds oil pipelines, and they were both totally excited that I was carrying the torch on an electric vehicle.

If we can raise the issues and have a positive conversation that invites people to join, if we can act from a place of openness and possibility instead of anger and fear, we're going to create a greater dialogue and a larger movement. If what we do and how we do it reaches only a small segment of the population, in the end we are simply having a conversation with ourselves. That said, as the stakes increase and fossil fuels and fresh water become scarcer, the opposition to clean energy and stronger laws is digging in its heels. BP recently announced plans to drill for oil in the fragile Arctic, despite the devastation of the oil spill in the Gulf of Mexico and a US government report on the spill that found systemic inadequacies in the way industry plans and reacts to an oil spill. BP is, of course, completely ignoring the National

Oceanic and Atmospheric Administration's (NOAA) report that 2010 was "an exclamation point on several decades of warming." Derek Arndt, chief of NOAA's Climate Monitoring Branch in the National Climatic Data Center of the US Department of Commerce, said that NOAA is tracking disasters like the floods in Brazil and Australia. "We are measuring certain types of extreme events that we would expect to see more often in a warming world, and these are indeed increasing."[5] I read that kind of stuff, and all I want to do is chain myself to BP's damn oil rig and stop them. There's no easy conclusion here to what the new role of environmentalism needs to be in an era when everyone claims to be green and the stakes are high, but I definitely know we don't have time to be protesting windmills instead of oil rigs.

The worry is, it's now a hell of a lot harder to separate the wheat from the chaff. So perhaps that's part of our role: clearly identifying the path forward, distinguishing between "green" and "greenwash" and building support for the right laws, the right policies and the leaders with the courage to stand up for them. That's going to take all the tools in our toolbox, from savvy boardroom negotiations to taking to the streets at the right moments.

And not being cynical is tough. When Coca-Cola committed to using energy-efficient, climate-friendly coolers and vending machines at the Beijing Olympics in 2008, Greenpeace gave them a "green medal." Since receiving that praise, Coca-Cola has developed a method to create part of their bottles from plant fibre instead of petrochemical plastic, an incredible innovation with the potential to have a serious environmental impact. Greenpeace received a lot of criticism for bestowing this award. And I totally understand where the criticism comes from. Coca-Cola is a company that uses the earth's finite resources to transport sugar water. We don't need it. They transform enormous amounts of fresh water into something that's unhealthy, and then use our finite fossil fuels to transport it all around the planet. But is it a good thing that they are using climate-friendly coolers around the world? You bet it is.

Walmart's announcement that it was going to carry organic produce changed industrial agriculture and the face of organic foods. Walmart makes organic food accessible to the people who aren't going to, or can't afford to, shop at their local health food store. But does that mean Walmart has improved its terrible labour practices and isn't promoting mass consumption of plastic goods?

How is change made if you're constantly alienating the majority of the population by telling them not to shop where they shop and not to buy what they buy? It's always about where you draw the line. If you feel the entire raison d'être of a company is reprehensible, you can't draw a line. I certainly struggle with this when it comes to oil companies and the tar sands.

IN BRITISH COLUMBIA'S 2009 election, I incurred the wrath of many of my friends and colleagues when the provincial NDP leader used the same "axe the tax" slogan created by the federal NDP to attack Stéphane Dion's proposed carbon tax, to challenge Gordon Campbell's carbon tax. What made this public denouncement particularly appalling was that only a year earlier, the provincial NDP included a carbon tax as part of its own environmental platform. When the NDP decided to reduce the debate over how to address the carbon crisis to a bumper sticker slogan, they also shredded their well-thought-out environmental programme in order to pander to fear and play on the old trope that environmental responsibility was toxic to the economy.

I sent a private e-mail to the party leader, Carole James. I told her that I felt betrayed by the NDP platform. That she was playing partisan politics with our children's futures. That her opposition to energy conservation policies such as smart meters had more in common with George W. Bush's Republican playbook than with the environmentalists who supported her in 2005.

But when I didn't hear back from her, I made a choice not to keep my concerns private. I joined with several other environmental groups, including the David Suzuki Foundation, in condemning the NDP's platform.

I can supply a roster of the Campbell government's environmental sins, but I believe the NDP's hypocrisy on the carbon tax outweighed them. Carbon is the issue we have to be voting on, and keeping silent about it in the hope that the NDP would do the right thing once elected would have been an act of cowardice.

I realize that global warming is not the only problem we face, but if we can't solve it, and the implications for food, water and security, and solve it quickly, nothing else will matter. I didn't support the provincial Liberal party—although I read in all sorts of blogs and online publications that I did—but I did support their carbon tax. After I presented Gordon Campbell with an award in Copenhagen, that photo appeared everywhere as proof that I was in the Liberal government's pocket.

That's one reason why I hesitated when the provincial Liberal's environment minister called and asked if I'd sit on its new Green Energy Task Force. The Task Force was established to look at environmental guidelines and rules around green energy and to make recommendations about the expansion of green energy in the province, to ensure that it's as ecologically responsible as possible. The offer led to a slightly contorted and stressful decision-making analysis about what my role is as an advocate, and how I could be most effective in ensuring strong environmental guidelines. I decided that I could play a role in strengthening those projects by sitting on the Task Force and making recommendations directly to cabinet and government.

I realized that I would face more criticism from the far left, that they'd say this was another example of how I was in bed with the Liberal government. But the fact is, if a government asks me to make recommendations that have the chance to become law, I'll do that, no matter who's in power.

One of my criteria for sitting on the Task Force was that there had to be at least one other environmentalist on the panel. The government had already invited Matt Horne from the Pembina Institute to the committee. Just before accepting the appointment, I talked to him on the phone to confirm that he'd accepted, and he urged me to do the same. He said, "You can help because you'll be persuasive in assuring the recommendations get accepted, and also, if there's criticism of the panel, you'll end up shouldering it as the lightning rod, and I can just go about my work."

—

PEOPLE ASK ME all the time, "Who should I vote for?"

And my answer is always the same: "You should vote for climate leadership." We do not have time to play partisan politics. We need to vote for whoever will do the most right now to shift our economy away from dirty fossil fuels and protect our kids. That's the bottom line.

In Canada's 2008 federal election campaign, the Liberal leader Stéphane Dion announced the greenest platform Canadian voters may ever see. Dion is a former federal environment minister who took global warming so seriously that he'd named the family dog Kyoto and made a carbon tax one of the key platforms of his campaign. As soon as he made the announcement, he was attacked from both sides.

There are two issues that we need to consider when any government addresses this challenge. One is how quickly they are reducing global-warming pollution, and what policy mechanisms they are putting into place to do that. And the other is how quickly they are scaling up the alternative in clean energy. In Canada our federal government under Stephen Harper has not come forward with a single policy to reduce global-warming pollution since they came into power. They've talked about cap-and-trade, but we have nothing on the books. Canada already has the worst record of any G8 country in terms of how quickly our global warming pollution is increasing. Some of the people I admire the most, who are doing the most on climate change, are from the right of the political spectrum—because it's not a right–left issue. Historically, environmental leadership in Canada, more often than not, hasn't come from the left. I find it surprising because I'm not sure how and why the left wing doesn't own this issue as an adjunct to the fight for social justice. The polemic that the right has pushed from the very beginning of modern environmentalism has been "it's either your jobs or it's the environment." And the right was very successful in ingraining that double bind into society, but almost every issue I've ever looked at shows that one does not negate the other. We can have more jobs with sustainable forestry because we're getting value-added manufacturing and more jobs per tree cut. We can have more jobs with renewable energy in Canada than we have from the oil and coal industries combined. According to surveys by the International Labor Organization and the United Nations Environment Programme, "the renewable energy programs in Germany and Spain are merely ten years old but have already created several hundred thousand jobs. . . . By the year 2020, Germany will have more jobs in the field of environmental technologies than in its entire automotive industry."[6]

In the end there is no easy answer for how to separate bright green (strong environmental positions, policies or initiatives) from pale green (incremental change) or even pea soup green (clean coal or "ethical" tar sands, anyone?). It requires a prioritization of the issues and a careful analysis along with a willingness to listen to your gut.

Those rules of the road and the encounters I have described culminated in 2010 with those who were angry at me over my vocal opposition to the NDP's "axe-the-tax" election campaign and my support of run-of-river, combined with those who were angry over my Olympics torch ride and those who were still angry with me over the Great Bear deal, all coming together in a kind of nightmare "we hate Tzeporah" coalition. Turns out I had taken on the sacred cows within the environmental left just one too many times. Friends called to tell me that a coalition was indeed forming, and that they were already having strategy calls. When Greenpeace International offered me the job to help run their climate and energy programme, the anti-Tzeporah coalition kicked into high gear. My return to Greenpeace after ten years just didn't fit the right-wing-corporate-sellout image of me that the coalition had. They wrote a letter to the Greenpeace board of directors and to executive directors around the world, alleging that I was a "Trojan horse for the biggest corporations on the planet" and that because I had been seen entering a clean-energy reception that was sponsored by General Electric I was in fact working for GE and would "destroy Greenpeace from within." The coalition even launched a website called savegreenpeace.org. Not exactly the way you want to be introduced to your new boss and start a high-profile, high-pressure job. Luckily for me I had a lot of support from those within Greenpeace who remembered me from the forest debates in the '90s and a lot from others outside Greenpeace who started a letter-writing campaign on my behalf. So I held on to my new job, and I have to admit I wasn't too sad to be once again getting the hell out of Dodge.

For many other reasons I was sad to be leaving home again. It was difficult to shut down our fledgling organization PowerUp Canada when I felt as if that work still held so much promise. It had been difficult funding the work, though; all too often it seemed that funders were more willing to support more studies and research than serious grassroots organizing or advocacy. Mentioning how we wanted to make the work relevant to election cycles so that we could show politicians that climate was a vote-determinative issue made the funders shy away from the work even more, as the rules around charitable giving restrict activity that is seen as political advocacy. In the end, though, it was not the funding or the fights within British Columbia that led me to leave for a while—it was the opportunity to learn from other campaigners around the world and to try to contribute to campaigns in the countries with the largest and fastest-growing emissions: the United States, India and China.

On a personal note, Chris and I were sad to leave because after years of dreaming and organizing, we were finally planning on building a truly green home for our family.

Chapter 17

LIVING GREEN
RECONCILING THE BIG STUFF
WITH OUR DAILY LIVES

*Living fully during a time of historic crisis for our planet
is possible, I believe, only if we are able to grasp how our
individual choices address its roots. . . . Spirals of power-
lessness are generated not only by laws on the books but
by the norms that our daily acts create. If we buy pesticide-
sprayed food, we're saying to the food industry, yes, yes
give me more of that. If we buy organic instead, we are
stimulating its production (why do you think McDonald's
serves organic milk in Sweden but not here?).*

FRANCES MOORE LAPPE[1]

PEOPLE OFTEN ask me how I try to "live green." While I think the
choices of how we vote are more important, I do believe that lifestyle choices have an impact both on the meaning and quality of our
lives and on whether we are able to chart a more sustainable course
for society.

I am asked what I eat, what I won't let near my plate, when and
how I travel and how I cope with the barrage of trade-offs and contradictions that surround maintaining a sustainable lifestyle.

Once again I am afraid to tell you that there are no easy answers.

That said, I think there are some easy guidelines to bring you
to your own answers. My decision-making process starts by asking

myself, Can I do without it? Can I get it local, used and/or organic? How far did this product travel? And, most important, could I proudly explain to my kids why I made this choice?

I grew up believing that eggs come in cartons, vegetables come in plastic and milk comes in bags. I also grew up thinking that animals come from zoos, and Indians were from the Wild West. In my first environmental studies class at the University of Toronto, our professor had us ask friends and family if they could name any indigenous plants. When I asked my sixteen-year-old brother, he looked at me for a minute, thought about it and answered, "Stelco?"

A factory! Not the type of plant our professor had in mind.

Most North Americans do not know where their drinking water comes from. Do you know? That's why we allow our watersheds to be logged or paved over or poisoned.

I am happy to say that the decision Chris and I made to live on Cortes Island means that Forrest and Quinn know what's allowed to go down the sink. They know about the water table, where their water comes from and where their waste goes. When Forrest was eight, we went to a restaurant off-island and he really wanted a hamburger. When the waiter came, he asked him if it was organic and if he knew whose farm the cow came from. He was shocked to discover that most of the time people don't know where their food was grown or how it was treated.

On the other hand, when Quinn was five and we went for our first lengthy trip to the city, he was shocked to discover that pizza could be delivered to your door. He not only didn't ask where any of the ingredients were from, he looked at me as if I had betrayed him and exclaimed in outrage, "You can get pizza delivered? And you don't even have to wait for the dough to rise? Why have you been keeping this from me?"

Growing up at my house we ate kosher and very traditionally— challah, chicken soup and matzo balls, and roast brisket. I grew up thinking that a meal was a big hunk of meat, potatoes and a vegetable. I didn't know organic food existed or why anyone would want it, since I had no clue that chemicals were routinely sprayed on my food. When I was eighteen and moved to Toronto to start university,

I became more exposed to other cultures and foods. I went to an Indian restaurant for the first time in my life, and when I started taking environmental studies, a lot of my new friends were vegetarian. I quickly became a vegetarian and, later, a vegan (meaning I didn't eat any animal products—including ice cream and cheese. That phase didn't last long). When I realized I didn't know how to cook vegetarian food, I took a job in a vegetarian restaurant.

I wanted to be vegetarian because of the environmental impacts of factory farming and eating higher up on the food chain, because it takes more resources to produce the same amount of protein and vitamins in meat as it does in the same amount of vegetarian food. It didn't hurt that at that time organic food was so expensive that eating vegetarian made economic sense because lentils are a lot cheaper than fish and meat.

Through all my work with First Nations in the Great Bear Rainforest, in Clayoquot Sound and on my travels to Japan when I helped Greenpeace start its Japanese forest campaign, I was a strict vegetarian. When I think about the number of First Nations people I offended during potlatches because I refused to eat salmon, I am slightly horrified that I was so dogmatic.

Then when I was about seven months pregnant with Forrest, I had the same dream every night for a month about eating chicken soup and matzo balls and pastrami sandwiches. At first I put it down to everything I was going through and wanting comfort food, the food of my youth. Then I started thinking, *I'm making bones in here. There's a baby growing inside me. Maybe I'm not getting what I need. Maybe I need more protein and iron.* Chris took up the challenge and started cooking more tofu, lentils and spinach. We were trying to cook everything we could think of that my body needed, and every night I was just craving pastrami on rye and chicken soup and matzo balls. Eight months into my pregnancy I couldn't stand it anymore. Chris took me to a Jewish deli in San Francisco, and I devoured four bowls of chicken soup and matzo balls and then proceeded to eat pastrami on rye. I was in heaven. That was my fall from vegetarian grace.

We still mostly ate vegetarian after that, but a few months following our move to Cortes Island I had a revelation while buying some outrageously expensive packages of tofu at the local food co-op. Every-thing that comes to Cortes has been on at least one boat. The tofu had probably also been on a plane, and the soybeans on a freighter, train or truck—maybe all of the above. I started wondering, how many miles has this travelled? Where were the soybeans grown? Where was this processed? Where was it packaged? What the hell is the carbon footprint of this tofu? As I stood holding the tofu in the store, I glanced up at the bulletin board and read, "My boat coming into the dock Saturday at four—prawns and halibut."

I realized we were barely contributing to the local economy. We had healthy, amazing food that people all over the world would kill for just showing up at our dock and we weren't eating it. I decided then and there that we were going to see how much local food we could grow, buy or trade.

We'd get a lamb from a neighbour once a year and beef from another neighbour. We bought prawns when the prawn boat docked and salmon when the salmon boat docked. After I'd been vegetar-ian for most of my adult life, it took me a while and some tips from the locals to figure out how to cook these things. We also had our moments of doubt, like the memorable day when I was at a meeting in San Francisco and Chris called my cellphone with a weird sound in his voice. "Ummm, your lamb arrived."

"Right," I said. "I asked Joy if we could have some, and I thought it would be nice for your parents when they come for the holidays."

"Okay," he said, still sounding dubious. "His name was Henry. It says it on the box. We have, um, all of him."

I had a lot to learn about ordering meat from the locals.

While living on Cortes we also tried to grow some of our own food and buy organic veggies from our neighbours. I found garden-ing meditative and loved watching the kids' delight and pride at what they grew. Quinn was so enamoured with the (very normal and average-size) squash he grew that he entered it in the local harvest festival. I remain indebted to the woman at the judging table who spon-taneously created a new category (Most Beloved Vegetable) and gave him a blue ribbon that he proudly pinned to his shirt and showed to anyone and everyone.

I canned the fruit from our trees. Every year I'd can at least sixty jars of applesauce and another forty jars of plum chutney. I would buy at least sixty pounds of local organic blueberries every summer and freeze them for the winter.

We've gone through whole winters on Cortes, with a family of four, when we have bought hardly any fruit because we had enough canned and frozen and local that we could eat from our own root cellar. It was incredibly satisfying, but from a global perspective it was a situation of rare abundance and privilege.

There's no question that cost and equity need to balance how we eat. It's an incredible luxury that on Cortes most fishers and farmers are willing to trade, so you can eat like royalty even if you don't have much money. People trade for work, for crafts. I've swapped home-made banana bread for prawns. I've traded foccacia for tuna. I recognize this system wouldn't work in most places in the world. But I think that we all have to find our own balance with trying to buy locally, both to support local economies and to ensure that we have a minimal carbon footprint.

British Columbia is famous for its orchards. So why the hell is it buying apples from New Zealand? Because they are cheap and someone got a good deal. Shipping food and relying on petrochemical fertilizers and pesticides is another waste of fossil fuel. Buying local and organic food as much as possible is absolutely critical.

Living in Amsterdam, we've gone back to a predominantly vegetarian diet because it's cheaper to eat vegetarian here and it's more accessible for our family. And in Amsterdam we don't know which beach the oysters are from, and the lamb isn't from Joy's farm. Ideally, you need to adapt your lifestyle to your environment and consider where your food and other products come from.

THE JOURNEY TO living on Cortes started almost a decade before we arrived.

When most of the younger activists ignored the invitation to Hollyhock, the founders regrouped to figure out what we needed most. The next invitation I received from Hollyhock read, "Come use our space. We'll fund your groups to come up here and hire a professional facilitator for a strategy meeting for your rainforest campaigns."

That didn't sound like a bad idea. So a bunch of environmental groups went to Cortes, and it was the best strategy meeting we'd ever had. There was a lot of infighting about positions and strategies, but the fights were easier to take where we had clean air to breathe, healthy food to eat and a new routine that introduced us to yoga and meditation. It was also inspiring to find ourselves surrounded by the nature we were trying to protect. At Hollyhock you're more likely to see deer on the road than vehicles. It wasn't long before everyone calmed down and started really listening and talking to one another.

Then one of the founders and now the board chair, Joel Solomon, and a few others realized that we didn't need just time and space, we needed skills. Most of us were drawn to the environmental movement because of the issues, and we often had issue-based knowledge, but you can't get an MBA in environmental campaigning. We didn't have any training in media skills or lobby work or organizational development or leadership skills. Hollyhock brought in Robert Gass, who teaches the art of leadership to corporations. We started applying those leadership skills to our work. Through Robert, I learned how I tended to react in tense situations and how I could be a more effective negotiator.

One day I was standing on the deck of Hollyhock with a number of other people when a pod of twelve orcas surfaced right in front of the beach. I thought, *This place is magical. If I could just stay connected to a place like this, it would give me the energy I need to continue this work.*

Six years later Chris and I were in San Francisco (he was working with Rainforest Action Network, and I was working with ForestEthics), and I realized I was pregnant with Quinn. I'd been travelling and living in Europe and San Francisco for most of the previous six years, and I missed home. I missed the connection to the forest and being able to see the ocean. I thought, *Our kids are growing up in cities and not knowing any of what we think is most important.* So Chris and I started talking about moving back to BC. I knew it was going to be tough to keep my job, but by this point we had staff all across North

America, and 70 percent of my time was taken up by e-mails and conference calls. I put together a chart showing how I spent my time, proposed the move back to BC to the executive director, committed to spending at least a quarter of my time travelling for meetings where I was needed in person, and ForestEthics agreed.

We started looking at where we wanted to live, and Cortes made the least sense. Compared with the other places we were considering, it was by far the most difficult to get to. If you're coming from Vancouver, you have to take the ferry to Nanaimo, then drive two hours to Campbell River, then take the ferry to Quadra Island and another to Cortes. There aren't many ferries to Cortes, and they don't always run in harsh weather. Around Christmas of 1999, we went back to BC and visited Bowen Island, Saltspring Island and Vancouver in search of a place that felt right for our growing family. We decided to visit friends on Cortes, even though we didn't think we could live so remotely. But when we arrived on Cortes, I felt I could really breathe for the first time in ages. It was so beautiful and, at the time, still so affordable.

I was on the board of Hollyhock because I'd been asked to help green their curriculum. I'd met a great couple there who invited us over for dinner. Their place was right on the lake and their children were so lovely—interesting, engaged and present. I remember turning to the mom and saying, "I have to learn about parenting from you guys. Your kids are amazing."

And she said, "Yeah, they are. But I would say it's just as much the school as it is us."

She told me that just down the road there was a school on an organic farm with only sixty students and an environment- and community-based curriculum.

Forrest was almost ready for kindergarten, and we had been struggling with where he would go to school, where we could afford the tuition and whether we could find a place that shared our values. The next day we visited Linnaea. Every morning they have a circle with all sixty kids sitting together and talking about their day. I remember walking into the circle, and there were Grade 7 and Grade 8 boys sitting with kindergarten kids on their laps. By choice. They were chatting while they waited for the circle to start. And I thought to myself,

When I was in kindergarten we were afraid of the Grade 8 boys. We didn't talk to them, let alone run over and sit in their laps. There was just something so moving about the way the older kids took care of the younger kids that I fell in love with the school.

We started looking around for places to live, and the house across the road from the school was for sale. It was on seven acres overlooking a freshwater lake and had an orchard with mature fruit trees. Bald eagles and herons nested in the trees. We bought it less than a week later and moved in a couple of months after that.

I knew we had made the right decision for two reasons.

The first day we pulled up in the moving truck, Forrest (who was four) stood on the front deck and said, "Is this a park, or is this my yard? Can I just go play here and I don't have to stay within your line of sight?" That had always been our rule in the city.

The second day we were on Cortes, Forrest walked into the kitchen and announced, "Mommy, I like this place." When I asked him why, he said, "I can drink the water right from the tap. And I'm sure there are no bad guys here."

"Why do you think there are no bad guys here?"

"'Cause nobody locks their doors and everybody leaves their keys right in their cars. So that must mean everybody likes each other and trusts each other."

I stood there thinking, *Oh my God, we made the right choice.* Parenting in a place like Cortes is a gift, because the kids spend 80 percent of their time outside. From the time Quinn could walk, he was outside with his brother. We would just ring a gong when we wanted to find them and they knew to yell to tell us where they were. These little boys know more about nature and natural cycles and the passing of the seasons and indigenous plants and ecosystem dynamics than I do. Because of the teachers at Linnaea, we'll walk through the forest and the boys will teach me things all the time. They understand farms and farming and where their food comes from.

THE ONE CATCH to living on Cortes with young children is that unless you're prepared to home-school them, you can't stay forever because there are no high schools. After seven glorious years, with Forrest approaching high-school age, we knew we had to start making plans to leave.

Chris and I had always wanted to live in Vancouver when our kids grew older, but the most appealing parts of Vancouver—where you have access to the beach and the forest and really good schools—are ridiculously expensive. Fortunately, Chris's parents had bought a little bungalow in Kitsilano forty years ago as an investment, and they'd been renting it out ever since. Chris and I started thinking. If you have that kind of asset in the family, how do you live your values and what do you do with that property?

We decided to get together with Chris's brother and his parents, remove the old single-family bungalow and develop an eco-density triplex. The house is a duplex in that there are two family homes side by side, but it's technically a triplex because underneath the two homes is a one-bedroom in-law suite—all on the same lot that used to have a little bungalow. Maximizing building density is part of what we need to do in cities to reduce sprawl and increase the potential of ecologically responsible shared services like district heating systems.

For a few years we explored how to build a "green" house and the meaning of "green." We based our thinking on a couple of core principles. We wanted to consume as little energy as possible, and we wanted the energy coming into the house to be fossil-fuel free. In order to have the most energy-efficient home possible, we spent the lion's share of our budget on triple-glazed windows, extra-extra insulation and the design of the house. Even in rainy Vancouver it turns out you can usually rely on solar energy if you have made the building envelope tight and designed it to capture the maximum amount of light (passive solar).

Since starting on the project, I have talked with people in Hamburg, Washington, DC, Ottawa and other places who have all built similar passive-solar houses, heated entirely from the sun, on a tight budget in even colder climates. We have a small fan system built into the walls and ducts so the warm air from the top of the house, near the skylights, circulates down through the walls and comes out through vents in the kitchen and the living room. The floors, especially in rooms with huge windows, are polished concrete, because concrete naturally holds heat. The central wall of the house is made with natural rock, because the rock will hold the heat and then release it slowly. In the coldest part of winter we might need a little additional heat, so we have baseboard heaters connected to the grid. Because BC is mostly on hydro power, even if you use electricity your power supply will still have a very, very low carbon footprint.

We've been able to build this house on a tight budget because we needed to (as I said, you don't do this work for the paycheque) and because we also wanted to prove that you could build a house like this in an affordable way.

The most challenging part of building the house came with the wood consumption and the finishings. The majority of the really green and attractive products are still specialty items and are super expensive. Seriously cool-looking recycled quartz countertops or recycled glass tiles are even more expensive. Local stone or tile is often twenty times as costly as beautiful ceramic or slate tiles from China.

We were diligent about every single purchase, asking ourselves, does this have the lowest ecological impact, is this the lowest carbon footprint, where did it come from, how much of it are we using?

I can see how people end up compromising their values to get the job done. I had no idea I would spend days agonizing over cupboards. The green options for the kitchen cupboards were wheat-straw waste board or natural wood plywood boxes that didn't contain toxic chemicals like formaldehyde, but were $5,000 more than conventional cupboards. And on our budget, $5,000 meant whether we could finish the kitchen. In the end we bit the bullet and went for FSC-certified plywood and laminate cupboards, but that meant we had to sacrifice hardwood floors and wool carpeting. We will stick with concrete floors and a couple of throw rugs.

I learned that you really need to know what you're asking for. I was shocked at how every supplier and every designer I met said, "We're eco and this is the greenest option," and it was clear they had no idea what they were talking about, or they were lying. Almost everything they were trying to sell me had a terrible carbon footprint, because it was from overseas or used toxic glues, or both. Or they'd say, "Yeah, it's sustainable wood that we're using because it's certified." Then I'd find out it was certified by the weak industry certification scheme Sustainable Forestry Initiative instead of the more socially and ecologically rigorous Forest Stewardship Council.

I love to cook and really wanted a kitchen with all the bells and whistles. I quickly realized that if we were going to spend the money for triple-glazed windows or solar water heating, we couldn't afford tons of drawers with fancy hardware. I was lucky to find a kitchen designer who shared my interests and convictions. She helped me solve the cost issue by building a pantry in the kitchen (dry wall and framing is a lot cheaper than cabinets). She also found material to make the hanging pantry barn door from recycled sunflower husks.

But when it came to the kitchen island we couldn't afford an FSC-certified wooden butcher block, and we couldn't find one made from reclaimed wood. Adhering to the premise that local is preferable, Chris talked to several people who work with wood, including an artist on Cortes who had found an old-growth maple that had washed up on the beach. That maple became our kitchen island, and also provided some much-needed hours of employment to locals in a rural community.

The kitchen stove was a challenge. I really wanted the convenience and efficiency of a fancy gas stove, but we had made a commitment to having a fossil-fuel-free house. After doing a bit of research I found out it's a bit of an outdated myth that gas is nicer to cook on than electric. Today's electric stoves heat in seconds and the burners react quickly to temperate change, just like a gas stove. The stove I finally decided on is also incredibly efficient, and those of you reading this who are cooks will appreciate that it has five burners and a warming drawer!

Because I knew the language, I was able to translate the faux-green jargon, but building this house made me realize just how difficult it is for most people to understand the options and do the best thing for their wallets, their families and the planet. You need to commit to constantly asking questions, dealing with the blank stares, and then asking more questions. Demand wood certified by the FSC, or reclaimed wood. Don't settle for toxic cabinet or carpet materials. Read the fine print. Ask where every product comes from and how far it travelled.

We all want to feel good about the choices we make in our daily lives, but there is one critical reason why I'm sharing this part of my personal journey: all too often I've learned that the market is more responsive and quicker to change than government. If we are clear about demanding FSC-certified cupboards and asking our grocery store managers why they don't have organic milk, as well as talking to our friends and family about our choices, we will contribute to the wave of sustainability that we have already experienced in our lifetimes.

When I was eighteen I had to become a member of a backroom co-op to buy organic food. There was no FSC-certified wood, and you couldn't buy recycled paper at Staples. I truly believe that our role as active citizens—engaging in advocacy with non-profit groups, participating in protests and writing letters to our politicians—is our most important role. But that doesn't mean that if we are doing one or all of these things, we should rest on our laurels and eat at McDonald's or buy a brand-new mahogany dining room suite, consequences be damned. One day I hope to live in our new passive-solar house in Vancouver, which now (thanks to friends, one of whom is a crazy-brilliant artist) has a twenty-four-foot cedar tree that was found on the beach on Cortes reaching up all three floors in the centre of the house and is being enjoyed by renters. In the meantime, we're back to being mostly vegetarian and exploring life as a car-free family in Amsterdam.

No discussion of living green would be complete without addressing flying. The fact is that you can live in a passive-solar house, walk to work every day and eat local and organic, and it will all be wiped out by one flight to Hawaii. Flying is by far the most polluting activity of our era. A single vacation flight to the other side of the world can dump ten to twenty tons of greenhouse gas emissions per person.[2] That's nearly a decade's worth of the climate damage that an average European emits from all other personal transportation combined.[3] Ten years' worth of carbon emitted from one flight! If we're going to reduce fossil-fuel emissions by 80 percent by 2050, which is what scientists from the International Panel on Climate Change, NASA and many others say will be required to stabilize the climate, then that one flight is more than forty years' worth of all climate damage a person will be able to emit from all personal transportation by 2050.[4] A fifty-thousand-mile-a-year frequent flyer will annually dump between twenty-two and forty-four tons of GHG into the atmosphere.[5] So it's pretty darn serious.

About eight years ago, inspired by two of our close friends who had made a commitment not to fly at all, Chris and I decided to restrict our flying to what was necessary for our work (even for work I fly a lot less today than I used to, by doing video conferencing instead of face-to-face meetings). Flying less has been one of the hardest things I have ever tried to implement in my personal life. It has meant the end of winter migrations from rainy BC to find sun. Yes, you can take a train or bus or drive to California or even Mexico, but we rarely have enough time off work and school to make that kind of trip. It has also been sad not to see our friends in California and other places around the world. One of the great bonuses of living in Europe for us has been the ability to jump on a train to show the boys different countries and cities and visit friends. We have broken our pact not to fly a couple of times to attend my niece's and nephew's bar and bat mitzvahs and once for Chris to go to a wedding in DC. George Monbiot in his book *Heat* calls these "love miles."

The bottom line is that we seriously need to work to restrict flying, and it's not going to be easy for those of us who have far-flung families and have gotten used to global mobility. Many people ask me about buying carbon credits if they fly. There are thousands of companies now that will take your money to assuage your guilt and put it toward projects that reduce fossil-fuel emissions, like building a wind farm to displace coal or diesel. The short answer is that if you do buy credits, make sure the company has a gold certification and check to see how it uses such revenue. Carbon trading is still a bit Wild West: without national and international registries, it's hard to know if a project is counted more than once or if it's even a good project.

Chapter 18

BACK IN THE MOTHER SHIP
RETURNING TO GREENPEACE INTERNATIONAL

One of the primary reasons big corporations want to be at our table is so they know they are not on our menu.

KUMI NAIDOO, EXECUTIVE DIRECTOR

OF GREENPEACE INTERNATIONAL

OUR DECISION TO move to Amsterdam so I could rejoin Greenpeace was not one we made lightly. It was the result of some serious soul-searching, evaluating how I could have the biggest impact, and some long heart-to-heart conversations with our family about what it would mean for all of us. The idea was sparked the night before I left Copenhagen to return to Cortes, when I met my old friend Steve Kretzmann, the founder and director of Oil Change International, at a bar. We drowned our sorrows in Danish beer while we talked about the future. "You know," I said, already a little tipsy from exhaustion and lack of food, "I bumped into old friends from Greenpeace who tell me that Greenpeace International is searching for a new climate director. You should apply."

Steve guffawed loudly, but then looked around to make sure no one was listening and said, "I have been thinking about it. It's an important position at a critical moment."

"I know," I said. "They have one of the strongest brands, an international reach, huge capacity and tools, and I hear the China office is growing fast. Besides, we both know that these are the critical years. Now is the time to pull out all the stops."

I pitched Steve hard because he's a great campaigner and would have been fantastic in the role. In the end he realized he just couldn't, as his co-parent would never agree to move to Europe, having just accepted a very exciting job in DC. Besides, his organization was just hitting its stride.

By our second beer Steve had turned the tables. "Wait a minute—why don't you apply? You have the experience. You would get the job in a heartbeat. You could have a huge impact. *Besides, we both know that these are the critical years. Now is the time to pull out all the stops."*

ONE THING I discovered by returning to Greenpeace is that there are Canadians all over the organization—which, I suppose, makes sense since the organization was born in Vancouver. The head of the forests campaign, the previous head of the climate campaign, the communications director for Greenpeace UK, the former executive director for Greenpeace Australia—all Canadians. Most of us are here because our experience originated with Clayoquot Sound. We learned by trial and error during the intense wilderness campaigns of the '90s and in the international work that gave us the knowledge and capacity to do other international work with Greenpeace.

These aren't just ex-pat Canadian protesters, though. Greenpeace International now comprises twenty-eight independent national/regional offices in over forty countries across Europe, the Americas, Africa, Asia and the Pacific.

It's a fascinating cast of characters. People like Paul Johnston, the Brit from the Science Unit in Exeter, who has been tracking climate change science since the days when the only people who'd heard about climate change were the scientists.

Zeina Al-Hajj, the fiery Middle Eastern woman who is determined to stomp on the toxic footprint of industry.

Anna Keenan, the cheerful young Australian whose size belies her strength. She literally has "climate justice" tattooed on her—on the back of her neck—and prior to and during Copenhagen she fasted for more than forty days. Given how small she is already, that hardly seems possible.

Joris Thijssen, the curly-haired Dutch campaigner who has an encyclopedic knowledge of coal financing and a fierce drive to expose corporate influence on climate policy.

The person I probably spend most of my time strategizing and planning with is my co-director (and my boss), Stefan Flothmann. Stefan is a brilliant strategist with an incredible work ethic and a drive for perfection. He doesn't suffer fools gladly and that combined with English being his second language (he is German) can result in some ruffled feathers. At first I was concerned that our styles would clash, but the more I worked with him the more I realized that our experience and management style are complementary. Stefan has been in senior positions within Greenpeace in several countries off and on for almost twenty years. He understands how the systems work and knows most of the players. In fact, he thinks in a way I can only describe as "systems theory." Whether we're planning to move new strategies or policies through the organization or trying to understand how to affect the investment climate for fossil fuels, he sees all the moving parts and players as one organism. Unlike many campaigners, Stefan is not distracted by media coverage or the engagement of senior decision makers. He forces me and others to constantly evaluate the tangible impact we're having in the world or how an event, action or tactic we're proposing fits into a larger theory of change. Since I naturally gravitate to grounded discussion of what we're actually going to do and how we're going to do it, I've had the feeling more than once that our work is stronger because of our collaboration.

I'm learning a lot from my co-workers and staff here. When I got this new job, my responsibilities included overseeing work on energy solutions. This work is run by Sven Teske, a brilliant, offbeat German engineer who works out of a cubbyhole in the Greenpeace Germany office in Hamburg. He has spent the past decade and a half analyzing global deployment potentials for renewable energy, founded Greenpeace Energy, the first green utility cooperative in Germany, and created the Energy [R]evolution series. My impression of Sven on the phone was that he is an incredibly smart, very detail-oriented engineer.

We agreed that we needed to spend a day face to face for me to better understand his work. He said he would come to Amsterdam while I was there. I was sitting in a café waiting to meet him when a guy came loping down the street toward me in a washed-out black rock-and-roll T shirt that had seen better days and a pair of ripped jeans. His hair was standing up in all directions, and he looked a lot like a German Mick Jagger. It was Sven, and here I was expecting someone with a crisp white shirt and a pocket protector. We spent a day together, and I learned an enormous amount about current global fossil-fuel consumption and how we can replace it with renewables.

One of the things that excited me most about returning to Greenpeace International was finding out about the years of research that the organization has done and all the engineers and scientists and experts it employs to analyze the art of the possible. The energy revolution documents and scenarios that Greenpeace has produced prove that it's entirely possible for the world to stop using polluting fossil fuels and to power our lives with energy-efficient and smart technologies supported by the sun, wind and water.

Decades ago we talked about how our cities could be run by wind-mills. But we didn't really know if it could work on a large scale. Today, thanks to Greenpeace studies, we do. These studies have been peer-reviewed by scientists and engineers around the world and supported by the International Renewable Energy Association. That's why the International Panel on Climate Change is issuing Greenpeace's Energy [R]evolution scenarios in its next report. This document examines every region of the world and every bit of energy produc-tion, and analyzes how fossil-fuel-dependent power can be replaced with the earth's capacity for renewable energy in each locale. The report also looks at how many jobs we could create by producing re-newable energy versus how many jobs we create with conventional energy. The Energy [R]evolution data prove that more jobs and more economic development would result from renewable sources.[1]

Sven and I met to brainstorm how to actually tell the world about the implications of this three-hundred-page report and get it covered in the media. It's a very dense modelling analysis, and I probably could count on one hand the number of people within Greenpeace—let alone the number of people outside of Greenpeace—who have read it in its entirety. We tried to figure out how to use the findings of the report to inspire people and show decision makers that what they need to do is technologically possible, economically feasible and will create more jobs and economic revenue. Working with others in the team, we broke it down to sixteen pages, then did a single-page summary for the media. We also produced a free Energy [R]evolution iPhone app, and Anna put together a great Al Gore–type slideshow with speaking notes that people can download free and present in their communities.

Despite all our best efforts, we still haven't been entirely successful in telling this hopeful story and getting widespread interest. It's sad, but the fact is that conflict, controversy, scandal and the cult of the celebrity are always far more appealing to media (and are more likely to go viral on Twitter and in the blogosphere) than concrete solutions. Maybe we need Brad and Angelina to break up due to a dispute about how many solar panels to install. We continue to work to find a way to tell the story of the energy revolution and influence governments to adopt policies that will make it a reality. It's hard sometimes, when reading the research, to understand why great numbers of people haven't already got the point.

The Energy [R]evolution scenario shows how to create about 12 million jobs (8.5 million in the renewables sector alone) by 2030 and 33 percent more jobs globally in the power sector, a significant contradiction of industry's constant complaint that environmental responsibility will come at the cost of jobs. Our research shows that the sustainable future of the planet is rooted in the investment in people and local communities who can install and maintain renewable energy sources rather than further subsidizing dirty and finite fossil fuels. Such investment not only creates jobs but means that energy sources are widespread and diversified—ultimately, millions of people who currently have no electricity will have access. The 2010 Energy [R]evolution report outlines the means to a 100 percent renewable, equitable, safe, clean energy supply for the world.

Again, a reason to hope. And a reason to be happy to be back inside what friends have called "the mother ship" and others have dubbed "Hotel California" because no one ever really leaves.

In our first meeting, Sven pointed out to me that for the past four years the only organization in the world that has been right on its predictions of how quickly renewable energy would grow and what would happen within each renewable energy technology has been Greenpeace. Clearly, it's now a much more sophisticated organization than when I left it over a decade ago, one with expertise in data analysis and in proving that solutions are possible while also kicking corporate and political ass. It uses the inside-outside strategy that I believe is the only way to achieve change—while creatively focusing on problematic environmental issues and negotiating in the halls of power, we're equally comfortable wearing suits as holding placards and linking arms to blockade trucks and tankers.

While most people know about Greenpeace in North America, its reputation is more established and impressive in the rest of the world. It's said that one in five families in the Netherlands are members of Greenpeace. In Germany there was a poll in the '90s asking what Germans value most; gold came first and Greenpeace came second. In many European countries, Greenpeace sets the agenda for environmental action.

When I told people in Canada that I'd taken a job with Greenpeace International, they said, "Oh, that's interesting." But in Europe, when people realize where I work, everyone from the bank manager to the clerk at the bakery thanks me. On my first day in Amsterdam, I mentioned what I was doing there to a café owner who then refused payment for my lunch. My work permit sailed through because I work for Greenpeace. Meanwhile, I'm still straightening out my ability to enter the United States because I worked for Greenpeace over a decade ago.

The changing face of Greenpeace clearly reflects larger global geopolitical realities. Already, over a year into the job, I'm seeing some of the debates play out that are the microcosm of the larger global debates around equity, and who pays for change. The fact is that the countries with the wealthiest Greenpeace offices are not necessarily those with the natural landscapes that most need protection, nor are they the countries that have to make the greatest change the quickest.

Greenpeace China is the fastest-growing office of Greenpeace International. China and India are the fastest-developing economies in the world. But while China is growing renewable energy capacity more quickly than any other country in the world, it also builds a new coal plant every couple of weeks. What we all need to figure out is how the country can bypass the fossil-fuel era it has avidly embraced—and that's going to require money and support from developed countries, which have been spewing pollution for the past hundred years.

One of the exciting things about working right now for Greenpeace is that the heads of national and regional offices, led by the new executive director, Kumi Naidoo from South Africa, have agreed to a "power shift" (millions of dollars are transferred from wealthier offices to Greenpeace offices in South Africa, China, India and the United States) to address these issues and ensure that offices in emerging economies have the ability to make a difference on key issues. That, combined with the capacity to connect the dots—to target a company in Switzerland (like Nestlé) for its impact on orangutan habitat in Indonesia, due to the Swiss consumption of palm oil (and run campaigns in both countries), or to oppose a coal plant in India and discover that it is being financed by a UK bank.

There have been numerous moments in the past year when I've been thankful for the experience I have under my belt and the ability to combine that with Greenpeace's global reach. I'm also excited to be working with a team of people around the world who are exploring the interplay between carbon and finance, and how that influences and is influenced by politics. We have been researching how much governments subsidize big oil and coal with taxpayers' money and how this holds back the expansion of renewables; in fact, Bloomberg reports that fossil-fuel subsidies are twelve times the subsidies given to renewable power globally.[2]

A MONTH INTO my new job at Greenpeace International, the cap blew off the BP oil well in the Gulf of Mexico, spewing as much as 100,000 barrels of oil into the ocean every day, according to some estimates.[3] The situation was disastrous, but I realized that with my experience coordinating shipboard responses, and being in my new position at Greenpeace, I was in the right place at the right time. There was a moment after the spill first started when Chris and I were talking about the best way Greenpeace could run a coordinated campaign to make sure this moment would become a turning point in global consciousness, when our society recognized the dangers of fossil-fuel development and the opportunity that exists to shift to clean energy. Chris said, "Don't they have people for that?" It hit me, it hit us both, and I said, "I am the people for that."

Initially Greenpeace responded quite quickly. We played a very traditional role in bearing witness. We had people on the shore and in our Zodiacs, out on the oily waters. We were finding oil on beaches and taking journalists to see the spill. Some of the best and most disturbing photographs of the spill from around the world were taken by Greenpeace photographers.

But about thirty days in, when plan after plan to stop the spill had failed, I started e-mailing my colleagues, saying, "We need a bigger response. This is a huge moment. We have to figure out how we can capture the outrage, the horror and the concern we're seeing around the world and use it to make change, to move beyond oil."

And that's when I was confronted with the downside of dealing with a massive organization: bureaucracy.

The benefit of working with Greenpeace is, of course, the brand—and the fact that if we need a ship in the Gulf we have one. There are times when Greenpeace practically feels like an independent country. The flip side is that when we want to move, we're not always nimble. There was some immediate response. Greenpeace US responded in the Gulf with its rapid response team. Greenpeace China also reacted quickly that year to the Dalian Oil Spill.

But Greenpeace International is, of course, a global organization, and as an international coordinator I have the job of listening to numerous voices calling for various actions around the world and trying to find some common ground. We had Greenpeace Austria advocating a boycott of BP. We had Greenpeace UK—the home of BP—saying, "No, no. We don't want to focus this on BP—they're just one company, and this is a much larger problem." I agreed. If we told our members to boycott BP, does that mean we were saying it's okay to buy their gas at Exxon or Shell? I believed we had to use the moment to talk about how our leaders had failed to protect us from disasters like this because their policies lead to fossil-fuel dependence. But many countries, building on their citizens' outrage at the spill and their desire for immediate action, wanted to harness that anger by boycotting BP. If BP was responsible for the spill, why not go to BP and campaign against them?

But to accomplish what?

"BP has to clean it up." But they're already cleaning up.

"BP has to agree to go beyond oil." What exactly does that mean? BP had already tried to rebrand itself "Beyond Petroleum" because they were putting some money into solar while investing in everything from the oil sands to drilling in the Gulf of Mexico, and causing some of the worst oil spills and environmental disasters in history.

The problem is that every campaign needs a bad guy. Positioning BP as the bad guy would have garnered an enormous amount of support, but I think it also would have resulted in a lot of criticism. The inevitable *New York Times* analysis would have been devastating, because they would've been right in denouncing a boycott. There was no endgame in going after BP. We needed to use the moment to create pressure for national legislation like vehicle efficiency regulations and clean energy development that would reduce our dependency on dirty fossil fuels. We needed to expose the ongoing plans of the oil industry and their inadequate safety and spill response plans. But how?

The internal fight went on for weeks. There are times when it seems that turning around an action or a policy is about as slow as turning around an oil tanker. For over a month I was up every day at 4:30 a.m. to negotiate with colleagues around the world on the best way to handle the spill. Meanwhile, the oil kept spewing. After a month on the job, I finally had authorization for a collective oil spill response strategy that we believed could harness the outrage at BP to create a wider conversation and a call for stronger laws. We lined up one of our largest ships, a helicopter and a trained team with a comprehensive media strategy and they arrived in the Gulf . . . the day BP capped the well.

I know it's wrong to even think this, but couldn't it have taken them just a few more days? We could (and did) still use our capacity in the region to take reporters into areas that they wouldn't have had access to, worked with scientists to assess the impact of the spill and continued to harness the concern about the impact for a call for more comprehensive legislation, but the urgency and interest in the issue seemed to be capped as well.

The spill was a reminder of how desperate we are for oil, because we're going to progressively less accessible places to drill for it. It is one of the most disgusting results of our industrial society that we're running out of easily accessible fossil fuels, so we're scratching the hard-to-reach places in really dangerous ways. It was also a reminder of the North American penchant for magical thinking when it comes to environmental issues. The moment the well was capped, so was the media coverage. A few stories came out with the US government and BP saying that the ocean was all better now because the oil had dispersed. Of course it had dispersed—BP had dumped tons of chemical dispersant in the water that is as toxic, if not more toxic, than the oil, and nobody knows what the long-term effects of that much oil or that much dispersant will be to the ocean, marine life and drinking water.

Part of my job at Greenpeace is to keep considering situations after the government passes approval and the media move on to the next disaster. So we sent in a scientific team to analyze the impacts of the spill on the ecosystems. Once we started looking into the BP spill and debating the correct response, Greenpeace woke up to tracking where deepwater drilling was happening around the world and examining the safety regulations. We found that in some of the most sensitive ecosystems on the planet—such as off the coast of Greenland—there are large drilling machines floating around. These unanchored, unstable pieces of equipment are the size of a city block, and they're drilling hundreds and in some cases thousands of feet below the surface. Not only could more spills like the BP disaster happen at any time, but the fact is that these spills are already happening and we don't know about them because they're in remote locations, not off the coast of New Orleans. So now we're starting to collect data on where the drilling is occurring and tracking spills wherever they are.

We discovered that as soon as Obama called for a moratorium on offshore drilling in the Gulf, many of the rigs just started drilling in other places around the world. We started planning an offensive off the coast of Brazil, and another off the coast of Malta. We have launched an international offensive against big oil, which is fascinating and satisfying to be in the middle of . . . and that's worth a few sleepless nights.

Our spill-response team grew. Now made up of campaigners in ten countries, two ships, several action teams, scientists, photographers, videographers and researchers, it works to expose the dangers of deepwater drilling, reveal the extensive damage of the Gulf spill and use the moment to call for legislation that would reduce our dependency on oil. Around the world from Turkey to New Zealand, from Austria to Canada, we have staged protests in front of government buildings with protesters covered in oil (turns out molasses looks just like oil, which works fine—except when there are bees). Our researchers found a company off the shore of Greenland planning one of the deepest drilling operations ever in one of the most fragile ecosystems of the Arctic. We looked at a huge map that covered a wall of our office, and put a little magnetic ship and a red pin in the point where they were drilling and said, "Let's go occupy that drilling rig and stop it." We sent out the *Esperanza*, with a crew of twenty trained climbers and spokespeople and the most high-tech communications equipment that exists, to a position two hundred miles off the coast of Greenland where big oil thinks no one else can get to them, or even see them. We successfully occupied a drill rig under the nose of the Danish navy and were able to raise awareness of Arctic drilling around the world as well as slow down the company's progress at the site. We also learned an enormous amount. I will never forget the day the footage came in showing oil company employees standing on the deck of the support ships, trying to clear a path for their rigs by spraying big hoses of hot water, actually melting icebergs. Unfortunately our team eventually had to leave the standoff because of bad weather and the company's threat of an injunction and expensive lawsuit.

Not to be outdone, less than two weeks later our intrepid "Go Beyond Oil" team stopped a Chevron drill ship in the North Sea by attaching a survival pod onto the side of the ship with activists inside doing media interviews on cellphones. When the pod had to be removed because of Chevron's claims that it was unsafe because of high winds, the activists took to the water in shifts, swimming in front of the mammoth drill ship, preventing it from moving to the well site. It was a memorable moment when the video came into the office that day with our lead campaigner and media spokesperson, the sassy yet articulate Ben Stewart, treading water, a tiny speck in the icy North Sea. Amazingly, on the video he is calmly explaining why they are there and the need for our society to move beyond dangerous oil and develop clean energy while the drill ship looms directly above him, blocking out the sky. The longer the confrontation went on, the more interest it generated in the media. Meanwhile, we were ensuring that the company's drilling window shrank.

In early 2011 Obama's National Commission released its report on the Gulf oil spill. The report concludes that offshore drilling is inherently dangerous and reinforced everything we have been saying about the inadequacy of the regulations that govern oil drilling, the risks associated with the spill and the lack of oversight, training and enforcement. Former senator Bob Graham (Florida), one of the commission's two co-chairs, said the *Deepwater Horizon* accident was "both foreseeable and preventable," and reflected a failure on the part of three individual companies and the federal government.[4] The report went on to recommend significant changes in planning, approvals and response. Despite the report, Obama has recently lifted the moratorium and given a green light to new deepwater drilling plans in the Gulf.

The report's authors also confirm that drilling in the Arctic is even more dangerous and risky and requires significantly more planning, and that adequate spill response and prevention scenarios currently do not exist.

One would think that this report, combined with the devastation in the Gulf, would be enough to slow down drilling, especially in the fragile Arctic region. It appears it may have been enough to slow down BP and Shell in the Arctic Ocean, which have announced a delay of a year or two. However, Cairn Energy and other companies are pushing forward with Arctic drilling, and BP has announced it is moving into

Russia and the Black Sea, where there may not be as much media interest, public outrage or controversy. The nice thing, however, about working in a global organization is that these companies can run but they truly can't hide. We continue to track them around the globe and are developing action plans, research and campaigns that we hope will not only slow them down but will make investors think twice before investing, and make politicians think twice before approving the controversial permits. Sadly, more and more oil spills continue to happen. As I write, some of my Arctic team on an expedition into the Russian Arctic are reporting that they have found literally thousands of oil leaks and spills that we believe may have never been reported. Back in Canada, our staff on the ground tell me that pregnant women and children are being evacuated from a Lubicon Cree community in Alberta because of the largest pipeline spill in Alberta's history. Here in the Netherlands, Greenpeace photographer Lu Guang has just accepted a World Press Photo award for his pictures capturing the death of firefighter Zhang Liang in the oily waters of the Dalian, China, oil spill that happened last year. The more oil spill and safety reports I read, the more I am convinced that unless we move quickly away from these dangerous fuels, our rush to get at the last of them will make us increasingly vulnerable to these disasters.

Conclusion

THE POINTY END

To be truly radical is to make hope possible rather than despair convincing.

RAYMOND WILLIAMS

THE MOST HEARTBREAKING question I get, and I get it all the time—at the end of my speeches, or from people calling in when I'm being interviewed on the radio—is "Do we have a chance?"

Sometimes people ask in other ways.

"Can we really do something about global warming?"

"Do you really think it's possible to move away from fossil fuels?"

And, "Is it too late?"

I always give the answer many people don't believe, but I still do. Yes, I think we do have a chance. We can win this fight. But there's a catch: only if we live every moment intentionally. Only if we organize.

We have to engage our friends and family, our synagogues, churches and schools. We have to acknowledge that we have the capacity and the right to demand that our politicians act, and we have to find a way to get to work. That's going to require widespread action and citizens' engagement. Together we can have a bigger impact than apart. But together for what? What are we actually doing? What are we calling for at any particular moment?

Years ago in a strategy meeting, Chris referred to our campaign's end goal and the need to focus and direct our efforts as "the pointy end." The term has always resonated with me because social organizing and campaigns should act like a funnel, and they need to funnel into something at every particular moment; if they don't, you've got a whole lot of good intentions and not much of anything else. Finding a clear focus for your work, a clear goal to set your sights on, that's "the pointy end" of the work. Without it we are all bark and no bite.

OFTEN WHEN WE talk about global warming and climate change, people's default reaction is guilt. And that makes sense because ultimately it is our lifestyle and our dependence on fossil fuels that have created the problem. So people automatically think, *Oh my God, I've got to change my light bulbs, I've got to walk to work, I've got to save for a hybrid. It's my fault, it's all my fault.*

What we see in social movement theory and psychological studies is that if a problem is so big that it cannot be easily understood, or the risks are overwhelming, people will make some changes to their lifestyle but try to forget about the actual problem. You're walking to work once a week, you're using your canvas bags for groceries, but the problem is getting worse. So eventually you get off your soapbox and go back to a "normal" life.

There are a million things you can do and, yes, you should do all you can to change your lifestyle. Yes, if you can afford it, you should drive a Prius—though it would be a lot better if you could cycle, take public transit or at least drive the car you already have until it's no longer fuel-efficient because building that shiny new Prius produces a whole lot of carbon. Yes, we should change our light bulbs. Yes, we should walk to work. All those energy-saving lifestyle tips are true.

But here's the thing: the majority of North America's as well as the globe's emissions come from heavy industry. So while we can and should change a lot of key aspects of our lifestyles, changing our individual actions alone is not enough to correct the course we're on.

One of the major fallacies of our age is that we are besieged with "environmental problems" that are overwhelming and unstoppable. The nature of the term denies human agency and distances us from individual and collective responsibility. It separates environmental issues from social issues in our minds, language and policy formation. I have come to realize that we do not have environmental problems, we have *human problems*. Human problems that create environmental disasters.

I have listened to foresters and corporate officials refer to "slope failures" and discuss technologies and restoration to overcome massive soil erosion. I have heard various Canadian environment ministers refer to "grave environmental problems" as if the environment itself were to blame. But the soil is not eroding on its own; it is washing down the slopes and into the salmon streams because humans have removed the trees and vegetation on the mountainsides. That is not a slope failure, it is a human failure. Yes, solving global warming is going to require some changes, but those changes are feasible. If the problem resulted from some bad human decisions, it stands to reason that some good ones can solve it. We need to remember that a problem without a solution is a tragedy. A problem with a solution that is not being implemented is not a tragedy, it's a scandal.

Once we realize the magnitude of the problems, we must cope with the stages of despair and denial—an emotional and intellectual trajectory. Stage one after my climate reckoning was that if it's one or the other, I'm going to choose a normal life because it's too soul wrecking to worry about what I'm doing or should be doing all the time. Then I went through my potato chips and *Battlestar Galactica* phase, when I tuned out the world, popped in DVDs and played Lego with my kids.

After that I tried to figure out my place in the problem, what I could do, how I could reach people, how I could find a community to have these discussions with. I found friends who were going through the same thing I was—and they were all relieved that they weren't crazy either, but freaked out that they weren't doing enough. Together we found some things to do that felt meaningful and, even better, we were all regularly inspired by stories of other organizations and groups around the world who were moving the dial too. Change is happening. In our homes, our schools, our workplaces and our legislatures.

In writing about this journey, I find myself flashing back to a speech I gave at a rally on the steps of the British Columbia Legislature. I was asked to "inspire the crowd," and right before I spoke I realized I had nothing left to say. I had spent the summer being horrified and depressed by the extent of clear-cutting logging I had witnessed and our seeming inability to even slow it down.

Closing my eyes to over a thousand people on the legislature lawn, I grabbed the microphone and gave it everything I had—lamenting the loss of these majestic thousand-year-old trees and decrying the tragedy of our ancient forests being destroyed to make phone books and toilet paper. I spoke from the heart and talked about how, at twenty-five years old, I was afraid to have children because I didn't want to bring them into a world where this kind of devastation was not only possible but predictable and acceptable. I talked about all the amazing people I had met that summer and how together I hoped we could make a difference. I opened my eyes and looked out at a sea of people whose fear, anger and caring were palpable. I ended my speech by saying, "I don't know what the future holds, but I know who holds it."

When I stepped off the stage I was shaking. Standing by the steps was an elderly couple, clearly moved. They stepped forward and told me they had known my mom and dad well and that my parents would have been very proud. That day I realized that beyond the pain, fear and anger was a place that sparkled with purpose, pride and honour.

Over the next decade I would remember that moment over and over again. I would remember how I channeled despair and anger into action and how good it feels to know you're part of a powerful community and contributing to something that will have an impact beyond your own lifetime.

In Bali and Copenhagen, Canada, the United States and Amsterdam, I have been reminded that despair is a powerful place from which to step forward. There are times when it feels too big, too overwhelming, and I feel too small and insignificant. But every day I look at my children and know that I need to find ways to contribute to raising awareness and finding solutions. I need to continue to find my voice and allow myself to feel the pain of despair to motivate a new strong commitment and voices for change.

—

CHOOSING TO COMBAT climate change is like deciding to exercise—we need to figure out how it becomes part of our daily practice. If I commit to exercise every day, whether practicing yoga or taking a walk, it becomes part of my life; if I don't, finding the time for it becomes impossible. If we are serious about making real change in the world, we have to treat our time like that; we have to be intentional about how we intervene. For a while I was telling myself I just had to write one letter a day—and on the days I didn't have time I would go to an environmental group's website and click where they wanted me to click. It was an incredibly satisfying feeling, and it was important to contribute. If we all started to make that commitment, to carve out a couple of hours a week to meet with a group of concerned people or an organization, or, better yet, created a daily habit of volunteering or engaging in the issues that became second nature like checking our Facebook page or a necessity like packing our kids' lunch boxes, imagine what a different world we'd have.

More important, you need to join an environmental group—especially a local one where you can take part in actions meaningful to your community—and interact with your elected decision makers. Send your support cheque to that group. Write those letters, make those phone calls. It takes only thirty seconds to click "send" every time one of the environmental groups working on vital issues initiates an e-campaign.

There's always a decision to be made about your own activities, about what you buy or don't buy, about whether you fly for pleasure or for work, or stop flying altogether. Ultimately environmentalism is about trying to figure out how we can each have the least possible impact. It's critical that we all do everything we can to eat locally and organically, to consume less, to use less energy.

I know we can't all work on these issues all day, every day. We have busy lives, bills to pay and our own individual fires to put out. But each of us can dedicate some of our ingenuity, some of our resources, some of our time. And we have to. Because today we're all responsible not only for what we do but for what we don't do.

—

HALF THE PEOPLE I talk to after my climate speeches say, "I feel like I'm going crazy. I had to stop reading about it."

I've met people who've stopped working on environmental issues because of climate change. I asked one friend why he'd walked away from a local climate campaign he had been working on, and he said, "Because my soul hurts too much." There are going to be climate-reckoning self-help groups in a couple of years. I've already heard of a counsellor in Canada who works with couples in crisis because one of them is more worried about the climate than the other.

When I had my climate reckoning, I delved into the writings of experts like George Monbiot, and I was the friend you didn't want at your dinner party. I remember New Year's Eve 2008 when someone asked me about the work I was doing. I started discussing the dramatic impacts of climate change that we are already seeing in vulnerable countries, my fear about the unsustainable path we're on. Before I knew it, the party had gone silent, and the two people beside me had tears running down their faces and I thought, *Oh crap, I'm the bummer girl. I'm the channel you change because you're too tired, so you flip to a rerun of* Friends.

It's true: you can't put the toothpaste back in the tube. Our world has changed permanently, and for many of us the way that we look at the world has changed forever. However, when I think of giving up, I remind myself that we have done this before. The Montreal Protocol worked. Today the holes in the ozone layer are smaller, and in some places they've even healed. I remind myself how much has changed for the positive in just the past couple of years and that we have the technology for economically viable solutions at hand.

New Scientist ran the numbers on what it's going to cost consumers to have a clean-energy transition and projected that radical cuts to the UK's emissions would cause barely noticeable increases in the price of food, drink and most other goods by 2050. Electricity and gasoline costs would rise significantly, but with the right policies in place, the modellers believe this increase need not lead to big changes in lifestyle. "These results show that the global project to fight climate change is doable," said Alex Bowen, a climate policy expert at the London School of Economics. "It's not such a big ask as people are making out."[1]

Though the results spoke directly to UK consumers, previous research came to similar conclusions for Americans. One study found that if Americans were to cut their emissions by 50 percent by 2050, prices of most consumer goods would increase by less than 5 percent as a result.[2] These findings were consistent with analyses by the Pew Center on Global Climate Change in Washington, DC. "Even cutting emissions by eighty percent over four decades has a very small effect on consumers in most areas," says Manik Roy of the Pew Center.[3]

How do we convince our governments that they have the social licence—that we will support them if they make these changes? We need to start with a vision.

A well-known pollster told me that travel agents don't talk about the cost or the flight to Hawaii; they talk about the beach. And one of the most inspiring speakers I know, Van Jones, is fond of saying, "There is a reason Martin Luther King never said, 'I have a kvetch, or I have a problem.' Because the problem rarely inspires action and commitment—it's the dream."

And that's why we need to talk about the dream.

Shock and horror rarely seed engagement. They seed helplessness in our souls. We need to stop talking about global warming and deforestation without talking about responsibility and identifying what we can do to create the world we want.

One of the most important pieces of theory behind my work has been Bill Moyer's "Movement Map," in which he outlines the stages of social movements. Moyer says that in order to move issues, goals need to be framed in terms of widely held values. When you speak to values, you go from having an issue that someone cares about to having a movement that a lot of people care about. It struck me when I started working on climate issues that the climate movement has been exclusive, complex and based on science and policy that speaks to policy wonks, not civilians. I've spent my adult life working on environmental issues, and it took me six months of intensive research to even begin to figure out what I was for. That's why I made it my goal to talk about these issues in a way that everybody can understand, and from that understanding, act.

Regardless of where you live, your government's inaction in the face of workable alternatives is a scandal, and we have to show that most governments are out of touch with widely held values of clean air, clean water and livable cities—that they are out of touch with our values.

In 2009, for the first time in human history, the combined new investment in renewables, wind, solar and water power was greater than the combined investment in dirty fuels—oil and gas and nuclear combined.

I dream of a world where we all have access to clean water, clean air and healthy food—a world where the rich countries that have been spewing pollution into the atmosphere for decades take responsibility and help the emerging economies leapfrog over the dirty-fossil-fuel era and develop renewable energy systems. I don't dream of us all going "back to the land" and living in cabins without running water and electricity. And I know we can't all live in places like Cortes Island. I dream of a high-tech world with sleek urban design, smart electricity grids, rooftop and community gardens, bike lanes and high-speed trains. I dream of a world where governments regulate and control pollution, never use taxpayers' money to subsidize dirty fossil fuels, and come together internationally to sign an emergency agreement for a fair, ambitious and binding treaty to protect what's left of our intact forests and stop climate change.

We need to create a collective vision that gives us all hope and inspires us to action. We need a process that creates a conversation. These are issues that need to be brought out of the domain of the experts, that cannot be addressed behind closed doors by stakeholder representatives. These are issues that will not be dealt with by one party, one government, one environmental group or any one person. We can no longer afford partisan squabbles that result in no climate legislation being passed. We cannot afford to wait and hope that any one government will do the right thing, because no one will have the courage to make the changes necessary without knowing we are all on the same page.

The changes required will not always be easy, or necessarily popular at the polls. People do not appreciate paying more for energy, do not like having their views altered or challenged, or seeing natural areas opened to clean energy production. It is our job to communicate the imperative. That's why we need far-reaching goals that everyone can understand and embrace. We need to stimulate tax breaks for renewables, we need access to low-cost capital renewables and low-carbon industry, and we need hard limits on pollution—and that means putting a price on carbon that polluters will actually notice. We need stronger regulations on buildings and vehicles. We have the technology to produce cars that don't pollute, so why aren't we producing them? Why don't we just outlaw the cars that do pollute?

Japan has an inspiring law that I think all countries should look at adopting, which translates as "the top runner law." The Japanese government looks at everything from dishwashers to ovens to tractors, and every three years it outlaws the bottom energy performers in each area. The result is truly dynamic competition and an industry and marketplace racing to be more efficient. That's why some of the most efficient appliances are from Japan.

Yes, we need entrepreneurship. Yes, we need financing. Yes, we need individual actions. But it's that law that's changing appliances around the world. Laws make a difference. We all need to become politically active and show our governments that the future of the planet means enough to us that it's the issue that must matter at the polls. I met with a Canadian government official recently who told me that while it's true that Canadians care, they don't care enough for climate policies to matter as an election issue. So the Harper government figures it is doing enough. That has to change, and not just in Canada.

American voters are frequently moved to the polls en masse by a single "wedge" issue, an issue some voters feel strongly enough about that it not only gets them to vote but determines their vote. Once the environment becomes that crucial issue, we'll see politicians of all stripes racing to turn green.

If there really is only one thing that you're going to do after reading this book, vote for climate leadership. Because ultimately we're not going to see change until politicians believe they have the money and votes to make the difficult changes that need to be made. It just makes sense to vote for the person who's going to save your ass.

And it's all within our grasp.

The United Kingdom has committed to ensuring that all new homes must produce zero carbon by 2016. China has stronger vehicle-efficiency regulations than Canada. The United States is putting one million plug-in hybrids on the road by 2015. The Pew Center on Global Climate Change has laid out three scenarios for the United States to achieve up to a 65 percent reduction in transportation-related GHG emissions by 2050;[4] however, the US government would have to stand up to the automobile lobby on fuel standards—another reason laws and lawmakers matter. Israel (population 7 million) has committed to an all-electric-car infrastructure. By the end of 2011 they plan to have electric cars in mass production and half a million charging stations.

Over one hundred countries, cities and other jurisdictions have joined the United Nations Climate Neutral Network and are implementing zero-carbon plans. Countries as varied as Norway, New Zealand and Costa Rica have committed to becoming carbon neutral. Sweden has promised to build an "oil-free society" and has already reduced oil for residential and commercial heating by 70 percent over the past thirty years.

It's clear that those of us who want to move away from a petrol state will have to prove to decision makers that we can create an economy that can and will fuel our needs with low-carbon energy, using sources that create jobs. We have to prove to our governments that this objective represents more than a niche market, and if we're going to do that, we have to figure out how to do it right, and stand up quickly.

SOME OF THE people with whom I work most closely, with whom I've had the biggest breakthroughs, have been people who work with logging companies, who want to do the right thing. Right now, some of the people who I think are most concerned about global warming in Canada work with energy companies. So yes, we need to call out bad decisions and name names in order to draw attention to a particular problem or intransigent decision maker, but through it all leave room for industry leaders to get creative and give bureaucrats the benefit of the doubt. We can't be so quick to stick a label on someone and limit his or her actions and our relationships.

That said, collaboration and relationship building work once everyone agrees there is a problem to solve. They work once it is clear that business as usual is not an option. Great shifts in history have always required citizen engagement and mobilization. That doesn't mean everyone needs to get out in the streets with a placard—though I hope some of you will—but it does mean you need to find a place that feels right for you and engage. It means there isn't a one-size-fits-all strategy or tactic, and in most cases the strongest campaigns are, like nature, diverse. It takes a lot of strands to make a strong web.

A few years ago I was at Bioneers and met Diane Wilson, the woman who scaled the Dow Chemical building with a banner in her backpack and used a bicycle lock to chain her throat to poles so she couldn't be dragged off by security guards or police.[5] She changed the face of negotiations with a behemoth chemical company. Diane reminded me of two things: how important it is to be bold, and how important civil disobedience and protest have been to every successful campaign I know of. She reminded me how easily we can become lost in engagement and negotiations and how the controversy, the willingness to put our freedom, and in some cases our lives, on the line can move the debate forward and increase our power by leaps and bounds.

Yes, we have to negotiate in the boardrooms and be prepared to use our power as consumers through boycotts, but we still need people who are willing to risk their freedom on the blockades. I know if we look back in ten years and admit that we didn't have the courage to stand with a placard in front of city hall, Parliament or the White House at a time when so many people and in fact our planet were threatened, we'll regret it.

It's not enough to sit back and let someone else decide the fate of our children's future. If you have the choice, you wouldn't let someone else decide where your kids go to school. You shouldn't let someone else decide what kind of air they're going to breathe. The world is changing. And it will change by default or design to a post-carbon economy. If we allow it to change by default, there will be far more casualties.

—

WHEN I STARTED this work, I thought I had all the answers. Now I know that no one does. The best we can do is really listen—to others and to ourselves. Then we need to make choices and act, guided by what we have learned, our capacity and resources, and our principles. There is no road map for social change and no single way to engage in these issues. In the end it is about creativity, commitment, courage and a little bit of luck or magic.

Global warming is real, its agents invisible, its schedule unaligned with daily human time frames. In a sense, we are all still sleepwalking through denial, unable to grapple with the enormity of the problem and the scale of changes needed. I am sympathetic to the difficulties of building a new generation of environmentalism, of coming to terms with the compromises we need to make and the speed with which they need to happen. But the laws of physics have no such sympathy. Either we make the change or we are on the sidelines while half the world's species and far too many of our fellow humans are sentenced to oblivion.

After attending the UN negotiations in Bali, I spent a week with my ninety-two-year-old grandmother, not long before she died. One day we were sitting in the hospital and I told her about my despair. She said, "I don't want to hear any more about how hard it is, how big it is, and that you don't know if it can work. When your mother was growing up, when I was having my seven children, we didn't have a phone, we had a party line. We didn't have a car. No one had their own car. We had just gotten electricity. We didn't have computers. We didn't have cellphones. No one had even thought of them yet—let alone this raspberry you're always holding," she said, looking at my ever-present BlackBerry.

"I never would have thought that in my lifetime I would be sitting here talking to my granddaughter about what the world was like, and it would be an entirely different world. The way we communicate is different. The way we move about the world is different. By the time I was an adult and having children, I had never met anyone who had been on a plane. You need to hold on to the fact that the world can entirely change in your lifetime."

So when I do this work every day, I'm holding on to the notion that one day I'm going to be sitting with my grandchildren telling them about this crazy time not too long ago when we were destroying some of the last of the world's old-growth forests to make catalogues and toilet paper, this crazy time in our history when we clawed at the earth to get at the last of the oil, a simply crazy time in our history when we used to fill our cars with gas. And they will barely believe me, because the world will be such a different place.

ACKNOWLEDGEMENTS

Tzeporah Berman

First and foremost, I want to thank my family, who have not only stuck by me through thick and thin but have also supported and encouraged me even when they thought what I was about to embark on might be lunacy. My partner (in every way imaginable), Chris Hatch, has inspired me with his work, his patience, his thoughtful analysis and clear strategic thinking. He has watched with a wry smile every time I got in too deep and has not only refrained from saying "I told you so," but has been willing to cast a line and help me wade out. I was shocked to learn that he came as a package deal with the best in-laws any girl could hope for. Ron and Veronica have made me dinner, offered a sympathetic ear, taken care of our children and simply bailed me out more times than I can remember. My children, Forrest and Quinn, have kept me grounded, reminded me how much joy can be found in everyday life and have brought surprising clarity to many of the issues I have struggled with. They have also forced me to keep going and giving it my all. From the time they flew across the country to keep me out of jail to their visits to Amsterdam, my sisters, Wendy and Corinne, and my brother, Steve, have been there to support me every step of the way. I love them and their huge, beautiful families more than I can say.

There's an adage that it takes a village to raise a child. In my experience, this is true, too, for creating a campaign . . . and a book. I am deeply indebted to the "villages" I have had the honour of working with over the years. Bruce Westwood and Carolyn Forde at Westwood Creative Artists knew I could do it even before I knew what "it" was. Amanda Lewis and Louise Dennys at Random House of Canada have been incredible mentors and thorough editors, from whom I have learned a great deal. In Clayoquot Sound I want to recognize Chief Moses Martin, Chief Francis Frank and Chief Councillor Nelson Keitlah, Valerie Langer, Joe Foy, Adriane Carr, Vicky Husband, Elizabeth May, Liz Barratt-Brown, Norleen Lillico, Kevin Pegg, Maryjka Mychajlowycz, Garth Lenz, Warren Rudd and many more from the Nuu-chah-nulth, the Western Canada Wilderness Committee, the Natural Resources Defense Council (NRDC), the Sierra Club, Friends of Clayoquot Sound and Greenpeace. The Great Bear Rainforest and boreal campaigns and the creation of the forest markets work in Europe, Japan and the United States would never have happened without the commitment of Patrick Anderson, Jim Ford, Bill Barclay, Christoph Thies, Phil Aikman, John Sauven, Michael Marx, Randy Hayes, Mike Brune, Marc Evans, Atossa Soltani, Karen Mahon, Tamara Stark, Ian McAllister, Wayne McCrory, Catherine Stewart, Steve Shallhorn, Merran Smith, Ross McMillan, Art Sterrit, Jody Holmes, Nicole Rycroft, Leah Henderson, Richard Brooks, Lorne Johnson, Steve Kallick, Cathy Wilkinson, Aaron O'Carroll, Peter Lee and many, many more at the Coastal First Nations, the Rainforest Action Network, the Ivey Foundation, Pew Charitable Trusts, the Tides Foundation, the Endswell Foundation, Greenpeace, the NRDC and the Canadian Parks and Wilderness Society. To Clayton Ruby for many years of mentoring, friendship and support. To Robert Gass for helping me to really see myself and then teaching me to get out of my own way. To Daniel Johnston for helping me to really listen and see people before positions, and to Avrim Lazar, Linda Coady, Patrick Armstrong, Mark Hubert, Ken Higginbotham, Bill Dumont and Bill Cafferata—what a journey we have been through together. Special thanks to the team at ForestEthics and in particular Todd Paglia, Liz Butler, Kristi Chester Vance, Candace Batycki, Lafcadio Cortesi and Aaron Sanger for your fierce friendship and awe-inspiring commitment and creativity. On my journey into climate and energy issues there were a couple of people who were particularly influential and remarkably patient with me as I charged about trying to get a grip on the issues and make sense of it all: Gillian McEchern, Tim Gray, Guy Dauncey,

Peter Ronald, Clare Demerse, Mathew Bramley, Marlo Raynolds, Rick Smith, Bruce Lourie, John Roy, Angus McAllister, Dr. Mark Jaccard, Neil Moncton, Natasha van Bentum, Steve Kretzmann, James Glave, Jim Hoggan, Kevin Grandia, Don Millar and Mike Wilson and many more at the Pembina Institute, Environmental Defence Fund Canada and FD Element. It has been an honour working with all of you. To Jenn Nelson who patiently kept me organized for seven years while I campaigned from Cortes Island and to my dear friends Sue Danne, Karen Mahon, Tom, Chloe, Ruben and Mia Gregg, Deena Chochinov, Eric Posen, Barry and Carrie Saxifrage, Mike Magee, Dana and Joel Solomon—no one could ask for more. Finally, I need to thank Mark Leiren-Young and his partner, Rayne, for helping me to unravel and try to make some sense out of the past two decades of my life and work—and for keeping me laughing while we did it.

ACKNOWLEDGEMENTS

Mark Leiren-Young

"It's a little cold," Tzeporah warned us right before we stepped into the water.

A little? When my girlfriend, Rayne, and I jumped into the bay on Cortes Island, I think my heart actually stopped for a moment.

"Don't worry," Tzeporah said, "you'll get used to it. My kids do this every day."

Great, I thought, *I'm not as tough as a five-year-old . . .*

As we stood in the water, Tzeporah told us how Quinn had been stung by a jellyfish that morning. I had no idea jellyfish could live in freezing temperatures. I'd thought jellyfish were a tropical thing. She said they never used to show up on Cortes but now . . . every once in a while . . . a few would appear. There was only one cure for a jellyfish sting I'd ever heard of—which was the one she and Chris knew about too—and it was seriously gross. Tzeporah told us that neither she nor Chris could bring themselves to pee on Quinn's sting to take away the pain, so they drafted a friend to do the deed. Apparently it worked. Quinn was on the beach, having fun, not swimming in water the temperature of a Slurpee.

Then Tzeporah explained how to catch the currents, dived in and whipped away like she was on a flume ride at the amusement park. Rayne and I copied her dive, and for however long it took to body-surf around the bay and out toward the Pacific Ocean, I was as lost in nature as I've ever been.

When I checked my e-mail later that night, I discovered that Alternet—an environmental news service I subscribe to—had sent me a story about how, thanks to climate change, jellyfish were moving into areas they'd never been seen before. I e-mailed Tzeporah and said we should start the book with her trying to pee on Quinn. And if she hadn't been hired by Greenpeace to save the planet from a world of rogue jellyfish, maybe we would have.

I wrote and directed *The Green Chain*, a movie about the battles in BC's forests, and when it was released in 2007 I started a podcast series (for thetyee.ca) to accompany it. When I put together my wish list for people to talk to about forestry issues, Tzeporah was near the top. From the moment I arrived for our interview at the ForestEthics office in downtown Vancouver, it was as though I'd known her for years. And in many ways I had.

I first heard about Tzeporah when everybody else in Canada did— during the "War in the Woods" in 1993. I vividly recall reading the front-page story about her being arrested, and wondering . . . how in the world did a nice Jewish girl from Toronto end up on the front-lines in BC's forests? I was across the street from Vancouver's Jewish Community Centre the day I saw the newspaper ad with some of Canada's most famous artists and activists calling for charges against her to be dropped.

After our podcast interview, I told Tzeporah that I thought it would be fun to try to write a movie about her adventures. She said she wasn't a big fan of being fictionalized, but she'd been approached about writing a book. She wondered if I'd be interested in working with her on it.

I went out for a one-day visit to Cortes Island—I hadn't realized how isolated it was—to see whether I'd get along with Tzeporah and her family and whether we'd have fun working together once it officially became more like work. The moment the ferry left Campbell River and sailed to Quadra Island, I knew this was somewhere I wanted to explore. After Chris, Forrest and Quinn approved of me, I knew this was a place I would be spending time and a story I wanted to tell.

And her story just kept getting better . . . I was at *The 11th Hour* premiere in Vancouver. I was with her the night she agonized over the decision to go public with her opposition to the BC NDP's cynical "axe the tax" campaign. I was on Cortes when she accepted a position on the BC government advisory board and the day Forrest pretty much ordered her to carry the Olympic torch.

We spent hours talking in Vancouver, on Cortes, in airports, in cars, on beaches and all over Hollyhock. We talked while she juggled questions, requests and demands from Forrest, Quinn and Greenpeace, and she shared some of my favourite stories while she was cooking for the kids. It's a pleasure to finally be sharing most of these stories here.

I owe thanks to several people especially Tav Rayne, Joan Watterson, Scott Hugh Garrioch, Julie Johannessen and Kennedy Goodkey for their work transcribing, researching and fact-checking; Warren Sheffer and Ian Ferguson for their help and advice; Bruce Westwood and Carolyn Forde for making the book happen with Knopf Canada; Louise Dennys for making this happen at Knopf Canada; Amanda Lewis for all her time, energy and patience; Chris, Forrest and Quinn for approving of me; and, most of all, to Tzeporah for encouraging me to jump into the racing water with her.

You were right—I did get used to it.

ACKNOWLEDGEMENTS *315*

IMAGE PERMISSIONS

© Greenpeace

© Adrian Dorst

Tzeporah Berman at the Peace Camp at Clayoquot Sound on August 15, 1993. (93-5713) © Peter Battistoni/*Vancouver Sun* [PNG Merlin Archive]

© Iain MacLeod/Greenpeace

© Lisa Tremblay

Photographer unknown. Courtesy of Corinne Berman.

Photographer unknown. Courtesy of Greg Blanchette.

Photographer unknown. Courtesy of Greg Blanchette.

Photographer unknown. Courtesy of Corinne Berman.

Photographer unknown. Courtesy of Corinne Berman.

© Greenpeace

© Louise Denis/*Vancouver Sun* (94-4482) [PNG Merlin Archive]

© Andrew Wright/www.cold-coast.com

© ForestEthics

© Greenpeace/Mark Warford

© Greenpeace/Philip Reynaers

© Steve Shallhorn

© Greenpeace/Bas Beentjes

© Greenpeace

© Michael Bezjian/ForestEthics.

© Richard Lam/*Vancouver Sun* [PNG Merlin Archive]

© Corinne Berman

© Daniel Beltrá/Greenpeace

Joel Pett Editorial Cartoon used with the permission of Joel Pett and the Cartoonist Group. All rights reserved.

NOTES

INTRODUCTION

1. Robert Socolow and Stephen Pacala, "Coming to Grips with Global Warming: The PEI at Work," President's Pages in *Princeton Alumni Weekly*, October 25, 2006.

2. President Obama speaking to the National Academy of Sciences, April 2009. Full text online at http://www.csmonitor.com/USA/Politics/The-Vote/2009/0427/obamas-teleprompter-commits-mutiny-during-major-science-speech.

3. Eric Pooley, "Senate Inaction Cedes U.S. Energy Race to China," http://www.bloomberg.com/news/2010-07-30/senate-inaction-cedes-u-s-energy-race-to-china-commentary-by-eric-pooley.html, July 2010.

4. See Malcolm Gladwell, *The Tipping Point* (New York: Back Bay Books, 2002).

5. For a succinct review of climate science that makes these conclusions, see Joe Romm, "A stunning year in climate science reveals that human civilization is on the precipice" (Nov. 15, 2010), http://climateprogress.org/2010/11/15/year-in-climate-science-climategate.

6. Ban Ki-moon said this in 2009: http://unfcccbali.org/unfccc/news-unfccc/news-unfccc/un-chief-says-climate-change-biggest-challenge.html.

7. Justin Gillis, "Figures on Global Climate Show 2010 Tied 2005 as the Hottest Year on Record," *The New York Times* (Jan. 12, 2011), A4.

8. *The Huffington Post,* Apr. 5, 2010. Also available at Climate Science Watch as "Hansen: Obama must defend climate scientists and 'facing the difficult truth of climate science'" (Apr. 5, 2010).

9. Jeroen van der Veer, "Two Energy Futures" speech, January 25, 2008, Delft University of Technology Symposium on Sustainable Solutions for Africa. http://www.shell.com/home/content/media/speeches_and_webcasts/archive/2008/jvdv_two_energy_futures_25012008.html.

10. Molly Bentley, "Climate resets 'Doomsday Clock,'" BBC News, January 17, 2007.

11. See above link to Van der Veer's 2008 speech.

12. A Christian Aid report, "Human tide: the real migration crisis, London, May 2007.

13. Lead author Anthony Costello (UCL Institute of Global Health), "Climate Change: The Biggest Global Health Threat of the 21st Century," *The Lancet* and UCL, May 14, 2009.

14. "Climate Change Is Hazardous to Your Health, Scientists Say," Union of Concerned Scientists: Citizens and Scientists for Environmental Solutions, July 8, 2010, http://www.ucsusa.org/news/press_release/climate-change-is-hazardous-0422.html.

15. Van der Veer, "Two Energy Futures."

16. *The Lancet*, May 14, 2009: 1701, col. 2.

17. For a fascinating and incredibly readable tour of real, inspiring solutions around the world that are working, see Chris Turner, *The Geography of Hope: A Tour of the World We Need* (Toronto: Random House Canada, 2007).

18. See, for example, George Monbiot, *Heat* (New York: Penguin, 2007), and Tim Flannery, *The Weathermakers* (Melbourne: Text Publishing, 2005). In addition, James Hoggan and Richard Littlemore's *Climate Cover-Up* (Vancouver: Greystone Books, 2009) provides an exhaustive account of the propaganda campaign that has manufactured dissent and uncertainty over the science of global warming.

19. Angus Reid poll, 1994.

20. Richard Black, "'World's Biggest' Forest Protection Deal for Canada," BBC News, May 18, 2010, http://www.bbc.co.uk/news/10123210.

21. Desertification, fires and flooding speed up the death and decay of forests. When a tree dies, it stops absorbing carbon dioxide and releases the carbon stored in its body. Damian Carrington, "Mass Tree Deaths Prompt Fears of Amazon 'Climate Tipping Point,'" *The Guardian* (London), February 3, 2011, http://www.guardian.co.uk/environment/2011/feb/03/tree-deaths-amazon-climate?cat=environment&type=article.

22. Associated Press, "Ban Ki-moon: World's Economic Model Is 'Environmental Suicide,'" January 28, 2011, http://www.guardian.co.uk/environment/2011/jan/28/ban-ki-moon-economic-model-environment.

CHAPTER 1

1. Aldo Leopold, *A Sand Country Almanac* (New York: Ballantine, 1966; orig. 1949).
2. Edward O. Wilson, *Biophilia* (Harvard University Press, 1984), p. 121.
3. Dirk Bryant, Daniel Nielsen and Laura Tangley, *Last Frontier Forests: Ecosystems and Economies on the Edge* (Washington, DC: World Resources Institute, 1997), p. 6.
4. Ibid., p. 19.
5. Ecotrust and Conservation International (CI), "Coastal Temperate Rain Forests: Ecological Characteristics, Status and Distribution Worldwide," Occasional Paper Series No. 1 (Portland: Ecotrust, 1992).
6. Bryant, Nielsen and Tangley, p. 22.

CHAPTER 2

1. Valerie Langer, "Clayoquot Sound: Not Out of the Woods Yet!" *Common Ground* (1993), http://www.commonground.ca/iss/0211136/13_clayoquot.shtml.

CHAPTER 3

1. While the government's and logging industries' PR materials were careful not to outright lie, the releases frequently avoided the truth by claiming the logging practices were "world class" and that "biodiversity was protected." I found the customers usually interpreted these lines to mean that the logging wasn't in old-growth forests or that the logging was not clear-cutting. Both assumptions were incorrect.
2. Canadian Council of Christians and Jews, *A Report of the International Conference of Christians and Jews* (1969), p. 21.
3. Andrew Ross, "Appendix 2: Clayoquot Sound Chronology" (University of Victoria, Oct. 1996), http://web.uvic.ca/clayoquot/files/appedix/Appendix2.pdf.

CHAPTER 4

1. *Kahtou News* (May 5, 1993). Tzeporah Berman, "Standing for Our Lives: A Feminist Journey to Clayoquot Sound" (master's thesis, York University, 1995), p. 24.
2. Friends of Clayoquot Sound, Greenpeace, the NRDC, Sierra Club and the WCWC.

CHAPTER 5

1. I am using a very broad "we" here. There is no question in my mind that the Pacific Bell campaign was a tipping point, and Linda Coady has since confirmed it in my discussions with her. However, a lot of the industrial logging by MacMillan Bloedel was stopped in Clayoquot Sound in the '90s because of the decades of local community activism, dozens of environmental organizations' efforts and thousands of people.

2. See Greenpeace Reports, *Chain of Destruction: The United States Market and Canadian Rainforests,* 1999, and *Consuming Canada's Boreal Forest,* 2007, as well as ForestEthics Report, *Bringing Down the Boreal,* 1999. In the past ten years, forest product exports have dropped significantly from $45 billion to $25 billion. The majority is still exported to the United States, most of the exports are pulp and paper, and most logging is in old-growth forests. Natural Resources Canada, *The State of Canada's Forests,* 2010.

3. Estimates vary, but according to the USDA in 2000 only 7 percent of forest cover in the United States could be considered century-old forest.

CHAPTER 6

1. "Living Landscapes," Royal BC Museum, http://www.livinglandscapes.bc.ca/thomp-ok/env-changes/land/ch2.html.
"Canada's Forests at a Crossroads: An Assessment in the Year 2000," Global Forest Watch, an initiative of the World Resources Institute, http://www.globalforestwatch.org/common/canada/report.pdf. In 2000 Canada logged 1,003,807 hectares, which is 2,750 hectares logged per day or 115 hectares per hour.

2. "Staples Inc. Now Offering FSC-Certified Paper: Staples Makes FSC the Standard Offering in All Copy & Print Centers," Forest Stewardship Council, United States, April 2008, http://www.fscus.org/news/archive.php?article=519&.

CHAPTER 7

1. In a statement for Canopy (formerly Markets Initiative).

2. Ecotrust, The Rainforests of Home: An Atlas of People and Place, 1995, http://www.ecotrust.org/publications/rain_forests_atlas.html.

3. George Hoberg, Scott Morishita, Adam Paulsen, "The Great Bear Rainforest: Peace in the Woods?" Forest Policy Resources, Department of Forestry

Resources Management, Faculty of Forestry, UBC, March 5, 2004, http://www.policy.forestry.ubc.ca/rainforest.html.

4. "The model for new environmentalism," ForestEthics, http://www.forest-ethics.org/great-bear-rainforest.

CHAPTER 8

1. Robert Matas and Patricia Lush, "How a Forestry Giant Went Green: When MacMillan Bloedel Stopped Thinking in Absolutes, It Rethought Clearcut Logging. Its Adversary Greenpeace Toasted the Firm in Champagne," *The Globe and Mail* (Toronto), June 15, 1998, A1, A6.

2. Justine Hunter, "MacBlo to end clearcutting in old-growth coast forests," *The Vancouver Sun,* June 10, 1998, A1.

3. Tom Stephens, interviewed in *Forest News Watch,* ca. 2003.

CHAPTER 10

1. Dirk Bryant et al., *The Last Frontier Forests: Ecosystems and Economies on the Edge* (Washington, DC: World Resources Institute, 1997) and A. Komonen, "Hotspots of Insect Diversity in Boreal Forests," *Conservation Biology* 17, no. 4 (August 2003).

2. For extensive statistics on Canada's forests and logging see the Natural Resources Canada, State of Canada's Forests Annual Reports. http://canada-forests.nrcan.gc.ca/rpt.

3. "ForestEthics and the Canadian Boreal Forest Agreement: A Historic Opportunity," May 18, 2010, http://www.forestethics.org/boreal-forest-agreement-media-kit; Bertrand Marotte, "Forum to keep forestry industry accountable," *The Globe and Mail* (Toronto), April 18, 2011; Marotte, "Keeping Tab on the Keepers of the Forest," *The Globe and Mail* (Toronto), April 19, 2011, B6.

CHAPTER 11

1. Jeremy Caplan, "Paper War," *TIME* magazine, December 11, 2005, http://www.time.com/time/insidebiz/printout/0,8816,1139834,00.html. Victoria's Secret mails about 395 million catalogues a year from Plunkett's Retail Industry Almanac, 2008.

2. Statistics from Tom Katzenmeyer speaking to Ontario government, Toronto, 2007.

CHAPTER 12

1. John Bermingham, "B.C. to Protect Caribou Habitat," *The Province* (Vancouver), October 17, 2007, quoted on Sierra Club's website: http://www.sierraclub.bc.ca/quick-links/media-centre/media-clips/b-c-to-protect-caribou-habitat.

CHAPTER 13

1. Germanwatch, 2011. Climate Change Performance Index 2011, http://www.germanwatch.org/ccpi.

2. Between 2000 and 2020, oil sands will have been responsible for adding nearly $800 billion to Canada's economy and $123 billion to government coffers through royalties and taxes. The tar sands will also result in 240,000 direct and indirect jobs. Read more: Barbara Yaffe, "Oilsands' Dirty Secret: They Add Billions of Dollars to Our Economy," *The Vancouver Sun*, October 21, 2010. http://www2.canada.com/story.html?id=3703920.

3. Richard Littlemore, "Bali: Leaked Canadian Documents Show Same Old Spin," Desmogblog.com, December 12, 2007, http://www.desmogblog.com/bali-leaked-canadian-documents-show-same-old-spin.

4. United Nations Millennium Ecosystem Assessment, Ecosystems and Human Well-Being, Island Press, 2005, www.MAweb.org.

5. Millennium Ecosystem Assessment, http://www.maweb.org/en/article.aspx?Id=58.

6. Edward O. Wilson, *The Future of Life* (New York: Vintage, 2003), prologue.

7. World Meteorological Organization, http://www.wmo.int/pages/publications/showcase/documents/1074_en.pdf http://www.sciencedaily.com/releases/2007/12/071213101419.htm

8. Intergovernmental Panel on Climate Change AR4. The Climate Change 2007 Synthesis Report, which was the fourth assessment report from the UN's Intergovernmental Panel on Climate Change, whose authors were jointly honoured with the 2007 Nobel Peace Prize.

9. Christian Aid, "Human Tide: The Real Migration Crisis," 2007 http://www.christianaid.org.uk/Images/human-tide.pdf.

10. Department of Defense, Quadrennial Defense Review, February 2010, http://www.defense.gov/QDR/QDR%20as%20of%2029JAN10%201600.pdf.

11. Environmental Protection Agency, "Endangerment and Cause or Contribute Findings for Greenhouse Gases under Section 202(a) of the Clean Air Act,"

December 7, 2009, http://www.epa.gov/climatechange/endangerment.html.

12. Bill McKibben, *Eaarth: Making a Life on a Tough New Planet* (Toronto: Knopf Canada, 2010).

13. McAllister Opinion Research, 2008, http://www.pembina.org/pub/1735.

14. Roland Berger Strategy Consultants, *Clean Economy, Living Planet: Building Strong Clean Energy Technology Industries.* Commissioned by WWF-Netherlands, November 2009.

15. David Boyd, *Canada vs. The OECD: An Environmental Comparison,* 2001, http://www.environmentalindicators.com/htdocs/PDF/CanadavsOECD.pdf.

CHAPTER 14

1. "Tailings," Government of Alberta, http://www.environment.alberta.ca/02011.html.

2. "What is the biggest dam in the world?" US Department of the Interior, Bureau of Reclamation, September 10, 2004, http://www.usbr.gov/lc/hoover-dam/History/essays/biggest.html.

3. Dawn Walton and Nathan Vanderklippe, "Syncrude Charged over Alberta Duck Deaths," *The Globe and Mail* (Toronto), February 9, 2009.

4. "Syncrude to Pay $3M penalty for Duck Deaths" CBC News, October 22, 2010, http://www.cbc.ca/canada/edmonton/story/2010/10/22/edmonton-syncrude-dead-ducks-sentencing.html.

5. Source for second-largest oil reserve: http://geology.com/nasa/athabasca-oil-sands/ http://athabasca-oil-sands.co.tv/.

6. According to a 2006 presentation by Richard Nelson at AERI, about 650,000,000 metres^3 of mature fine tailings (MFT) have been generated and stored in the tailings ponds since 1968. According to Figure 2 in Maria V. Colavecchia, Peter V. Hodson and Joanne L. Parrott ("CYP1A Induction and Blue Sac Disease in Early Life Stages of White Suckers [*Catostomus commersoni*] Exposed to Oil Sands," *Journal of Toxicology and Environmental Health, Part A,* 69:967–94, 2006), the total PAH (TPAH) in one of the larger of these ponds is 1.3 mg/g sediment, which is likely MFT. Assuming the density of the MFT is around 2 g/cm^3 (2,000 kg/m^3), the product of these two factors gives a TPAH load of 1.7 x 10^12 g TPAH (i.e. 650,000,000 m^3 x 2,000 kg/m3 x 1,000 g/kg x 0.0013 g TPAH/g MFT). Regarding the *Exxon Valdez,* at least 41,000 m^3 of oil leaked out of the vessel, with a TPAH concentration of about 0.015 g/g oil, and at a density of about 0.9 g/cm3. This is equivalent

to 41,000 m^3 x 900 kg/m^3 x 1,000 g/kg x 0.015 g TPAH/g oil = 5.6 x 10^8 g TPAH. The ratio of the TPAH values calculated above is three thousand.

7. Government of Canada, 2010, National Inventory Report, http://unfccc.int/ national_reports/annex_i_ghg_inventories/national_inventories_submissions/items/5270.php.

8. Environmental Defence 2008, *Canada's Toxic Tar Sands: The Most Destructive Project on Earth*, http://environmentaldefence.ca/reports/ canadas-toxic-tar-sands-most-destructive-project-earth.

9. Canada has "won" the Colossal Fossil Award four years running, including Cancun 2010. The Colossal Fossil is an award granted to the country that has done the most to disrupt or undermine the UN climate talks. The winner is selected through voting among more than 500 international organizations. Climate Action Network Canada, 2010, "Can't'nada Wins Fourth Straight Colossal Fossil Award," http://www.climateactionnetwork.ca/e/news/2010/ release/index.php?WEBYEP_DI=80.

10. UN Framework Convention on Climate Change, World Resources Institute, US Department of Energy's Carbon Dioxide Information Analysis Center, 2007.

11. "An Estimate of Recoverable Heavy Oil Resources of the Orinoco Oil Belt, Venezuela" USGS, 2010, http://pubs.usgs.gov/fs/2009/3028/.

12. "Fact or Fiction? Oil Sands Reclamation," Pembina Institute, May 26, 2008, http://www.pembina.org/pub/1639.

13. Pembina Institute, Oil Sands Fever, 2005, http://pubs.pembina.org/reports/ OSF_Fact72.pdf.

14. Joe Romm reviews both studies at Climate Progress, 2010, http://climateprogress.org/2010/11/12/ ccs-carbon-sequestration-study-leaks-contaminate-drinking-water/.

15. Mitch Potter, "U.S. Opening Up to 'Dirty Oil from Canada,' Clinton Hints," *Toronto Star*, October 20, 2010, http://www.thestar.com/news/world/ article/878399—u-s-opening-up-to-dirty-oil-from-canada-clinton-hints?bn=1.

CHAPTER 15

1. Climate Progress, 2009, http://climateprogress.org/2009/03/23/ obama-we-can-remain-the-worlds-leading-importer-of-foreign-oil-or-become-the-worlds-leading-exporter-of-renewable-energy-we-can-allow-climate-change-to-wreak-unnatural-havoc-or-we-can-cr/.

2. In 2010 Bill McKibben and his group 350.org approached President Obama about putting the solar panels back, and the president agreed to put them up.

3. Barack Obama, speech to National Academy of Sciences, April 29, 2009.

4. The protests around the world were organized by 350.org and included more than four thousand events in 170 countries worldwide over one weekend, 2009, http://www.guardian.co.uk/environment/gallery/2009/oct/27/350-campaign-climate-change-protest.

5. The agreement was written in 1987 and is "perhaps the single most successful international agreement to date," said Kofi Annan, former secretary-general of the United Nations, quoted in "The Montreal Protocol on Substances that Deplete the Ozone Layer," http://www.theozonehole.com/montreal.htm. Very important in climate context is that the Montreal Protocol commits developed countries to act first to phase out CFCs and other ozone-depleting chemicals, followed by phase-outs by developing countries.

6. The *Stern Review on the Economics of Climate Change* is a seven-hundred-page report prepared for the British government on October 30, 2006.

7. Jane Taber, "Yes Men Pull 'Very Good' Prank on Stephen Harper," *The Globe and Mail* (Toronto), January 28, 2010, http://www.theglobeandmail.com/news/politics/ottawa-notebook/yes-men-pull-very-good-prank-on-stephen-harper/article1447953/.

8. Climate Change Performance Index 2011, www.germanwatch.org/ccpi.

9. "Secret Cap-and-Trade Proposal Confirms that Canada Has No Intention of Meeting its 2020 Greenhouse Gas Target: Leaked Cabinet Documents Show Government Plan for Massive Increase in Oil and Gas Emissions by 2020," Climate Action Network Canada, December 15, 2009, http://www.climateactionnetwork.ca/e/news/2009/release/index.php?WEBYEP_DI=44.

10. The G-77 is a caucus organization that helps developing states pursue common goals and develop leverage in United Nations deliberations.

11. *Review of Policy Research* 27, no. 6 (November 2010): 795–821; first published October 20, 2010, online at http://onlinelibrary.wiley.com/doi/10.1111/j.1541-1338.2010.00472.x/full.

12. "Koch Industries Still Fueling Climate Denial," www.greenpeace.org/usa/en/campaigns/global-warming-and-energy/polluterwatch/koch-industries/.

CHAPTER 16

1. Smart meters have proven in many jurisdictions to be one of the simplest and easiest ways to encourage energy conservation. They tell you how much energy you're consuming and how much it will cost in real time.

2. "Even in Canada where we make abundant use of hydro power, almost 80 percent of our energy still comes from fossil fuels. Transitioning our energy system on that scale is a massive undertaking. And it must be done with unprecedented speed." "Canada's Fossil Energy Future: The Way Forward on Carbon Capture and Storage," Natural Resources Canada, 2008, http://www.nrcan-rncan.gc.ca/com/resoress/publications/fosfos/fosfos-eng.php.

3. Bill McKibben, "The Fierce Urgency of Now," *Toronto Star,* March 29, 2009.

4. Quoted in *Recharge,* June 12, 2009.

5. Linsey Davis and Jennifer Metz, "Raging Waters in Australia and Brazil Product of Global Warming," January 3, 2011, http://abcnews.go.com/International/extreme-flooding-world-caused-climate-change-scientists/story?id=12610066&page=2.

6. "Silver Lining to Climate Change—Green Jobs," United Nations Environment Programme, December 6, 2007, http://www.unep.org/Documents.Multilingual/Default.asp?DocumentID=523&ArticleID=5717&l=en.

CHAPTER 17

1. Frances Moore Lappe, "Every Day We Choose" in *Hope Beneath our Feet: Restoring Our Place in the Natural World,* ed. Martin Keogh (Berkeley: North Atlantic Books, 2010).

2. "The Emissions Calculator," using Seattle–London–Delhi: 10 tons = coach; 20 tons = first class. Note that you can burn much more than 20 tons on this flight, depending on what aircraft you fly on. A person can dump 50 or more tons of CO_2 by flying halfway around the world and back in a Cessna Citation 3, for example. See https://www.atmosfair.de/index.php?id=5&L=3.

3. 1.9 tCO_2 for EU per capita average for all transportation from World Resources Institute CAIT database using latest year (2007) and selecting "transportation" and EU(27), http://cait.wri.org/cait.php?page=compcoun&url=form&pHints=shut&pOne=open&pTwo=shut&pThree=shut&pFour=&lmenu=-27&rmenu=500&year=2007&sector=trans&co2=1&update=Update&start2=1950&limit2=1&emit2=1&year3=2003. Only 60 percent transport GHG is "personal transport," with

40 percent freight and other transport (the math: 1.9 tCO_2 60% = 1.14 tCO_2 for EU personal transport). See also http://www.internationaltransport-forum.org/Pub/pdf/10GHGTrends.pdf

The math for "nearly a decade's worth of the climate damage": 10 tCO_2 from flight divided by 1.14 tCO_2/year = 9 years.

4. Starting with 1.14 tCO_2 for EU per capita personal transport today, needing 80% GHG cut by 2050 to meet climate goals (might need more than that): 1.14 tCO_2 20% = 0.23 tCO_2 per person per year in 2050: 10 tCO2 from flight divided by 0.23 tCO_2/year = 44 years = "more than 40 years' worth."

5. https://www.atmosfair.de/index.php?id=5&L=3. This calculation is based on a large pool of round-trip flights each totalling 3,600 km (2,237 miles). The average worked out to about 1 tCO_2 for coach per 3,600 km, 1.5 tCO_2 for business class and 2.0 tCO_2 for first class. The math: 50,000 miles (1 tCO_2/2,237 miles) = 22.4 tCO_2 coach. Double for first class. FYI: In addition, Atmosfair lets you choose various aircraft to see different GHG profiles for the same flight. GHG for my sample 3,600 km flight can range from 0.8 tCO_2 up to 4.3 tCO_2, depending on aircraft model. Using 1.14 tCO_2 per year today for EU average person for all personal transport: 22.4 tCO_2 / 1.14 tCO_2 = 20 years for coach = two decades' or more worth.

CHAPTER 18

1. The Energy [R]evolution, Greenpeace http://www.greenpeace.org/energyrevolution.

2. Alex Morales, "Fossil Fuel Subsidies Are Twelve Times Renewables Support," Bloomberg New Energy Finance, Energy Subsidies Report, July 29, 2010, http://www.bloomberg.com/news/2010-07-29/fossil-fuel-subsidies-are-12-times-support-for-renewables-study-shows.html.

3. Ernest Scheyder, "BP Estimates Oil Spill Up to 100,000 Barrels Per Day in Document," Reuters, June 20, 2010, http://www.reuters.com/article/idUSN1416392020100620.

4. National Commission on the BP *Deepwater Horizon* Oil Spill and Offshore Drilling Final Report, January 11, 2011, http://www.oilspillcommission.gov/final-report.

CONCLUSION

1. Kenneth P. Green and Aparna Mathur, "A Green Future for Just Pennies a Day?" *The American,* February 19, 2010, http://www.american.com/archive/2010/february/a-green-future-for-just-pennies-a-day.

2. Richard J. Goettle and Allen A. Fawcett, "The structural effects of cap and trade climate policy," *Energy Economics,* 31:2 (Dec. 2009), 244–53. Cited in Tzeporah Berman, "Cost of the Clean Transition? 'Barely Noticeable,'" *The Vancouver Sun,* December 9, 2009.

3. Green and Mathur, "Green Future."

4. Dawn Fenton, "U.S. Can Reduce Transportation GHG by 65%, Report Says," *Environmental Leader,* January 13, 2011, http://www.environmentalleader.com/2011/01/13/u-s-can-reduce-transporation-ghg-by-65-report-says/.

5. Living on Earth, June 5, 1998, http://www.loe.org/shows/shows.htm?programID=98-P13-00023.

RECOMMENDED WEBSITES

350.ORG
www.350.org
350.org is building a global grassroots movement to solve the climate crisis. Their online campaigns, grassroots organizing and mass public actions are led from the bottom up by thousands of volunteer organizers in over 188 countries. To preserve our planet, scientists tell us we must reduce the amount of CO_2 in the atmosphere from its current level of 392 parts per million to below 350 ppm. But 350 is more than a number—it's a symbol of where we need to head as a planet.

BIONEERS
www.bioneers.org
As a non-profit organization, Bioneers provide solutions-based education and social connectivity through national and local conferences and programmes, including a radio series, an anthology book series, television programmes and an online community. Their materials are used by colleges, schools and organizations.

CLIMATE FEEDBACK: THE CLIMATE CHANGE BLOG
http://blogs.nature.com/climatefeedback
Climate Feedback is a blog hosted by the Nature Publishing Group to facilitate lively and informative discussion on the science and wider implications of global warming. The blog aims to be a forum for debate and commentary on climate science in the *Nature Climate Change* journal and in the world at large.

CLIMATE PROGRESS

www.climateprogress.com

Climate Progress is a blog dedicated to providing a progressive perspective on climate science, solutions and politics.

THE DESMOGBLOG PROJECT

www.desmogblog.com

The DeSmogBlog Project began in January 2006 and quickly became the world's number-one source for accurate, fact-based information regarding global warming misinformation campaigns.

THE DIRTY ENERGY MONEY CAMPAIGN

www.dirtyenergymoney.com

The Dirty Energy Money Campaign aims to end all government handouts to oil, coal and gas companies and persuade our elected representatives to reject campaign contributions from these dirty energy industries.

ENVIRONMENTAL DEFENCE

www.environmentaldefence.ca

One of Canada's most effective environmental action organizations, Environmental Defence works with governments, businesses and individuals to ensure a greener, healthier and prosperous life for all. They seek to create a world Canadians are proud to pass on to their children.

ÉQUITERRE

www.equiterre.org

équiterre helps build a social movement by encouraging individuals, organizations and governments to make ecological and equitable choices, in a spirit of solidarity. It sees the everyday choices we all make—food, transportation, housing, gardening, shopping—as an opportunity to change the world, one step at a time.

FORESTETHICS

www.forestethics.org

Founded in 2000, ForestEthics is a non-profit environmental organization with staff and board members in Canada and the United States.

Its mission is to protect endangered forests and wild places, wildlife and human well-being. Climate change, which threatens to undermine all conservation efforts, is also one of its campaign focus areas. ForestEthics catalyzes environmental leadership among industry, governments and communities by running hard-hitting and highly effective campaigns that leverage public dialogue and pressure to achieve its goals.

GLOBAL FOREST WATCH
www.globalforestwatch.org
Global Forest Watch is an initiative of the World Resources Institute (WRI). The WRI is an independent research and policy institute created in 1982 with a mission of moving human society to live in ways that protect the earth and its capacity to provide for the needs and aspirations of current and future generations. The WRI provides—and helps other institutions provide—objective information and practical proposals for policy and institutional change that will foster environmentally sound, socially equitable development.

GREENPEACE
www.greenpeace.org
Greenpeace is a forty-year-old action-based, independent, global environmental organization. They take action to protect oceans and forests, eliminate the use of harmful chemicals and transition to a world powered by clean and unlimited energy sources like the wind and sun.

HOW TO BOIL A FROG
www.howtoboilafrog.com
How to Boil a Frog is a comedic documentary about Overshoot: too many people using up too little planet much too quickly.

INTERNATIONAL BOREAL CONSERVATION CAMPAIGN
www.interboreal.org
The International Boreal Conservation Campaign is an initiative of the Pew Charitable Trusts (PCT), with major support from the William and Flora Hewlett Foundation and the Lenfest Foundation. For over

fifteen years, PCT has been supporting conservation of old-growth forests and wilderness in North America. This website is a great resource for scientific reports on the boreal forest and tar sands.

NATURE
www.nature.com
The Nature Publishing Group (NPG) releases high-impact scientific and medical information in print and online. The NPG publishes journals and manages online databases and services across the life, physical, chemical and applied sciences and clinical medicine.

THE PRICE OF OIL: OIL CHANGE INTERNATIONAL
www.priceofoil.org
Oil Change International campaigns to expose the true costs of fossil fuels and facilitate the coming transition toward clean energy. It is dedicated to identifying and overcoming barriers to that transition.

RAINFOREST ACTION NETWORK
www.ran.org
Rainforest Action Network envisions a world where each generation sustains increasingly healthier forests, where the rights of all communities are respected and where corporate profits never come at the expense of people or the planet.

THE SIERRA CLUB
www.sierraclub.org
Since 1892, the Sierra Club has been working to protect communities, wild places and the planet itself. They are the largest and most influential grassroots environmental organization in the United States. They are committed to a safe and healthy community, smart energy solutions and an enduring legacy for wild places.

TCKTCKTCK
http://tcktcktck.org/
TckTckTck is part of the Global Campaign for Climate Action (GCCA), an alliance of more than 270 non-profit organizations all over the

world with a shared mission to mobilize civil society and galvanize public support to ensure a safe climate future for people and nature, to promote the low-carbon transition of our economies, and to accelerate the adaptation efforts in communities already affected by climate change.

RECOMMENDED READING

Broecker, Wallace, and Robert Kunzig. *Fixing Climate: What Past Climate Changes Reveal about the Current Threat—And How to Counter It.* New York: Hill and Wang, 2009.

Dyer, Gwynne. *Climate Wars.* Toronto: Random House Canada, 2008.

Flannery, Tim. *The Weathermakers: The History and Future Impact of Climate Change.* Melbourne: Text Publishing, 2005.

Friedman, Tom. *Hot, Flat and Crowded: Why We Need a Green Revolution—And How It Can Renew America.* New York: Farrar, Straus & Giroux, 2008.

Hoggan, James, and Richard Littlemore. *Climate Cover-Up: The Crusade to Deny Global Warming.* Vancouver: Greystone Books, 2009.

Homer-Dixon, Thomas, ed. *Carbon Shift: How the Twin Crises of Oil Depletion and Climate Change Will Define the Future.* Toronto: Random House Canada, 2009.

Jaccard, Mark, Nic Rivers and Jeffrey Simpson. *Hot Air: Meeting Canada's Climate Change Challenge.* New York: Random House, 2008.

Jones, Van. *The Green Collar Economy: How One Solution Can Fix Our Two Biggest Problems.* New York: Harper One, 2009.

Leonard, Annie. *The Story of Stuff: How Our Obsession with Stuff Is Trashing the Planet, Our Communities, and Our Health—And a Vision for Change.* New York: Simon & Schuster, 2010.

Lovelock, James. *The Vanishing Face of Gaia: A Final Warning.* New York: Basic Books, 2009.

Marsden, William. *Stupid to the Last Drop: How Alberta Is Bringing Environmental Armageddon to Canada (And Doesn't Seem to Care).* Toronto: Vintage Canada, 2008.

May, Elizabeth. *Global Warming for Dummies*. Hoboken: Wiley, 2008.

McKibben, Bill. *Eaarth: Making a Life on a Tough New Planet*. Toronto: Knopf Canada, 2010.

Monbiot, George. *Heat: How to Stop the Planet from Burning*. New York: Penguin, 2007.

Patel, Raj. *Stuffed and Starved: The Hidden Battle for the World Food System*. Brooklyn: Melville House Publishing, 2008.

Pollan, Michael. *In Defense of Food: An Eater's Manifesto*. New York: Penguin, 2008.

Rand, Tom. *Kick the Fossil Fuel Habit: 10 Clean Technologies to Save Our World*. Austin: Greenleaf Book Group Press, 2010.

Rose, Chris. *How to Win Campaigns: 100 Steps to Success*. London: Earthscan, 2005.

Rubin, Jeff. *Why Your World Is About to Get a Whole Lot Smaller: Oil and the End of Globalization*. Toronto: Random House Canada, 2009.

Tertzakian, Peter. *The End of Energy Obesity: Breaking Today's Energy Addiction for a Prosperous and Secure Tomorrow*. Toronto: John Wiley & Co, 2009.

Turner, Chris. *The Geography of Hope: A Tour of the World We Need*. Toronto: Random House Canada, 2007.

Vasil, Adria. *Ecoholic: Your Guide to the Most Environmentally Friendly Information, Products and Services in Canada*. Toronto: Vintage Canada, 2007.

Weaver, Andrew. *Keeping Our Cool: Canada in a Warming World*. Toronto: Viking Canada, 2008.

INDEX

Dion, Stéphane, 205, 268

Domini Social Investments, 180

Dumont, Bill, 108, 153–55

ecology, lack of protection for, 79

economic issues (world), 7, 13, 15, 79,
    205, 217, 238, 248

economics

    binge, 93

    green, 148, 215, 241, 254, 256, 258,
        306

    pitted against environmental
        sustainability, 51, 72, 79, 82,
        85–87, 108, 140, 155, 238,
        250–51, 266, 268

Ecotrust Canada, 94

The 11th Hour (film), 184, 187–88, 192

Emerson, David, 158

employment, sustainability of, 27, 126,
    162, 169, 217, 247, 258, 268–69,
    281, 287–88

Energy [R]evolution (papers/reports),
    286–88

"energy security," 5, 220, 227, 230, 234

the environment, carelessly defined,
    224

environmental buildings, 279–82

Environmental Defence (NGO), 217,
    221

the environmental movement, crises
    within, 260–61

"ethical oil," 220

Evans, Mark, 101

"externalities" (freely available
    resources), 224–25

ExxonMobil, 247, 292

Exxon Valdez (oil spill), 221

Finlay, Colin, 219–20

First Nations (Canadian), 88–94,
    124–25

    angered at environmentalists,
        82–88, 104, 131–34

    join in conservation efforts, 107,
        126

    unjust treatment of, 82, 92–94

fishing, unsustainable, 116–18

Flothmann, Stefan, 286

flying. See air travel

food, "local," 7, 274–75

ForestEthics, 10, 81, 118, 120, 139,
    146, 151, 158–62, 166–67,
    171–77, 180–84, 192–93,
    197–98, 203, 213, 221, 226,
    240, 276–77

ForestEthics Chile, 159–60

Forest News Watch, 151

Forest Practices Code (British
    Columbia), 55

Forest Products Association of Canada
    (FPAC), 168

forestry, the profession in the future,
    169

Forest Stewardship Council (FSC),
    112, 178, 252, 281

Fort Frances, Ontario, 163

Fort McMurray, Alberta, 219–21, 227

the Fossil Award (Canada's), 206–7

fossil fuels. See also climate change;
    greenhouse gas (GHG) emissions

Harper, Stephen, and his government, 205–7, 213–15, 225–26, 234, 240, 268, 305

Hatch, Chris (author's husband), 66–67, 90, 109, 147–48, 213–14, 270, 279–81, 283, 291, 297

commutes from San Francisco to Bowen Island, 136–37

as a husband, father and supporter, 69, 71–74, 76–77, 165, 257, 272–74, 276

joins the Clayoquot campaign, 44–45, 115

joins PowerUp campaigns, 213–14, 270

joins RAN campaigns, 101, 135–37

promoted to executive director of RAN, 137

Hawken, Paul, 148, 186

Hayes, Randy, 102

health issues (world), 5–6, 15, 79, 212

Hesquiaht (First Nations), 82–83, 85

Hilton, Paris, 3, 192–94, 198

Hinton, Alberta, paper mill, 171, 175, 178

Hollyhock (retreat centre), 74, 154, 179, 275, 277

Holmes, Dr. Jody, 153

Home Depot, 107, 109–10, 129, 160, 165, 252

hope, as possible and reasonable. *See primarily* Berman, Tzeporah, hope and optimism felt by, 8, 230, 238

Horne, Matt, 267

Human Footprint and *Last of the Wild* (studies), 113

humour, its value in campaigns, 120

Husband, Vicky, 90

index, puzzling self-reference to, 337

injustice, 60, 66, 68–69, 89, 246

Interfor (logging company), 91–93, 130, 147, 151, 153

Intergovernmental Panel on Climate Change (IPCC), 212, 243

Interim Measures Agreement (British Columbia), 89–90

International Forest Products. *See* Interfor

International Herald Tribune, 68, 151

International Paper Corp., 173–75, 179

International Renewable Energy Association, 287

International Woodworkers of America (IWA), 51, 72, 168

Isaak (logging company), 90

Israel, 306

Jacobs, Jane, 76

James, Carole, 266

Japan, 135, 240, 273, 305

Jewison, Norman, 77

jobs. *See* employment

John, Elton, 153–54

Johnston, Daniel, 168

Johnston, Paul, 285

the Joint Solutions Project, 151, 160

Jones, Van, 184, 186, 188, 192, 303

junk mail (waste paper), 106–7, 167

justice. *See* "climate justice"; laws, decisions to disobey; injustice

Kallick, Steve, 221
Katzenmeyer, Tom, 171, 177–83
Keenan, Anna, 285
Kelly, Petra, 35, 60
Kelly, Steve, 231–33
Kennedy, Robert Jr., 77, 82, 89
Kilmer, Val, 190
Kimberly-Clark Co., 167
King, Martin Luther Jr., 35, 60, 303
Kingsolver, Barbara, 209
Kitasoo First Nations, 131–33
Koch Industries, 247
Krawczyk, Betty, 61
Kretzmann, Steve, 208, 284–85
the Kyoto Protocol, 205, 207, 221, 236–38

Landers, Nicole, 184, 191
Langer, Valerie
    activism of, 36, 43, 47, 52–53, 55, 87, 89, 109, 129
    advice and support given by, 34–35, 37–38, 41, 84, 87, 109
    introduced and described, 9, 34, 37–38, 87
languages (indigenous), destroyed, 85, 94
Lappe, Frances Moore, 271
The Last Frontier Forests (report), 113
Lawrence, Sharon, 192
laws, decisions to disobey, 33, 39, 41, 45–46, 60, 69, 127, 307
Lazar, Avrim, 168–69

Lenz, Garth, 42, 46
the Liberal Party (Canada), 205, 207, 234, 267
lifestyle choices, considerations of, 6, 205, 210–11, 217, 271–75, 298–300
Limited Brands (holding company), 177–78, 182–83
Linnaea school (Cortes Is.), 277–78
L.L. Bean, 172
logging. *See primarily* boreal forest campaign; the Clayoquot campaign; clear-cutting in forests; Forest Stewardship Council; Great Bear Rainforest; *Guide to Ecologically Responsible Forest Practices*
Los Angeles Times, 20
Loudermilk, Linda, 188
Love Canal, 35, 186, 261
Lubicon Cree (First Nations), 296
Lucas, Chief Simon, 82–83

the Mackenzie River, 221
MacKinnon, James, 138
MacMillan Bloedel (forestry company), 54, 58, 62, 67, 82, 100–102, 108, 130, 138, 145, 148, 152–53, 182
    dialogues and cooperation with, 90, 145–52
Maguire, Tobey, 190
Mahon, Aedan Magee, 76, 145
Mahon, Karen
    activism of, 42–43, 52–55, 58, 67, 123, 129, 145–46, 148, 151, 155

increasing likelihoods of, 264–65, 295–96

Unocal Corp. drilling platform Alpha (1969), 20

Ondaatje, Michael, 76

overfishing campaign. *See* fishing, unsustainable

Pacala, Steven, 2

Pacific Bell (phone utility), 101–3

Pacific Environment and Resources Center, 101

Pacific Wild (organization), 128

Paglia, Todd, 161, 177, 220

Paparian, Michael, 20

paper, sources of, 58, 101, 106, 163–64, 166

Pedersen, Larry, 107

Pembina Institute, 217, 267

Penner, Barry, 118

Pew Center on Global Climate Change, 303, 306

Pinchot, Gifford, 148

Poitras, George, 220

pollution, 3–4, 7, 14, 16, 22, 35, 205, 217, 225, 240, 268, 290

fined or taxed, 225, 255, 304–5

Pootlass, Chief Lawrence, 91

PowerUp Canada, 146, 214, 232, 239–41, 249, 256–57, 270

pragmatism, the importance of, 27, 114, 229, 250–53

Princess Royal Island (B.C.), 128, 137

problems, human vs. environmental, 298–99

puffins, 117–18, 122, 129

Pulp, Paper and Woodworkers of Canada (PPWC), 126

the Raging Grannies, 45, 49

Raincoast Conservation Society, 128

Rainforest Action Network (RAN), 24, 101–2, 111, 130, 135–37, 276

Reagan, Ronald, 230

Rebick, Judy, 176

Reid, Walter, 27

rights (civil, environmental and human), 15, 40, 77, 85, 112, 132

Robertson, Gregor, 196

Robinson, Svend, 48

the Rockwood Institute, 154

Roderick Island (B.C.), 131–32

Rose, Chris, 117

Rosen, Harry, 22

Roy, Manik, 303

Ruby, Clayton, 37, 63

run-of-river power proposals, 235, 254, 256–58, 269

Rycroft, Nicole, 167

Ryerson University, 22–23

Saltspring Island (B.C.), 277

Sauven, John, 117

Scheer, Hermann, 260

Schuyler, Arent, 20

Schwarzenegger, Arnold, 233, 238, 255

Scott Paper Co., 58, 100–101

Sears (company), 172

Sea Shepherd Conservation Society, 33

TZEPORAH BERMAN is a founder of ForestEthics and PowerUp Canada, and is currently Greenpeace International Climate and Energy Co-Director. She has been designing and managing environmental campaigns for almost twenty years. She is known for her role in coordinating the largest civil disobedience in Canada's history, the logging blockades in the rainforests of Clayoquot Sound in 1993, during which she was arrested and charged with 857 counts of criminal aiding and abetting. She is also known for her work in creating unlikely alliances with the logging industry and major paper and wood consumers that have resulted in the permanent protection of millions of acres of old-growth forests. She was one of the experts in Leonardo DiCaprio's documentary, *The 11th Hour*. The Royal BC Museum has included her in a permanent exhibition as one of the 150 people who have changed BC's history. She has been lauded as "Canada's Queen of Green" in a cover story in *Reader's Digest* and was recognized by the *Utne Reader* as one of 50 Visionaries Who Are Changing Your World. www.tzeporahberman.com

MARK LEIREN-YOUNG is the author of *Never Shoot a Stampede Queen*, winner of the 2009 Stephen Leacock Medal for Humour, and *The Green Chain—Nothing Is Ever Clear Cut*. He wrote, directed and produced the award-winning feature film *The Green Chain*, and wrote and produced the EarthVision award-winning TV comedy special *Greenpieces*. His stage plays have been produced throughout Canada and the US and have also been seen in Europe and Australia. As a journalist he has written for such publications as *TIME*, *Maclean's* and the *Utne Reader*. He's half of the comedy duo Local Anxiety and has released two CDs—*Greenpieces* and *Forgive Us We're Canadian*. For more on Mark, please visit www.leiren-young.com.